Abraham Lincoln and Robert Burns

➤─◆─○─◆─◄

Abraham Lincoln
and
Robert Burns

>━I━◆❯━❍━❮◆━I━◄

Connected Lives and Legends

Ferenc Morton Szasz

>━I━◆❯━❍━❮◆━I━◄

Southern Illinois University Press / *Carbondale*

Southern Illinois University Press
www.siupress.com

22 21 20 19   4 3 2 I

Cover illustrations: Mathew P. Brady, "Abraham Lincoln," February 9, 1864,
cropped. Courtesy of the Lincoln Museum, Fort Wayne, Indiana. No. 0-92.
Alexander Naysmyth, *Robert Burns*, 1787, cropped. By permission of the
Scottish National Portrait Gallery, Edinburgh.

ISBN 978-0-8093-3765-1 (paperback)

The Library of Congress has cataloged the hardcover edition as follows:
Szasz, Ference Morton, 1940–
Abraham Lincoln and Robert Burns : connected lives and legends /
Ferenc Morton Szasz.
p. cm.
Includes bibliographical references and index.
ISBN-13: 978-0-8093-2855-0 (cloth : alk. paper)
ISBN-10: 0-8093-2855-0 (cloth : alk. paper)
1. Lincoln, Abraham, 1809–1865—Ethics. 2. Lincoln, Abraham, 1809–1865—
Political and social views. 3. Lincoln, Abraham, 1809–1865—Influence. 4. Presidents—
United States—Biography. 5. Burns, Robert, 1759–1796—Ethics. 6. Burns, Robert,
1759–1796—Political and social views. 7. Burns, Robert, 1759–1796—Influence.
8. Poets, Scottish—18th century—Biography. 9. United States—Intellectual life—
1783–1865. 10. Scotland—Intellectual life—18th century. I. Title.
E457.2.S96 2008
973.7092—dc22   2008005349

Printed on recycled paper. ♲

For Margaret, who loves history, Scotland, and
travel in about equal proportions

And to Richard W. and Betty Smith, who started it all

Contents

Illustrations

Following page 86
Burns's birth cottage
Lincoln's log-cabin birthplace
Murdoch Instructing Burns
Lincoln studying by firelight
American engraving of Burns (1859)
Vanity Fair cartoon of Lincoln (1861)
Boy Scout wreath-laying ceremony
Forgery of Lincoln document by Joseph Cosey
Stamps honoring Burns and Lincoln
Statue of Burns in Central Park
Statue of Lincoln in Edinburgh
Lincoln Memorial Statue with Children

Acknowledgments

No historian works alone, and I have many people to thank for this project. My indebtedness to the past and present scholars of Robert Burns and Abraham Lincoln may be seen in the endnotes and bibliography.

I begin by thanking my Aberdeen colleagues and friends for their many kindnesses: Grant Simpson and Anne Simpson, Rosemary Tyzack, Paul Dukes, David Ditchburn, Roy Bridges and Gill Bridges, Louise Boudreau, Allan Macinnes, Thomas Devine and Katherine Devine, Marjory Harper and Andrew Shear, Donald Meek, Chris Fraser and Beth Fraser, and Colm O'Boyle and Frances O'Boyle.

Special thanks, as well, to the librarians at the Queen Mother Library and especially to Iain Beaven and Myrtle Anderson-Smith of Special Collections. I would like to also credit Ian Nelson of the Edinburgh Central Library, the staff at the Dublin (Ireland) Public Library, Paul Cowley of the Robert Burns House in Dumfries, and Alistair Macleod of the Central Library in Inverness. Thanks also to Donald Nelson, director of the famed Burns Manuscripts Collection at the Mitchell Library in Glasgow.

Both Donald Nelson and Deborah Harper Rouse of the Special Collections Division of the Robert Manning Strozier Library at Florida State University in Tallahassee deserve special mention. After asking me to don white gloves, they each let me hold their lone copy of the Kilmarnock edition of *Poems, Chiefly in the Scottish Dialect*. Although it betrays me as a bit of a romantic, I have to confess that leafing though those two volumes, which Burns himself may well have handled, set a genuine thrill up my spine. Such, I guess, are the unexpected benefits of archival research.

Thank yous also to Kim Bauer, curator of the Lincoln Collection of the Illinois State Historical Library in Springfield; Wayne Temple, former editor of the *Lincoln Herald*; Jim Patton, chief interpreter at Lincoln's New Salem Village; and the National Park rangers at the Lincoln Home in Springfield, Illinois; Lincoln City, Indiana; and the Lincoln birthplace monument near Hodgenville, Kentucky.

I would also like to credit Patricia Maus, manager/curator of the Manuscripts Collections for the Northeast Minnesota Historical Center, Duluth, and Cindy Van Horn, librarian at the Lincoln Museum Research Library in Fort Wayne, Indiana. As always, the staff at the Library of Congress in Washington, D.C., proved immensely helpful as well. Sharon Karpinski aided my research in the *Scottish American Journal*. Thanks, too, to Helen McIntyre for gifting me her collection of Lincoln books and to Helen M. Connell for giving me her father's extensive collection of Lincoln materials. For their gracious reading of sections of the manuscript, I owe a great deal to Daniel Feller of the University of Tennessee Knoxville, Lucas Morel of Washington and Lee University, Marjory Harper of the University of Aberdeen, Scotland, and Margaret Connell Szasz of the University of New Mexico, Albuquerque. I am, as always, deeply in debt to the superb staff of the Paul A. Zimmerman Library at the University of New Mexico.

My daughters, Maria S. Szasz and especially Chris G. Bradley, helped with both the research and the typing. Kelly Van Andel also assisted with the typing.

Any errors of fact or interpretation, of course, remain my own.

Abraham Lincoln and Robert Burns

Introduction

With the onset of winter 2009, Scotland and the United States will lift the curtain on two major national celebrations. On January 25, 2009, Scots will mark the 250th anniversary of the birth of their famed poet Robert Burns; seventeen days later, on February 12, 2009, Americans will mark the 200th anniversary of the birth of their favorite president, Abraham Lincoln. Although the national planning for these events has been extensive, few on either side of the Atlantic Ocean seem aware of the multifaceted connections between these two historic figures. And that is what this book is about.

As Burns is to Scotland, so is Lincoln to the United States: the ultimate symbol of the nation. As a Scottish commentator recently noted, Burns's classic verses extolling equality and religious tolerance are as germane today as when he first wrote them.[1] Similarly, a spokesperson for the U.S. Bicentennial Commission remarked that Lincoln's goal was not only to save the American Union but also, via the emancipation of the slaves, to make the Union worthy of such saving. If ever a nation could be embodied in a single individual, Burns and Lincoln do precisely that.

In the pages that follow, I link two life stories that most people would not connect in a month of Sundays: Robert Burns (1759–96) and Abraham Lincoln (1809–65). At first glance, this would seem to be a bit of a stretch. Burns gained fame as an eighteenth-century Scottish peasant poet who voiced the aspirations of his embattled underclass and his equally embattled nation, while Lincoln is remembered as the most able person ever to occupy the White House, the man who guided the Union victory over the Confederacy in a bloody and seemingly endless Civil War. The thirteen-year gap between their lives assured that they never could have met. Apples and oranges, one might say; surely chalk and cheese.

The lives and the legends of Burns and Lincoln parallel and intersect one another on a variety of fronts. Both were born into poor farming families that often barely kept the wolf from the door. Both tried a number of professions—including farming and surveying—before finding their callings. Each battled depression on a regular basis and experienced great difficulties in dealing with upper-class women. Although each remained a child of the Enlightenment, with firm faith in the power of reason, each had a strong sense of the supernatural. When a young adult, each agonized over questions of destiny as framed by his respective Reformed faith. Both spoke out briefly for the rights of women. Each became an avid reader and eventually rose to fame through the strength of his personality and the power of his words and deeds. Neither has lacked for detractors, but "the people" elevated each man into a transcendental icon after his tragic death. Indeed, one cannot think of the history of either Scotland or the United States without having Burns or Lincoln flash to mind.

The parallels continue. Each man became victimized by an earlier biographer. Dr. James C. Currie's account of Burns's life (1800) suggested that the poet had turned into a confirmed alcoholic who could never contain his passion for attractive women. In his 1888 biography of Lincoln, William Herndon, his former law partner, suggested that the president's father, Thomas Lincoln, had been a shiftless idler and that Lincoln may have been illegitimate; that Lincoln had fallen madly in love with Ann Rutledge in New Salem, Illinois, had never recovered from her death, and had only tolerated his wife, Mary Todd; and, especially shocking for the time, that he was, at heart, a confirmed Freethinker in religion. These accusations set the terms of scholarly debate for going on a century and a half.

But the parallels between their lives take a backseat to the Lincoln/Burns intersections. These are directly related to the numerous links between Scotland and America, connections that began in the seventeenth century, expanded dramatically in the decades surrounding the American Revolution, and continue to the present day. Although they might share the same island, Scottish and English societies do not share the same cultural norms. In many areas—especially the belief in widespread public education, the popularity of the Reformed tradition of Protestantism, and respect for individual worth rather than inherited social class—the Scots were much closer to the avowed goals of the new American Republic than their southern neighbors. Compare, for example, the sentiments expressed in a popular Church of England hymn,

> The rich man at his castle
> The poor man at his gate
> God made them high and lowly
> And ordered their estate.

with the popular Scots image of the "lad o' pairts," the young man trudging off to the university with a bag of oatmeal and dried herring under his arm to rise as far as his abilities would allow him. Historian Douglas Sloan maintains that unlike the English, the Scots have never feared an educated populace. Thus, Scots were always far more sympathetic to the idea of public-supported education for the ordinary citizen. If the emerging American educational system had British roots, Sloan argues, they trace back to Scotland far more readily than they do to England. Even the alleged "shortcomings" of the Scots and Americans overlapped, for critic Thomas Carlisle once noted how both enjoy "elbowing their way" through the world.[2] Indeed, for many citizens of post-Revolutionary America, Scotland's social goals and America's social goals were viewed as identical.[3]

Consequently, when the poems of Robert Burns reached the shores of the newly created United States in the late 1780s, they became immensely popular. Perhaps due to lack of rivals, Burns took on the role during the early nineteenth century as not only the chief poet of Scotland but also "America's poet" as well. His verses extolling love, drinking, contempt for religious hypocrisy, democracy, and faith in equality seemed to many to voice the goals of the new federal republic. Young Lincoln's discovery of Burns's verses in southern Indiana during the 1820s proved a turning point in his life. He quickly memorized many of the most famous lyrics and throughout his days praised Burns as his favorite poet. Without the impact of Robert Burns and Scotland, Abraham Lincoln would not have emerged as the Lincoln that we now recognize.

Sometime in my early teens, long before I ever dreamed that one could earn a living as a professional historian, I picked up an inexpensive eight-by-ten photograph of Abraham Lincoln and placed it prominently on my desk at home. How I happened upon it I do not now recall, nor do I know its fate after the family house was sold. But the Lincoln image sat in front of me for over five years, a constant reminder of America's most famous citizen.

This reproduction once sparked a comment about the Civil War from my mother, Mary Plummer Szasz (1902–2002), for she well remembered her grandfather John A. Morton, who had served four years in the Union Army. Born in 1836, Morton joined Company H, Fifteenth Illinois Infantry, in 1861, because, as a good Northern Baptist, he felt slavery to be a mortal sin. Captured by Confederates at Acworth, Georgia, on October 4,

1864, he was dispatched to the infamous Andersonville Prison in that state, where he spent the remainder of the conflict. One of his duties there was to bury the Union dead. Grisly though this assignment must have been, it allowed him to leave the premises with regularity, where, family legend has it, he was able to beg, bargain, or steal enough food to allow him to survive. Even so, when he returned to his Midwestern farm, he weighed under ninety pounds; it was years before he could put in a full day's work. As my mother recalled, he never liked to discuss his war experiences.[4]

My interest in Lincoln and the Civil War era was further enhanced by Professor Richard W. Smith at Ohio Wesleyan University in Delaware, Ohio, for Smith's total commitment to the field forever enticed me into the study of history. My graduate-school training at the University of Rochester in New York, however, bent me along a slightly different path, and I concentrated on what was then called American social and intellectual history. Over the years, this emphasis led me into the study of the history of American religion and the early history of the atomic age. But I never completely lost my interest in Lincoln. My first history department chair at the University of New Mexico urged all junior faculty to develop community outreach programs, so I hastily cobbled together a "Myths about Abraham Lincoln" lecture. During my three decades in Albuquerque, I have delivered a version of this talk to scores of service clubs, women's groups, retired teachers' associations, and the like. And each time I drew this assignment, I found an excuse to read one more book on my favorite historical character.

I ran across Robert Burns much later in life. In 1991–92, my wife, Margaret Connell Szasz, a historian, negotiated a teaching exchange with Ted Ranson of the University of Aberdeen, Scotland. Because I was on sabbatical leave, I used the year to explore the excellent holdings of the Queen Mother Library there. This year in Aberdeen—plus an additional three summers when Margaret taught University of New Mexico students in an Aberdeen setting—gradually enticed me into exploring the connections between Scotland and America, which, I discovered, were extensive. It was while doing this research that I stumbled upon Lincoln's fascination with Robert Burns, a fascination, I have to admit, that I soon came to share.

Finally, my interest in these two master wordsmiths must surely be linked to growing up in a multilingual home. My father, Ferenc P. Szasz, an immigrant from Austria, spoke five languages fluently—a talent his son did not inherit—and my mother taught American and British literature on the secondary level throughout the upper Midwest. Thus, many a family discussion dealt with the power of words. No writers had better command of that power than Robert Burns and Abraham Lincoln, whose classic phrases reach across the generations to touch both head and heart. At their best, their words simply cannot be improved upon. In a contemporary world of endless electronic babble, this is a rare gift, indeed.

In the course of my research on this theme, which has now stretched over two decades, almost everyone I asked ranks Burns and Lincoln among the most famous figures of the Western world. Scottish maps label the Ayrshire region as "Burns Country," and heroic statues of the bard dot the High Streets of virtually every Scottish city of any size. Burns's handsome visage has come to symbolize the essence of Scotland.

Similarly, the state of Illinois terms itself "the Land of Lincoln," and his profile appears on millions of license plates. His homely, brooding image graces over fifty U.S. postage stamps, the five-dollar bill, and, after 1909, the lowly penny. Since 1922, the towering figure of a seated Lincoln has gazed across the Washington, D.C., Mall. Daniel Chester French's majestic white-marble statue is the most impressive of the over eighty U.S. Lincoln statues. Except, perhaps, for the White House and the Capitol building, the Lincoln Memorial has become the architectural symbol of the American nation.

Each man changed the world through the power of his words. But Robert Burns wrote only a single book, *Poems, Chiefly in the Scottish Dialect*, 612 copies of which appeared, largely by subscription, from Kilmarnock printer John Wilson in 1786. A second Edinburgh printing followed the next year, a third in 1793, and then the deluge began. By 1898, publishers had brought out 696 editions of his poetry in Great Britain alone.

In addition to *Poems, Chiefly in the Scottish Dialect*, Burns also collected, modified, or wrote approximately three hundred songs for two Edinburgh publishers, James Johnson, *The Scots Musical Museum* (six volumes, 1787–1803), and George Thomson, *A Select Collection of Original Scottish Airs for the Voice* (five volumes, completed 1818). His verses sold so well that during most of the nineteenth century, some critics deemed him more popular than Shakespeare.[5] By 1986, printers had produced about two thousand editions of Burns's poetry and songs, an average of ten a year since the first Kilmarnock edition. His verses have been translated into over fifty languages and are especially popular in contemporary Russia and China. A move is even under way to change the name of the Prestwick airport, south of Glasgow, to Robert Burns International Airport.

Sometime during the early nineteenth century, Burns evolved into legend, the very symbol of Scotland itself. For Scots, both at home and abroad, he represented a variety of shifting positions: vigorous drinker, sexual libertine, critic of religious hypocrisy, admirer of nature, patriotic voice of a "stateless nation," defender of the Lowland Scots' language, rival to Shakespeare (and more beloved as a man), exponent of equality, and romantic exemplar of the enduring power of love.

Burns's message especially resonated in the United States. Over the years, countless American travelers sought out his birthplace in Alloway, Ayrshire, to pay homage. The list of noted Americans who made pilgrimages to the various Burns sites include Andrew Carnegie, Jefferson Davis, Ralph Waldo Emerson, Nathaniel Hawthorne, Robert G. Ingersoll, Helen Keller, Mary Todd Lincoln, and Roy Rogers and Dale Evans, just to name a few. In 1959, a former Burns Cottage curator in Dumfries noted that people of color were especially interested in the poet's message.[6] Perhaps the most poignant story comes from Tom Sutherland, a Colorado State University professor who was temporarily teaching in Lebanon when Islamic militants kidnapped him and held him prisoner for five and a half years (1985–91). Sutherland had memorized numerous Burns lyrics when he was young, and while he was imprisoned, he later wrote, the constant repetition of those poems "occupied *hundreds* of hours and helped keep me sane in that most trying of times."[7]

During the last half of the nineteenth century, the W. and A. Smith Company employed four hundred people—the largest employer in Ayrshire—to produce an endless array of Mauchline Ware, or, as it was later known, Burnsiana: snuffboxes, jugs, plates, wall hangings, engravings, cups, lithographs, tea towels, and the like. Even so, the company could barely satisfy tourist demand. The company has long since closed its doors, but contemporary visitors to Scotland may still purchase similar endless mementoes from an expanded Burns Heritage Trail that now includes not only his Ayrshire birthplace but also his homes in Dumfries and Edinburgh as well.[8] Numerous collections of Burnsian quotations seek to apply his words to the dilemmas of modern life.[9] Robert Burns has become, in a sense, a timeless spokesperson for Scottish social ideals.

The scholarly interest in Burns has grown at a similar pace. From Currie's initial biography, written to provide funds for Burns's widow, Jean, and their children, to the flood of sophisticated analyses surrounding the two-hundredth anniversaries of his birth and death (in 1959 and 1996, respectively), critics and defenders have delved into every aspect of his life. There is an estimate of nine hundred biographies of the man.

Catherine Carswell's pioneering study, *The Life of Robert Burns* (1930), paved the way for a reinvigorated scholarly reappraisal, as seen in the classic accounts by David Daiches, *Robert Burns and His World* (1953/1971), and Thomas Crawford, *Burns: A Study of the Poems and Songs* (1960). In 1985, noted American Burns expert G. Ross Roy of the University of South Carolina produced the standard compilation of the poet's extensive letters. Seven years later, James MacKay of the Burns Federation published a massive, if highly controversial, biographical defense of the man. The annual *Burns Chronicle* (founded 1892) remains devoted to publishing every scrap of information about him.

In 1996, the bicentenary of his death produced a dazzling array of Scottish museum exhibits, speeches, pamphlets, and scholarly reassessments. The best of the list include Alan Bold, *A Burns Companion* (1991); Ian McIntyre, *Robert Burns: A Life* (1995; 2001); Hugh Douglas, *Robert Burns: The Tinder Heart* (1996); Gavin Sprott, *Robert Burns, Pride and Passion: The Life Times and Legacy* (1996); a reissue of Carol McGuirk, *Robert Burns and the Sentimental Era* (1985), and the fine edited works by Robert Crawford and Kenneth Simpson. Literary critic Crawford also places Burns at the center of his *Devolving English Literature* (1992/2000).[10] In *The Canongate Burns* (2001), Andrew Noble and Patrick Scott Hogg added to the accepted canon a number of new poems that, the editors argue, Burns had been forced to publish anonymously for fear of political reprisals.[11] A comprehensive *Burns Encyclopedia*, edited by Maurice Lindsay and now in its third edition, explores every aspect of the poet's brief but productive life. Peter J. Westwood has recently completed a fifteen-volume facsimile compilation of all letters sent to and from Burns. Red Rose provides the latest film version of his life, and Linn Records has made available all 368 Burns songs in a set of twelve compact disks. The proposed "Homecoming Scotland" venture for 2009, by the Scottish Executive, has frankly showcased the Burns story in an appeal to the approximately 10 million people of Scots or Scotch-Irish ancestry in the United States and the 40 million or so worldwide.

Although Scotland's incomparable scenery, famed golf courses, and cultural events all play a role in this campaign, there is general agreement that the bard remains the most-recognized Scot today, a "global cultural icon."[12] Patricia Ferguson, Scotland's tourism and culture minister, once estimated that the Robert Burns "brand" has generated about £160 million for the Scottish economy. Truly Burns ranks among Scotland's "greatest cultural assets."[13]

In short, the world of popular, governmental, and academic Burnsiana is simply overwhelming. The University of Aberdeen Library, for example, lists over 140 books by Burns and over 190 about him; the Edinburgh Central Library contains more than 450 total references. In the 1960s, a bibliographer compiled 1,352 Burnsian listings. Today, the Mitchell Library in Glasgow, which holds the world's largest collection of Burns materials, contains over four thousand items. A 2008 Internet search revealed 1,050,000 hits. In July 2007, Glasgow University opened a new research center for Robert Burns studies. Given this abundance, one can sympathize with the dilemmas of famed Burnsian expert George F. Black of the New York Public Library. In the 1920s, Black attempted to compile the definitive listing of all editions of Burns's works but became so overwhelmed by the variations that he suffered a nervous breakdown and had to abandon the project. If one includes newspaper articles and the countless amateur speeches delivered at the annual Burns's Day Suppers (on every January 25) around the world, it may safely be said that more people have sent forth more words on Robert Burns than on any other writer in the world, including Shakespeare.[14]

The only person to approach Burns in this level of popularity is Abraham Lincoln. Burns wrote only a single volume (plus numerous letters), but Lincoln's literary output proved much more extensive. His written words, now available in a nine-volume collected works, with two supplements, exceed that of the Bible and Shakespeare combined. His biographers have been equally fulsome. The studies range from hastily written campaign accounts to William Herndon's *Life of Lincoln* (1888) to the popular six-volume study by Carl Sandburg in the 1930s to Benjamin P. Thomas's still-classic *Abraham Lincoln* (1952) to a cornucopia of contemporary books.

Given this proliferation, people have wondered for years if anything new remained to be said about either man. Burns's Day speakers voiced this concern as early as the 1820s; Lincoln biographer L. P. Brockett raised it as early as 1865, well before the six men who had known him best—Herndon, Ward Lamon, Isaac N. Arnold, Henry Clay Whitney, and John Hay and John Nicolay—had penned their own accounts. (Hay and Nicolay's study runs to ten volumes.)[15] When journalist Ida Tarbell began her Lincoln research in the 1890s, Nicolay flatly told her that nothing remained to be said. When she interviewed Robert Todd Lincoln, he gave her essen-

8

tially the same advice.[16] All throughout the twentieth century, one finds numerous comments that "the Lincoln theme is complete for our generation." Perhaps the most famous statement in this regard came from noted University of Illinois historian James G. Randall. In 1934, Randall wrote his classic essay "Has the Lincoln Theme Been Exhausted?" Although he concluded, somewhat reluctantly, one suspects, that work remained to be done, the doubting Thomases held sway for years. The Lincoln story, they confidently asserted, had been told for their generation.

Never were such predictions so far off the mark. Because Lincoln lies at the heart of the American experiment, each generation has revisited his career—what he did and what he did not do—in light of the urgent questions of the day. Moreover, the rapid growth of the historical profession plus the active role played by scattered city Lincoln groups, the National Park Service, and various governmental agencies has helped lay the groundwork for this seemingly inexhaustible public interest.

During the grim Cold War years, the world of Lincoln scholarship received a gigantic boost from the national celebrations surrounding the 1959 sesquicentennial of his birth—also, of course, the bicentennial of the birth of Burns. The subsequent centennial commemoration of the Civil War only added to the interest. Given this proliferation, the studies predictably varied in quality. They ranged from Stefan Lorant's superb *Lincoln: A Picture Story of His Life* (revised edition, 1957) to a great deal of popular-magazine rubbish, including some from the pen of respected Civil War expert Bruce Catton. Because the Cold War remained much in evidence, the United States Information Agency commissioned a comic-book biography of Lincoln for distribution overseas. The book described him: "To Americans and to the peoples of many nations, Abraham Lincoln is the beloved symbol of humanity and democracy. His faith in people, in freedom, in the goodness of man is the very core of America's creed. To study the life of Lincoln is to reach out and touch the soul of a nation." The comic book was published in classical Arabic, Hindi, Indonesian, Nepalese, Singhalese, Tamil, Thai, and Vietnamese, among other languages. Although exact numbers are not available, it seems safe to say that the USIA's *Abraham Lincoln* reached millions of readers across the globe.[17]

In spite of the ongoing Civil Rights movement, the tone of the books and articles of the late 1950s and early 1960s remained remarkably neutral. The overall tone of the Civil War centennial literature could well have been borrowed from the pages of St. Louis novelist Winston Churchill's best seller on the war, *The Crisis* (1901). Said Churchill in a "factual afterword" to his work, "There is no side but Abraham Lincoln's side. And this side, with all reverence and patriotism the author has tried to take. Abraham Lincoln loved the South as well as the North."[18]

The decade of the 1990s introduced a revived wave of Lincoln scholarship, similar to the outburst of Burnsian studies in Scotland during the same period. As the 1909 celebration of Lincoln's birth helped produce the Lincoln penny and (eventually) the Lincoln Memorial in Washington, D.C., the current U.S. Bicentenary Commission is considering the following: a redesigned penny and five-dollar bill, various academic conferences, traveling exhibitions, postage stamps, and possibly a rededication of the Lincoln Memorial. The commission has encouraged the American public to participate through an interactive Web site.[19]

The caliber of recent Lincoln books is high. Just a partial list includes Mario Cuomo and Harold Holzer, eds., *Lincoln on Democracy* (1990); Garry Wills, *Lincoln at Gettysburg* (1992); Philip B. Kunhardt Jr., Philip B. Kunhardt III, and Peter W. Kunhardt, *Lincoln: An Illustrated Biography* (1992); Mark E. Neely Jr., *The Last Best Hope of Earth* (1993); Michael Burlingame, *The Inner World of Abraham Lincoln* (1994); Merrill D. Peterson, *Lincoln in American Memory* (1994); Philip Shaw Paludan, *The Presidency of Abraham Lincoln* (1994); Wayne C. Temple, *Abraham Lincoln: From Skeptic to Prophet* (1995); David Herbert Donald, *Lincoln* (1995); Allen C. Guelzo, *Abraham Lincoln: Redeemer President* (1999); and Kenneth J. Winkle, *The Young Eagle: The Rise of Abraham Lincoln* (2001).

The first years of the new century have even accelerated the trend: Gabor S. Boritt, *The Lincoln Enigma* (2001); William Lee Miller, *Lincoln's Virtues: An Ethical Biography* (2002); David Herbert Donald, *"We Are Lincoln Men": Abraham Lincoln and His Friends* (2003); Jennifer Fleischner, *Mrs. Lincoln and Mrs. Keckly: The Remarkable Story of the Friendship between a First Lady and a Former Slave* (2003); Thomas Keneally, *Abraham Lincoln* (2003); Matthew Pinsker, *Lincoln's Sanctuary: Abraham Lincoln and the Soldiers' Home* (2003); Daniel Mark Epstein, *Lincoln and Whitman: Parallel Lives in Civil War Washington* (2004); Allen C. Guelzo, *Lincoln's Emancipation Proclamation: The End of Slavery in America* (2004); Harold Holzer, *Lincoln at Cooper Union: The Speech That Made Abraham Lincoln President* (2004); Geoffrey Perret, *Lincoln's War: The Untold Story of America's Greatest President as Commander in Chief* (2004); C. A. Tripp, *The Intimate World of Abraham Lincoln* (2005); John Channing Briggs, *Lincoln's Speeches Reconsidered* (2005); Joshua Wolf Shenk, *Lincoln's Melancholy* (2005); Doris Kearns Goodwin's prize-winning *Team of Rivals* (2005);

Richard J. Carwadine, *Lincoln* (2003); Richard Striner, *Father Abraham: Lincoln's Relentless Struggle to End Slavery* (2006); Gabor Boritt, *The Gettysburg Gospel: The Lincoln Speech That Nobody Knows* (2006); Douglas L. Wilson, *Lincoln's Sword: The Presidency and the Power of Words* (2006); and Andrew Ferguson, *Land of Lincoln: Adventures in Abe's America* (2007). The list could easily be extended.

As of 2008, the Library of Congress housed over four thousand entries on Lincoln. Rhode Island Chief Justice Frank J. Williams is compiling a bibliography of Lincolniana that exceeds sixteen thousand entries, with more added each year. What the two hundredth anniversary of Lincoln's birth year will produce is anyone's guess.

Paralleling the *Burns Chronicle*, three periodicals, the *Journal of the Abraham Lincoln Association*, *Lincoln Herald*, and *Lincoln Lore*, seek out all the nooks and crannies of his life. A marvelous *Lincoln Log: A Daily Chronology of the Life of Abraham Lincoln*—now available online[20]—allow us to follow his activities in greater detail than any other American president, including such modern figures as Ronald Reagan, William Jefferson Clinton, or George W. Bush. The popular compilations *Lincoln on Leadership* (1992), *The Words Lincoln Lived By* (1997), and *Bite-sized Lincoln* (1998) apply his observations to contemporary dilemmas. In the latest example of this genre, *Why Lincoln Matters* (2004), former New York state governor Mario M. Cuomo creates a speech that Lincoln might have delivered to the 2004 Congress. Like the various compilations of Burns's observations, Lincoln's words have taken on a timeless quality. Liz Dulaney, long-term University of Illinois Press editor, once observed, "There can't be too many books on Abraham Lincoln." Taking her comment to heart, in the following chapters, I hope to explore an aspect of Lincoln's life that few have examined before—his fascination with the words of Robert Burns, his interaction with the important Scots and Scottish émigrés of his day, and the forgotten overlap between their emerging national mythologies.

Because most contemporary Americans are likely to be somewhat hazy on Burns's life, chapter 1 briefly sketches out the career of Scotland's most famous poet. Chapter 2 examines the role that his songs and verse played in early America, and I argue that while his poems became incredibly popular with ordinary citizens, for a number of writers he became virtually a "category of thought." The culmination of this popular sentiment occurred in the winter of 1859, when over sixty American cities on January 25 formally celebrated the centenary of his birth. Springfield,

Illinois, joined in the festivities, and Lincoln gave a brief speech there. This nationwide festival provided the last gasp of national unity in the United States for over half a century. In chapter 3, I show how Lincoln first met Burns's lyrics and, perhaps more speculatively, suggest how they might have influenced his views of society. Lincoln's early fascination with satire, his skepticism of organized Christianity, and his basic sense of equality, I argue, very likely had Burnsian roots. Chapter 4 examines the impact that six of Burns's fellow Scots had on Lincoln, from poet William Knox to Presbyterian pastor James Smith to detective Allan Pinkerton, among others. I discuss how William Knox's rather pedestrian verse helped shape much of Lincoln's early attempts at poetry. I also suggest that the American version of the primarily Scottish idea of a "covenanted nation" probably lay behind Lincoln's requests for national Fast Days and Days of Thanksgiving during the war years.

The final chapter discusses the overlap between the respective legends of Burns and Lincoln. After their deaths, each man evolved into myth through similar means: pilgrimages to their birthplaces and tombs, the erection of heroic statues, the delivery of countless speeches, and the annual celebration of their birthdays. Equally important, until after the Second World War, many observers considered American and Scottish social goals as virtually "interchangeable." Thus, it is no surprise that in 1893, Scotland erected the first heroic statue to Lincoln outside of the United States or that about twelve American cities similarly established heroic statues to Robert Burns. To honor one was, it seems, to honor the other as well. Many of Lincoln's early biographers readily acknowledged this overlap, but the connection began to disappear during the early 1930s. By this time, widespread appreciation of Burns's poetry had begun to fade from American public memory. Instead, it became largely restricted to the Scottish-American community. Today, the average American citizen would be hard pressed to identify any of Burns's verses, a far cry from the situation of, say, 1859. The epilogue explores the dilemmas of democratic fame, and I suggest that the numerous contradictions embodied in the lives of Burns and Lincoln have enabled Scots and Americans of each succeeding generation to search their words for answers to the problems of the present day. One was a poet whose message was laced with politics, and the other a politician whose message was laced with poetry. In a sense, both Burns and Lincoln have become timeless spokespersons for social goals that their societies, at least in their better moments, have long sought to realize.[21]

1
Robert Burns: A Brief Biography

In the early nineteenth century, so the story goes, a blue-ribbon Edinburgh committee planned to erect a memorial to Robert Burns. So, they sought out Sir Walter Scott's advice on the best inscription. Said Scott, "Simply place on the monument, 'Burns.' Who does not know the rest?"[1]

Although Scott's observation has held for over two centuries in Scotland, as well as in much of the former British Empire, Burns's reputation has faded considerably in the United States. Most Americans today are not half as familiar with Scotland's greatest poet as their great-grandparents would have been. From 1908 to 1909, when Harvard President Charles Eliot compiled his famed fifty-volume *Harvard Classics*—the books a person needed to master to become "educated"—he devoted an entire volume to Burns. Contemporary Americans, on the other hand, might recognize an odd Burnsian phrase but likely would be hard pressed to identify the source. When I spoke to a junior colleague (sporting a fresh Ph.D. from an Ivy League university) about this project, he confessed that he had never heard of Robert Burns. Thus, it is probably best to start with a brief sketch of his life, and there is no better place to begin than with the words of Burns himself.

In August 1787, shortly after his first visit to Edinburgh, Robert Burns wrote a letter to John Moore, a distinguished London physician and author, in response to Moore's praise of his verse. This lengthy missive provides our chief understanding of Burns's early life. A relevant section follows.

Mauchline, 2nd August 1787
Sir
. . . I have not the most distant pretensions to what the pyecoated guardians of escutcheons call, A Gentleman.—When at Edinburgh last winter, I got acquainted in the Herald's Office, and looking through that granary of Honors I there found every name in the kingdom; but for me,

"—My ancient but ignoble blood
Has crept thro' Scoundrels ever since the flood"—

. . . Irascibility are disqualifying circumstances: consequently I
was born a very poor man's son.—For the first six or seven years of
my life, my father was gardener to a worthy gentleman of small estate in the neighbourhood of Ayr.

Had my father continued in that situation, I must have marched
off to be one of the little underlings about a farm-house; but it was
his dearest wish and prayer to have it in his power to keep his children under his own eye till they could discern between good and
evil; so with the assistance of his generous Master my father ventured
on a small farm in his estate.

. . . —In my infant and boyish days too, I owed much to an old
maid of my Mother's, remarkable for her ignorance, credulity and
superstition.—She had, I suppose, the largest collection in the
county of tales and songs concerning devils, ghosts, fairies, brownies,
witches, warlocks, spunkies, kelpies, elf candles, dead-lights, wraiths,
apparitions, cantraips, giants, inchanted towers, dragons and other
trumpery.—This cultivated the latent seeds of Poesy; but had so
strong an effect on my imagination, that to this hour, in my noctur-
nal rambles, I sometimes keep a sharp look-out in suspicious places;
and though nobody can be more skeptical in these matters than I.

. . . This kind of life, the cheerless gloom of a hermit with the un-
ceasing moil of a galley-slave, brought me to my sixteenth year; a little before which period I first committed the sin of RHYME.—You
know our country custom of coupling a man and woman together
as Partners in the labors of Harvest.—In my fifteenth autumn, my
Partner was a bewitching creature who just counted an autumn less.

. . . Thus with me began Love and Poesy; which at times have been
my only, and till within this last twelvemonth have been my highest
enjoyment.—My father struggled on till he reached the freedom in
his lease, when he entered on a larger farm about ten miles farther in
the country.—The nature of the bargain was such as to throw a little
ready money in his hand at the commencement, otherwise the affair
would have been impractible.—for four years we lived comfortably
here; but a lawsuit between him and his Landlord commencing,
after three years tossing and whirling in the vortex of Litigation, my
father was just saved from absorption in a jail by physical consump-
tion, which after two years promises, kindly stept in and snatch'd
him away—"To where the wicked cease from troubling, and where
the weary be at rest."—

. . . I threw off six hundred copies [of *Poems, Chiefly in the Scottish Dialect*], of which I had got subscriptions for about three hundred and fifty.—My vanity was highly gratified by the reception I met with from the Publick; besides pocketing, all expences deducted, near twenty pounds.—This last came very seasonable, as I was about to indent myself for want of money to pay my freight.—So soon as I was master of nine guineas, the price of wafting me to the torrid zone, I bespoke a passage in the very first ship that as to sail, for

"Hungry ruin had me in the wind"

. . . I need relate no farther.—At Edinburgh I was in a new world: I mingled among many classes of men, but all of them new to me; and I was all attention "to catch the manners living as they rise."—[2]

Robert Burns was born on January 25, 1759, about two miles south of the Scottish town of Ayr in a clay cottage that his father had built with his own hands. About two weeks later, a fierce storm blew the roof off, and all had to flee to a neighbor's house until it could be repaired. Burns's birth occurred only thirteen years after the infamous battle of Culloden, where the Hanoverian army under the Duke of Cumberland destroyed the rival Stewart's hopes of reclaiming the British crown, as well as shattering the power of the Highland clans. As a Lowland Scot, Burns never fully shared either the Gaelic language or the Highland culture, although he later displayed a romantic Jacobite sentiment that was vaguely linked with his father's family home in Kincardineshire. What Burns did share with the Highland clans that went "out" in the Jacobite rising of 1745, however, was a distinct sense of a Scottish identity. Whether Lowland or Highland, eighteenth-century Scots were conscious that they occupied the unique role of a "nation-within-a-nation" in Great Britain. The Scotland of Burns's youth boasted its own legal and education systems as well as its own established Presbyterian church, even as it functioned as an integral part of Britain and the Empire, which were headquartered in London.

Burns's first language was Scots—a linguistic cousin of English—both of which had evolved from Middle English. Scots words, phrases, and intonations borrowed heavily from the Scandinavian, French, and Dutch, for Scottish ships could reach those foreign lands far more easily than an Edinburgh coach could travel to far-off London. The Scots language had once held its own on a rough par with English, but it had begun by the early eighteenth century to lose its centrality and to splinter into dozens of regional dialects.[3] The reason was straightforward: English had slowly but steadily emerged as the lingua franca of commerce, religion, and politics. The most popular translation of scriptures, the Authorized or King James Version (1611), had triumphed as the Bible most used in Scotland,[4] and ever since the Union of the Parliaments in 1707, the handful of Scottish members of Parliament all traveled to Westminster for vital political discussions. With these influences, English gradually began to supersede Scots as the language of the upper and middle classes. Edinburgh's Lord Braxfield (1722–99) has gained fame as the last Scottish judge to speak Scots during the trials held in his court. But, the Scots tongue remained very much alive among the peasants of the countryside, and every region, sometimes every village, boasted a distinct accent.

It was within this world that Robert Burns grew to maturity, the firstborn son of William Burness and Agnes Broun. (The name was initially pronounced "Bur*ness*," and the *e* was dropped only with William's death in 1784.) As farmer/gardener to Ferguson of Doonholm, William displayed a thorough knowledge of agriculture. He may have introduced several plants to Ayrshire: basil, carrots, cauliflower, leeks, marjoram, onions, parsnips, spinach, and turnips, which were added to everyone's basic garden of cabbage or kale.[5] Still, William's market garden business never succeeded financially; neither did the various Burns farms. "We lived," Robert remarked, "very poorly."[6]

In spite of the poverty, William Burness insisted that Robert and his siblings all be educated. When Robert was six, he attended a small school at Alloway Mill. Shortly afterwards, William joined with four neighbors to engage John Murdoch to establish another small school, which Robert and his younger brother Gilbert both attended. After two and a half years, the family moved to a new farm at Mount Oliphant, where the boys were taught by William himself. In all, Robert Burns had three short periods of formal study—perhaps a little over three years' worth of grammar, theology, Alexander Pope and Henry Bolingbroke, some Latin, and a bit of French. The fundamental teaching tools always remained the Hebrew Bible and the New Testament, from which he quoted throughout his life. Indeed, his voluminous letters are replete with biblical phrases.[7]

Burns harvested oats when he was thirteen and at fifteen served as his father's chief farm worker. But he also tried his hand at other professions. In 1781, he moved to Irvine, on the coast, to master the trade of flax dressing (preparing flax for spinning into linen) and also briefly studied surveying. Gifted with a sense of destiny, he seems to have suffered from periodic depression as he searched for a vocation worthy of his talents. In 1782 he returned to his father's farm in Lochlie to assist in facing severe financial problems concerning arrears in rent; two years later, after his father's death, the family moved to Mossgiel, Mauchline. He stood about five feet ten and had a slight stoop. As the numerous portraits show, he was very handsome with dark eyes and a high forehead.

Ever ambitious, the young Burns constantly tried to improve himself. He was an avid reader—contemporaries often found him with his nose in a book—even while walking or at table, and he helped to organize two young men's debating societies. The first was the Tarbolton Bachelors' Club, which was limited to sixteen men, all of whom had to be "a professed lover of one or more of the female sex." When farming at Mauchline, he joined a young men's society to debate the issues of the day and (surely) to pursue the "belles of Mauchline."[8]

Although he started rhyming at age fifteen, he did not begin to pen serious poetry until 1784 while he and his brother Gilbert farmed at Mossgiel. The initial impetus came not from love or democracy but from a quarrel among factions in his local Presbyterian kirk (church). As one contemporary wryly observed, "Every Scotch peasant who makes any pretension to understanding is a theological critic."[9] Indeed, Burns's intellectual world was dominated by the established Kirk of Scotland. From 1707 to 1999, Scotland was without a national parliament. Thus, the endless quarrels and controversies of the established Kirk in a sense reflected the divisions of social class, philosophy, and region that might well have been political had the parliament remained in Edinburgh. The Kirk had its hands full. In spite of strenuous effort, the clerics had never been able to quash the omnipresent pagan past of witches, warlocks, kelpies, and second sight that lurked just below the Christian surface. As his letter to Dr. Moore showed, Burns learned of this world first hand from his mother's relative Betty Davidson, but he must have bumped into it through hundreds of local songs, stories, and place names as well.

The Presbyterian Kirk had even greater difficulties in controlling the sexual mores of a peasant society that revolved around breeding cattle and sheep and where the houses were so compact that the men and women lived in one another's laps. Managing fornication and illegitimacy proved especially challenging. Ever resourceful, the Presbyterian leaders devised numerous public rituals to allow the offenders to acknowledge their errant ways, be forgiven, and return to the church fold. Proper public confession of sins, followed by some form of humiliation in front of the congregation, meant a full restoration to fellowship. In many cases, because the Kirk had a legal dimension to it as well, the decision also involved the law. Still, if the Burns case is in any way representative, such procedures did little to alter sexual behavior.

Intense theological discussion proved much a part of Burns's youth, for the Ayrshire church of his day had divided along New Licht versus Auld Licht factions regarding Calvinist theology and acceptable behavior. Burns's family belonged to the liberal, or New Licht, group, but the Mauchline pastor William "Daddy" Auld, abetted by the infamous hypocrite William Fisher, held to the stricter perspective. In one quarrel, Burns's friend Gavin Hamilton found himself accused of breaking the Sabbath—allegedly by asking his servant to pull potatoes on Sunday—and Burns entered the theological fray by writing the satirical "Holy Willie's Prayer." This witty attack on William Fisher, one of Hamilton's overly pious accusers, passed from hand to hand in manuscript form amidst howls of glee. Even after two centuries, critics still rank it as one of the most devastating satires on record. Verse seven:

> O Lord! yestreen, Thou kens, wi' Meg—
> Thy pardon I sincerely beg,
> O! may't ne'er be a living plague,
> To my dishonour!
> And I'll ne'er lift a lawless leg
> Again upon her.

In other verses, Burns poked fun at revivals in "The Holy Fair" and at the Presbyterian clerics themselves in "Twa Herds." The local kirk session held several meetings to discuss these poems.[10] So popular were the poems that Hamilton advised Burns to seek publication by subscription, and Burns found a Kilmarnock printer, John Wilson, willing to do so.

All of this coincided with the first of what would prove to be a rather long list of awkward entanglements with women. Burns later admitted to fathering nine illegitimate children by several women, although the two sets of twins borne by Jean Armour were not technically so. Still, he had already fathered a child by Elizabeth Paton, which produced the tender poem "A Poet's Welcome to His Love-Begotten Daughter," and he now learned that his "Bonnie Jean" was expecting.

When Jean's father, Master Mason James Armour, an Auld Licht of Mauchline, first discovered the situation, he fainted. Scots law of the day allowed for various forms of unorthodox marriage, and Burns had given

Jean a private, written document to that effect, which, in the eyes of the law, made their marriage legal. Her father, however, had Robert's and Jean's names excised from the paper and forced Jean to cease all contact with a man he considered an irresponsible idler and first-rate troublemaker. Then he set the law after him for child support.

Wounded to the quick, Burns rebounded into the arms of a farm servant, Mary Campbell—Highland Mary—and the couple exchanged promises to marry. He gave her a Bible to pledge his troth and she the same, and they laid plans to emigrate to Jamaica, where Burns planned to serve as a bookkeeper on an estate. Had they actually done so, it is quite possible that Robert and Mary might eventually have emigrated to the United States.[11] But then fate entered in. Mary died suddenly in Greenock, Scotland, either from taking care of her brother, who had typhus, or from bearing Burns's son, who died shortly thereafter, probably the latter.[12]

To considerable acclaim, 612 copies of *Poems, Chiefly in the Scottish Dialect* appeared in July 1786, and this success began the slow process of reconciliation with Jean's parents. In addition, the popularity of *Poems* brought Burns to the attention of the Scottish literati in Edinburgh. Drawing on the prevailing eighteenth-century concept of the "noble savage," they began to lionize Burns as "the heaven-taught plowman" or "Caledonia's Bard." As Burns later wrote of this period, he could never have known "all the powerful circumstances that omnipotent necessity was busy laying in wait for him."[13]

After an expanded 1787 Edinburgh edition of *Poems* appeared, with a print run of 2,800, the Burns name became a household word among Edinburgh upper-class Scots. They sought him out for an extended round of dinner engagements, where he met many of the major figures of the Scottish Enlightenment. The Edinburgh literati of the Athens of the North were delighted with the peasant poet from Ayrshire. At last, they had found the long-lost voice of Scottish cultural nationalism.

The social gap between the Ayrshire peasantry and the drawing-room culture of Enlightenment Edinburgh proved cavernous. The first portrait of Burns, painted by Peter Taylor in 1786, reveals a moderately well-dressed farmer sporting a decidedly bewildered look.[14] Thus, it should not be surprising that Burns made some social blunders. The problem usually revolved around attractive women. As biographer James C. Currie phrased it, "In the gamester's phrase, he did not always know when to play off and when to play on."[15] Still, by most accounts, Burns generally carried himself well in these elevated circumstances. He dressed neatly and plainly and, aided by his valuable Masonic connections, dazzled Edinburgh society with the power of his verse and the brilliance of his conversation. Virtually all who met him marveled at his charm of manner. An aristocratic woman of Edinburgh confessed that she had never met a man "whose conversation so completely carried her off her feet."[16] A later observer noted that when "kindled up in conversation, his countenance assumed a very pleasing aspect, and his manner was altogether irresistible."[17] Maria Riddell, who had known him well, said in the *Edinburgh Courant* shortly after his death, "*None* certainly ever outshone Burns in the charms—the *sorcery* I would almost call it, of fascinating conversation, the spontaneous eloquence of social argument, or the unstudied poignancy of brilliant repartee."[18]

The second edition of *Poems* came from the press of well-known Edinburgh publisher William Creech, and it made Burns a moderately wealthy man. He used the profits for both editions, plus the sale of the copyright, to make an extensive tour of the Lowlands and then another of the Highlands, to wrangle the lease of a farm at Ellisland, about six miles above the port of Dumfries, and later to accept a government job as an excise man, a "gauger." After a passionate, if platonic, relationship with the middle-class "Clarinda" (Agnes McLehose) in Edinburgh, Burns officially married Jean Armour, who was again pregnant, having lost her first set of twins.[19] The couple returned to Ellisland to farm but soon moved to Dumfries, where Burns devoted his attention to the excise duties.

Although Burns wrote relatively few poems after his Edinburgh years, in 1791 he penned—in a single day—his masterpiece, "Tam O' Shanter," at his farm in Ellisland. A number of phrases from this classic—which many Scottish schoolchildren memorized by heart—have entered common parlance.

> Whare sits our sulky, sullen dame,
> Gathering her brows like gathering storm,
> Nursing her wrath to keep it warm.

or

> Nae man can tether Time nor Tide,
> The hour approaches Tam maun ride;

But if Burns wrote relatively few verses after 1787, his creativity remained undiminished as he devoted most of the rest of his life to collecting the poetry of ordinary Scots, to which he added or modified (sometimes both) a number of lines. It took a poet's sensibility, as well as a deep knowledge of the folk tradition, to recast these ancient songs. Sometimes he had only a chorus or a half-remembered set of lines to work with. In 1787, he wrote to Reverend John Skinner that he found "a wild happiness of thought and expression" in the old Scots songs that marked them as vastly different from similar English verses.[20] As he later confessed to his friend James Candlish, "I have collected, begged, borrowed, and stolen all the songs I could meet with."[21] Burns has been credited with compiling, writing, and/or improvising nearly four hundred Scots songs, producing during a nine-year period what one scholar has termed an incredible collection of "tone poetry."[22] In essence, he condensed much of Scotland's rich folk wisdom into song.

When most people think of Burns's works, they rarely distinguish between his original compositions such as "The Cotter's Saturday Night," "Holy Willie's Prayer," "Twa Dogs," and "Tam O' Shanter" and the reworked folk songs such as "Green Grow the Rashes, O," "My Heart's in the Highlands," "The Birks O' Aberfeldy," and "Comin' thro the Rye." Moreover, a number of his poems—"Scots Wha Hae," "A Man's a Man for a' That," and "Ae Fond Kiss," just to name a few—were soon matched with traditional Scottish tunes, which propelled them even further into the popular mind.

In many cases, Burns took the bawdy lyrics of the original verses, deeply rooted in a Scottish peasant world as they were, and "softened" them. By so doing, he steered these ribald Scots lyrics from the pubs and alehouses into parlors and mixed company. In essence, he universalized them. Some examples: the current version of "Green Grow the Rashes, O" contains the verse "The sweetest hours that ere I spent/Were spent among the lasses, O." One original read, "A feather bed is no sae saft/As the bosoms o' the lassies, O."

Similarly, the classic old-woman's love song to her husband of many years, "John Anderson, My Jo," now reads:

> John Anderson my jo, John,
> When we were first acquent
> Your locks were like the raven,
> Your bonie brow was brent;
> But now your brow is beld, John,
> Your locks are like the snaw;
> But blessings on your frosty pow,
> John Anderson my jo.

John Anderson my jo, John,
We clamb the hill thegither;
And monie a cantie day, John,
We've had wi' ane anither:
Now we maun totter down, John,
And hand in hand we'll go:
And sleep thegither at the foot,
John Anderson my jo.

Gone is the original line that complained of Mr. Anderson's declining sexual prowess. Finally, the central verb *kiss* in

Gin a body meet a body
Comin' thro' the rye
Gin a body kiss a body
Need a body cry?

was initially a good deal stronger. But the tradition of Scots Bawdy did not completely die. Burns compiled a collection of these earthy songs that later broke into print under the title of *The Merry Muses of Caledonia* (1811).[23]

Both in song and verse, Burns drew from the Scots idiom to touch the very core of human existence. He sympathized with all of nature, especially with the daisy that he accidentally cut down in the field and with the mouse whose nest he upturned with his plow. In "To a Mountain Daisy on Turning One Down with the Plough in April 1786," he wrote:

Wee, modest, crimson-tipped flow'r,
Thou's met me in an evil hour;
For I maun crush among the stourie
Thy slender stem:
To spare thee is now past my power,
Thou bonny gem.

Although written in Scots Doric, most English readers could comprehend his verse with minimal difficulty.[24]

Burns especially loved "the art of loving," and many of his classic poems deal with romance, final farewells, or tragic losses. Among his most widely recognized love songs is:

O, my luve's like a red, red rose,
That's newly sprung in June.
O, my luve's like the melodie,
That's sweetly play'd in tune.

When he bid farewell to his beloved Clarinda (Agnes McLehose), he wrote:

Ae fond kiss, and then we sever!
Ae farewell, and then forever!
Deep in heart-wrung tears, I'll pledge thee
Warring sighs and groans I'll wage thee.

The words of "Mary Morison" (perhaps a lament to his lost Highland Mary) reflect a poignant longing for one who is no longer here.

Tho this [woman] was fair,
And that was braw [fine]
And yon the toast of the town,
I sigh'd and said amang them a':
'Ye are na Mary Morison!'[25]

Burns's skill with words captured the heart of the Scottish imagination and a number of his phrases turned into instant proverbs.

O wad some Power the giftie gie us
to see oursel as ithers see us;

Facts are chiels that winna ding
And downa be disputed;

The heart's ay the part ay
That makes us right or wrang;
Man's inhumanity to man makes countless thousands mourn.

And the poignant.

The best-laid plans o' mice an' men
Gang aft agley

Burns's "Selkirk Grace," dashed off in a moment to Lord Selkirk, has also become a classic.

Some hae meat
An canna eat
And some wad eat
That want it;
But we hae meat
And we can eat
Sae let the Lord
Be thankit.

His "Scots, Wha Hae," set to the tune "Hey, Tutti Taitie," which Scottish soldiers allegedly marched to when they faced the English at the Battle of Bannockburn in 1314, has evolved into the symbol of Scottish military commitment:

> Scots, wha hae
> Wi Wallace bled,
> Scots, wham Bruce has aften led,
> Welcome to your gory bed
> Or to victorie!
> Now's the day,
> And now's the hour;
> See the front o' battle lour,
> See approach proud Edward's power
> Chains and slaverie!

Then of course came "Auld Lang Syne" (Old Times Past), perhaps the most recognized of all his songs. Here one sees his genius at work. The original, which dated from the seventeenth century, was decidedly stodgy.

> Should old acquaintance be forgot,
> And never thought upon,
> The flames of love extinguished,
> And freely past and gone?
> Is thy kind heart now grown so cold
> In that loving breast of thine,
> That thou canst never once reflect
> On old-lang-syne.

Burns reworked these words into the popular contemporary rendition. Now belted out all over the world every New Year's Eve, "Auld Lang Syne" vies with "Happy Birthday" as the most widely sung song on the planet.

> For auld lang syne, my dear
> for auld lang syne,
> We'll tak a cup o' kindness yet
> For auld lang syne.

This song has been described as "the world's doxology."[26]

From 1786 to 1787, Burns emerged as *the* poet of eighteenth-century Scottish cultural nationalism. Said an early biographer, J. G. Lockhart, the son-in-law of Sir Walter Scott, "On one point there can be no controversy: the poetry of Burns has had the most powerful influence in reviving and strengthening the national feelings of his countrymen."[27] But Burns's nationalism reflected as much of the Scottish past as it did the Scottish present. As a youth, he read Blind Harry's *A Life of Wallace*, the first Scottish hero, and biographer Catherine Carswell believed that this book inspired him to cast his life in the same heroic mode.[28] Certainly, he knew well where he fit in the historic Scottish bardic tradition. When he first visited Edinburgh, he helped erect a plaque in the Canongate Churchyard over the grave of Scottish poet Robert Fergusson. When he visited the tomb of Robert the Bruce in Dunfermline, he bent over to kiss the stone. He visited England only twice and then but briefly, kissing the soil of Scotland upon his return.

Burns could serve as the voice of historic Scottish nationalism with relative impunity. But when it came to voicing his views on contemporary political issues, such as republicanism and social equality, he had to tread more cautiously. While in Edinburgh, he bitterly chafed at the condescension he received from "Squire Something" and "Sir Somebody." Like many youth of his day, he became enthralled by the success of the American Revolution. In 1784, he penned a satirical ballad that lampooned the blunders of the British military leaders in the war with the American Colonies, which had now won their independence.[29] In addition, he gave public toasts to George Washington, composed an "Ode to General Washington's Birthday," and wrote an antislavery poem, "The Slave's Lament." The promises of the early years of the French Revolution fascinated him, too. He read Thomas Paine's *Rights of Man* with enthusiasm and in 1793, while riding through a storm in the wilds of Kenmore, created his stirring "Scots, Wha Hae." Perhaps his most famous lines were written in January 1795, "Is There for Honest Poverty" (and soon put to the tune "For a' That").

> For a' that, an' a' that!
> It's comin' yet for a' that,
> That man to man the world o'er
> Shall brithers be for a' that.

These lines reveal his commitment to republican equality, but because of his government job as an excise man, as well as the prevailing conservatism of the Dumfries area, he cast his message in universal rather than in local, specific terms.[30]

Even so, he almost lost his livelihood. Three years previously, in October 1792, he joined in singing the chorus to the radical French anthem

"Ça Ira." An informer (probably) turned him in to authorities, and he barely survived the investigation. (He may or may not have purchased four cannonades from a captured smuggler's ship to send as a present to the French Assembly in 1793.) When rumors spread of a possible French invasion of the British Isles, he wrapped himself in the flag to pen "Does Haughty Gaul Invasion Threat?" He also joined the Dumfries militia, which helped restore his reputation with the authorities. Because of this local tension, however, all his statements regarding equality and democracy remained "coded."

In spite of or perhaps because of his fame, Robert Burns did not live a long life. When he fell desperately ill in the spring of 1796, his friends in Dumfries worried aloud, "Who do you think will be our poet now?" Burns died of endocarditis caused by rheumatism on July 21, 1796, probably as a combination of overwork and overconsumption of alcohol. He was only thirty-seven.[31]

His death left his wife and four children in dire straits, and under the urging of local citizenry, Liverpool physician James C. Currie collected his poems and letters and added a brief biographical sketch. Published in four slim volumes in 1800, the book went through four editions in four years and raised enough to provide the family with a modest income. Because Currie had lived in Virginia for about five years as an employee of a Glasgow-based tobacco firm, he was undoubtedly aware of potential book sales among American Scottish émigrés. Although a loyal Scot who greatly admired Burns's lyrics, former alcoholic Currie was also a strong advocate of temperance. Moreover, he had met Burns on only one occasion. Thus, the most important early biography of the man who would eventually become the representative figure of Scotland made no attempts to hide his faults. Currie stressed Burns's melancholy, his inability to control his passions for women and alcohol, and his inability to save himself from ruin: "He saw his danger, and at times formed resolutions to guard against; but he had embarked on the tide of dissipation, and was borne along its stream."[32]

Over the years, a number of critics proved eager to join the chorus. Not surprisingly, those who had been wounded by his biting satire were pleased to return the favor. "Holy Willie" Fisher's response has not survived but Reverend William Peebles, whom Burns satirized in several poems, denounced the Greenock Burns Club in 1811, "What call you this? Is it Insomnia? / I'll coin a word, 'tis Burnomania."[33]

Although Burns retained a few clerical supporters, most of the so-called "Black Legion" of Church of Scotland clerics mounted a steady stream of criticism against him for the next century and a half. Perhaps the apex came in 1847, when a Presbyterian cleric depicted Burns's last days: "His eloquence, once so pure, even its wildness and mirth, was now a hideous compost of filth and fire. Death never did a more merciful act when he closed the most lying lips that ever spake in Scotland—the lips of Robert Burns."[34] Scotland's divines argued that their nation should never make a national icon out of a theological heretic, alcoholic, and sexual libertine.

But the clerical response proved to be a minority report. Although Burns's early biographers all noted his faults, they placed far more emphasis on his "natural genius." Said Robert Heron in 1797, Burns had a "wonderful power to transport every imagination, and to agitate every heart."[35] Similarly, J. G. Lockhart noted that by the poet's capacity to influence the minds of men and women and, thus, their conduct, Burns had a greater influence on humanity than any contemporary statesman. Inexpensive chapbooks, intended primarily for the working class, made his verses available to the peasantry.[36] It was not long before virtually every Scottish home, from castle to hovel, acquired its prized copy of Burns verse, often placed next to the Bible as the two chief books of the household. Perhaps part of his appeal lay with the fact that he contained within himself a jumble of contradictions: Burns was (simultaneously) political radical, democratic wordsmith, prolific song maker,   Scottish cultural nationalist, and libertine, rake, and heretic.

Whatever one thought of the man himself, his words soon became common property. The many editions of *Poems, Chiefly in the Scottish Dialect*, plus the songs he contributed to James Johnson's six-volume collection and George Thomson's five-volume compilation, all coincided with the great Scottish Diaspora. From the late eighteenth century forward, thousands of Scottish émigrés sought economic betterment in the United States, Canada, and later in Australia and New Zealand. Countless more were driven away by the infamous Highland clearances of the same era. As men and women readied their trunks for the long sea voyages, they packed Burns's songs, in books and in memories, and it was not long before the power of his words began to spread around the globe. His earnest supporters soon labeled the Ayrshire ploughman as the greatest lyric writer of his day. Some have even argued that the worldwide popularity of Scottish song is simply "the lengthened shadow of Robert Burns." In essence, the best of Burns's lyrics embodied both a "portable Scotland" as well as a broader paean to the themes of love, equality, and democracy. And they would have an enormous impact on the fledgling republic of the United States of America.

2

Burns's Poetry Comes to America

Robert Burns wrote from the heart of an eighteenth-century Scottish culture poised to send its citizens to the four corners of the globe. Many, of course, landed in the new American nation. By the 1780s, New York City and Philadelphia already contained active Scottish émigré communities that kept abreast of the Scottish literary scene. American booksellers advertised *Poems, Chiefly in the Scottish Dialect* within weeks of the publication of the 1787 Edinburgh edition. Although the Philadelphia newspaper *Pennsylvania Packet* printed a few verses, émigrés Peter Stewart and George Hyde of that city published the first American edition of Burns in 1788, emphasizing the comic brilliance of "the Celebrated Ayrshire Ploughman." Glasgow-born Archibald McLean brought out a New York edition that same year, heralding Burns's poem in praise of the American Revolution.

In 1788, the Constitution was one year old, and the capitol of the United States still located in New York City (it later moved to Philadelphia for a decade and eventually to the District of Columbia in 1800). As a copy of the New York edition of Burns's poems was discovered in George Washington's library upon his death, it is likely that the president—who surely knew of Burns's support for the patriot cause—acquired it shortly after publication. Three American editions of Burns's verses appeared before 1800. Thomas Jefferson's Aberdeen-born tutor at William and Mary even suggested that because Americans would surely develop a dialect of their own, Burns might serve as a "model." When *American Universal Magazine*, published in Philadelphia, noted the poet's death in 1797, the publication became the first of thousands of American tributes to Scotland's national bard.[1]

The Scottish community in Philadelphia proved especially responsive. As there was no international copyright, Philadelphia printers republished Dr. John C. Currie's four-volume study (1800) and R. H. Cromek's *Reliques of Robert Burns* (1808) within a year of their appearance in Britain. The finding of a previously undiscovered Burns verse or the setting of one of his songs to music usually merited comment by American newspapers. Eighteen years after the actual event, the *Salem* (Massachusetts) *Gazette* reprinted the 1796 account of his death. In 1823, a blind Scottish émigré made his living by traveling through New England soliciting subscriptions for a new six-hundred-page edition of Burns's works. While visiting Baltimore in 1834, Charles Augustus Murray was delighted to discover a museum with statues to Burns's most famous characters, Tam O' Shanter and Souter Johnny.[2]

In 1811, Robert Walsh, editor of the *American Review of History and Politics*, argued that the poetry of Burns was more widely read and understood in the States than in England. Americans were not "a mere tilling and shopkeeping race," he said (somewhat defensively). Instead, they greatly admired the scientific and literary achievements of Scotland and acknowledged Edinburgh as "the metropolis of genius and learning."[3]

By 1860, American publishers had brought out at least twenty-four editions of Burns's verses. In 1848, Samuel Tyler, a Scottish-born Baltimore lawyer, added a biography of his own: *Robert Burns: As a Poet and as a Man* (New York, 1848), the first full-length American tribute, which carefully avoided mentioning his sexual activities. In addition, all through the early decades of the new century, newspapers drew on Burns's poems as fillers to round out their columns.

On his deathbed, Burns said to his wife, Jean, that his name would be far more appreciated after he was gone than during his lifetime. He proved prescient. When the poet died in Dumfries in 1796, a crowd of several hundred admirers marched in the funeral cortege. The *London Herald's* obituary described him as possessing "the vigour and versatility of a mind guided only by the light of Nature and the inspiration of genius."[4]

Around 1801, a Greenock group decided to commemorate Burns's birthday with a ceremonial dinner. Similar gatherings in Paisley, Dumfries, Irvine, Kilmarnock, and Dunfermline soon followed. By 1815, Edinburgh had formed a Burns club as well.

In addition to celebrating his birthday, Burns admirers began to erect a variety of civic memorials throughout Scotland. Greenock officials dedicated a monument to Highland Mary in 1842, but the most dramatic celebration occurred two years later. August 6, 1844, was declared a Scottish national holiday to correlate with a major celebration of his life at the unveiling of an impressive new Burns monument in Ayrshire. Burns's two surviving sons attended as honored guests as the Earl of Eglinton presided over a demonstration that drew thirty thousand people to the banks of the River Doon. Many came from abroad, including a number of Americans. All through the day, the crowds sang Burns's most popular songs—especially "Ye Banks and Braes O'Bonnie Doon" and "Auld Lang Syne"—with the greatest enthusiasm. John Wilson, famed editor of *Blackwood's*, spoke of the "moral in every man's life," and the crowd heard one son confess that (alas) poetic genius did not seem to be hereditary.[5] As an American observer noted, Burns would probably best be remembered through his songs, for his music now stretched from the banks of the Ganges and the Tiber rivers to the Ohio River Valley.[6]

In the new American nation, the steady stream of Scottish immigrants—about five thousand a year for most of the nineteenth century—kept the Burns's flame equally alive. Wherever they settled in sufficient numbers, these émigrés established Presbyterian churches with St. Andrew's Day (November 30) celebrations and/or various Caledonian clubs that often commemorated his birthday (January 25). Virtually all official U.S. gatherings that celebrated Scottish culture involved a ceremonial reading of Burns's poems. Although organized chiefly for Scots, non-Scots frequently attended as well.[7] These gatherings usually revolved around three themes. Cooks prepared an abundance of Scottish traditional foods and speakers offered an endless round of toasts that often stretched into the wee morning hours. Haggis—an authentic food of the poor—always figured prominently in the festivities. The orator of the day usually noted that the social goals of Scotland and the emigrants' adopted nation overlapped extensively. Fulsome though the speeches may have been, they pointed to a basic truth. More than virtually any other European nation of the early nineteenth century—France, Spain, Ireland, the German principalities, Holland, Sweden, among others—Scotland celebrated universal, widespread education, a respect for the self-made man, and a rough, pragmatic form of social equality. Moreover, ever since the mid-eighteenth century, Scotland and America had felt themselves "culturally inferior" to England and its glittering capital of London.[8] The annual celebration of Robert Burns allowed Scots to declare a type of cultural independence, and Americans found much to admire in this message.

It is not clear when the first American official celebrations began, but they were common by at least 1820. In 1819, Glaswegian John M. Duncan attended a St. Andrew's Day gathering in a posh New York City hotel that was appropriately festooned with Scottish flags and memorials, both inside and out. The lengthy dinner involved much drinking and singing, all accompanied by bagpipes and, in this case, backed by a full American orchestra. The focus revolved around the ceremonial reading of Burns's lyrics, in a wide variety of first-, second-, and third-generation accents.[9] Because many Scots vowel and consonant sounds do not exactly correspond with English, large differences soon began to appear between the lyrics as printed on the page and those read aloud by a nonnative speaker.[10] It was these differences that bothered the fastidious Duncan. So appalled was he at the pronunciation that he helped silence a third-generation reader by loud applause.[11]

As the years passed, however, the Scottish American celebration of January 25 shifted from concern over correct pronunciation to extolling the virtues of Scotland in general and Burns in particular. The Baltimore gathering of 1831 mingled toasts to the memory of Washington with those to the memory of Burns, Robert the Bruce, and William Wallace. They saluted not Britain per se but "her present endeavors in the cause of national reform."[12] Speakers at the New York celebration of 1836 ranked Burns with Christopher Columbus and Washington as a benefactor of the human family. William Carr, president of the society, interpreted Burns's message as a call to contemporary Americans to strive for the public good and make the welfare of the human race their ultimate concern.[13] Five years later in Louisville, Kentucky, a reporter celebrated Burns's universal genius, reminding his audience, "You all know the history of Burns. The world knows it by heart."[14] Such comments, from both north and south of the Mason-Dixon Line, suggest that Burns's life and lyrics had been well integrated into the antebellum American world view.

The Lack of Rivals

One reason for the appeal of Burns's poetry in the states may well be because he faced virtually no poetic rivals. From the Revolutionary era until about 1840, the offerings of American poets proved thin, indeed. Boston Black poet Phillis Wheatley achieved modest fame for her *Poems on Various Subjects, Religious and Moral* (1773). After the Revolution, two graduates of the College of New Jersey (later Princeton), Philip Morin Freneau and Hugh Henry Brackenridge, created "A Poem on the Rising Glory of America," and fellow patriot Timothy Dwight of Connecticut wrote "The Conquest of Canaan; a Poem in Eleven Books" in 1785. Dedicated to George Washington, it compared Joshua's leading of Ancient Israel to the promised land to Washington's leading the colonials to create a new nation. But none of these or any other early American poems resonated in the popular mind. Wheatley could not find a publisher for a second edition, and "A Poem on the Rising Glory of America" never penetrated the American backwoods.

A similar fate awaited the Hartford Wits, the first serious group of writers who consciously tried to forge an appropriate poetic literature for the new republic: Dwight, John Trumbull, Joel Barlow, David Humphreys, Lemuel Hopkins, and Richard Alsoe. Earnest though they might have been, the Wits' poems were laced with obscure classical and political allusions, and their fame never extended much beyond their hometown.[15] Some examples follow, the first from Trumbull's one-hundred-page poem, "M'Fingal."

> The Town, our hero's scene of action
> Had long been torn by feuds of faction
> And as each party's strength prevails
> It turn's up different, heads or tails.

From Dwight's "The Conquest of Canaan":

> With anguish Caleb saw her fading charms,
> And caught the favorite in his hastening arms
> Reviv'd with piercing voice, that froze his soul,
> She forc'd the big, round tear unwish'd to roll;

Such offerings helped confirm British writer Sydney Smith's famous 1820 sneer: "Who in the four corners of the globe reads an American book?"[16]

For three generations, American intellectuals were mortified at the absence of a first-rate national epic poem. By all rights, complained John Knapp in 1818, the American Revolution should have called forth a burst of poetic greatness. He viewed the lack thereof as an "undoubted forerunner of national decline." Historian Russell B. Nye concludes that all American literature from 1776 to 1830 was either imitative or derivative.[17] An 1861 writer for the *North American Review* charted what he considered the failures of the generation of poets who had lived through the American Revolution. The writer lamented about these poets, the first to attempt a democratic literature in America: "There is not one of them whose reputation outlived his age. . . . Barlow's 'Columbian' and Dwight's 'Conquest of Canaan,' died by their own weight; it is hardly possible that any persons except their mothers should have had patience to read them through. In leaden dullness and heaviness they have been seldom equaled, never surpassed." Thus, for at least two generations, the United States had an authentic "poetry vacuum," a genuine "poetry gap." And into this gap flowed the poems and songs of Robert Burns.[18]

Early-nineteenth-century Scots and Americans, however, tended to view Burns through very different lenses. For the former, the poet embodied the integrity of Lowland Scots as a language and the long-term struggles of Scottish cultural nationalism within the British Empire. Scottish nationalists often used Burns's popularity as a stick with which to beat Shakespeare and other English writers. But American readers showed little interest in these themes. In the States, Burns took on a far different role. Americans read Burns quite selectively. Admittedly, a good many of the lyrics would have been unintelligible to them, as, for example, the following.

> My Lan' afore's a gude auld has been,
> An' wight an wilfu' a' his days been.
> My Lan' ahin's a weel gaun fillie,
> That aft has bore me home frae killie[19]

And, only a small minority—but one in which Lincoln was prominent—celebrated the biting religious satires. Instead, Burns's verses extolling nature, equality, intellectual honesty, and universal democracy appealed to most Americans for these echoed the aspirations of the young republic. It is not too much to say that for much of the early nineteenth century, Robert Burns served almost a subcategory of American republican thought.

Americans had no trouble finding "proof texts" in Burns's poems. Although few cited his 1794 "Ode for General Washington's Birthday," several other verses fit perfectly with the stated goals of the Revolution. Some examples:

> O wad some Pow'r the giftie gie us
> to see oursels as ithers see us!

or

> Princes and Lords are but the breath of Kings,
> An honest man's the noblest work of God.

or

> The rank is but the guinea's stamp,
> The man's the gowd for a' that.

And, especially,

> A man's a man for a' that!

These phrases received constant repetition and eventually evolved into idioms of American English.

The belief that Burns voiced the heart of American hopes remained in place throughout the century. In 1892, Wallace Bruce, a minor poet himself, noted that Burns's songs of love and hope "filled a great want in our literary life." Five years later, John G. Dow, a Scottish immigrant to Madison, Wisconsin, stated that Burns was known and loved in America as much as in his native land. He attributed this to Burns's celebration of democracy as "the new creed and gospel of humanity. . . . In this, Burns is more in sympathy with American than with Scottish life."[20] As late as 1925, W. R. Bonney, the American consul to Edinburgh, told a local gathering of Scots, "Robert Burns is ours as well as yours. His philosophy is woven into the warp and woof of our Bill of Rights, and his vision of man's estate is part and parcel of our American ideals of democracy and justice."[21]

Songs

As many Burns Day speakers noted, the poet reached countless early-nineteenth-century Americans largely through the power of his songs. As he himself might have phrased it, Providence had selected his skill with words to convey the folk wisdom of the Scottish people to the wider world. A near-contemporary, Irishman Thomas Moore, similarly wrote and/or modified a number of Irish lyrics that he set to traditional Irish folk tunes. The first volume of *Moore's Irish Melodies* appeared in 1808 and the last of the ten volumes in 1832. Combined with the steady flow of Irish immigration, these songbooks also helped introduce the "wild" Irish lyrics to American audiences.[22] Yet, there was a subtle difference between the early Irish and Scottish melodies. The Scottish and Scots-Irish music arrived in the eighteenth century with the earliest immigrants, many of whom settled on the American frontier, where they may have constituted as much as ten percent of the population. Sustained Irish immigration, however, did not occur until the Great Famine of the late 1840s, and although the Irish immigrants also hailed largely from peasant backgrounds, they became primarily an urban people in the states. Consequently, excluding Moore's "Oft in the Stilly Night," most of his other songs, such as, "Last Rose of Summer" and "Believe Me, If All Those Endearing Young Charms," did not reach out to ordinary citizens. Instead, they remained restricted to the nation's urban stages and music halls. Unlike Burns's classics, "John Anderson, My Jo," "Scots Wha Hae," or "Green Grow the Rashes, O" they never became an integral part of antebellum folklife. In addition, the

Irish songs of patriotism may have served to rally Irish Americans to the incipient Irish independence movement, but the Scottish patriotic songs seemed to align themselves with the success of the American Revolution. (The Scottish devolution issue would not gain a mass following until the late twentieth century.) Thus, the Scottish/Scots Irish songs had deeper roots in America than did Moore's Irish compilations.

Part of Burns's genius lay in his ability to tap the inherited wisdom of traditional, Scottish music. Some critics have argued that the truest expression of a nation rests with its folk songs, for these represent the authentic soul of a people.[23] As Dundee Presbyterian minister George Gilfillan later phrased it, Burns's songs had set the pulse of the human heart to music.[24] Gilfillan's contemporary Principal Shairp agreed: Burns's "songs are not like many modern songs—set to music; they are themselves music."[25] And this music formed very much a part of Ohio River Valley frontier life.

In spite of the increasing sophistication of oral history, estimating the impact of songs or poems on a culture has always remained problematic. Still, one can point to a number of places where Burns's lyrics overlapped with the emerging democratic American culture. Parodies of two of his poems found their way into the election of 1828, which pitted Tennessee lawyer Andrew Jackson against incumbent president John Quincy Adams. According to the Jacksonians, Adams had dipped into public funds to purchase a billiard table for the White House (in fact, he had used his own monies, but that was beside the point). One form of attack came in a parody of "John Anderson, My Jo," which had been put to music in 1824. To succeed, parody demands a widespread familiarity with the original. Because the Jacksonian appeal lay largely with urban workingmen in eastern cities and raw farmers on the moving frontier, Jackson supporters must have assumed that hearers would recognize the lyrics.

> John Adams Q
> My Joe, John
> Now don't you think 'twas rash
> For billiard balls and cues, John
> To spend the people's cash
> For billiard tables too, John
> Alas, by doing so,
> You've "holed" yourself
> You're on the shelf
> John Adams Q, my Joe.

In another parody, the Jackson men tapped the ubiquitous "Auld Lang Syne."

> Let auld acquaintance be forgot,
> And never brought to mind,
> And Jackson be our President
> And Adams left behind.

In a similar fashion, local temperance groups came up with "John Alcohol, my foe, John," which they used to bolster their cause throughout the century.

The poetry of Robert Burns also echoed throughout the successful Texas revolution in 1836 against Mexican rule. Shortly after the first shots were exchanged at Gonzales, radical Texan William H. Wharton passed out an inflammatory broadside at Brazoria. The leaflet opened with a call to arms and a line (without attribution) borrowed directly from Burns's "Scots Wha Hae":

> Freemen of Texas
> To Arms!!! To Arms!!!
> Now's the day, and Now's the hour!

Four Scots also perished at the battle of the Alamo. Aberfeldy-born piper John McGregor is still viewed as a hero in contemporary Texas. Part of his fame came from his notorious duet with legendary frontiersman Davy Crockett, who played the violin. There is also a persistent—if dubious— legend that the unflattering Mexican term for Americans—*gringo*—derived from Robert Burns's "Green Grow the Rashes, O," which Mexicans heard American soldiers and cowboys sing.[26]

A number of Burnsian phrases worked their way into American English. In the 1830s, Abraham Lincoln studied surveying (as had Burns) and when he felt himself competent, approached John Calhoun, the chief surveyor of Sangamon County, Illinois, for an assignment. After Lincoln departed, Calhoun's sister-in-law, who had witnessed the conversation, scoffed at Lincoln's homeliness and unkempt appearance. Calhoun responded in a Burnsian idiom, "For all that he is no common man."[27] Another story has Mary Todd Lincoln upbraiding her husband's self-doubt by quoting Burns back to him.

> O wad some power
> the giftie gie *you*
> to see yousel' as
> Others see you.[28]

Widespread use of Burnsian imagery continued to flourish through the Civil War era. Edward Bates, Lincoln's attorney general, whose son served in the Confederate Army, often cited Burns in his diary.[29] An 1860 Republican campaign song contained the verse:

> John Anderson, my Jo, John
> Ye fill my heart wi' joy.
> A farm upon the prairie, John,
> For ilka darling boy!
> "Old Abe" will help them split the rails
> to fence them in, ye know.
> And ye ken they'll keep out slavery too,
> John Anderson, My Jo.

The Virginia *Richmond Dispatch* printed an anti-Lincoln ditty to the same tune.

> Old Abraham, my jolly Abe,
> When we were first acquaint,
> I thought you were an honest man,
> But nothing of a saint;
> But since you wore the
> Spanish [Scottish] cloak,
> You love the negro so,
> And hate the white man, so you do,
> My jolly Abe, my Jo.[30]

After the initial firing on Fort Sumter in 1861 that sparked the beginning of the war, "Columbia" delivered this tribute to Major Robert Anderson, the commander of the federal-held post.

> Bob Anderson, my beau, Bob, I really don't know whether,
> I ought to like you so, Bob, considering that feather,
> I don't like standing armies, Bob, as very well you know;
> But I love a *man that dares to act,*
> Bob Anderson, my beau![31]

The tune of "Auld Lang Syne" was similarly used by both sides in a variety of parody versions. Because the nineteenth century abounded with parodies of Burns songs, one can fairly assume that they were quite familiar to ordinary citizens.

Visitors to Ayrshire

A surprising number of American travelers to Britain made a special pilgrimage to the "auld clay biggin" where Burns was born, and several of their descriptions were later printed in local newspapers in both America and Scotland. One American lieutenant visiting Ayr allegedly could recite a part of every one of Burns's poems.[32] In 1846, a New Hampshire tourist defied any visitor to stand at the Auld Brig o' Doon and not picture the witch Cutty Sark frantically chasing after poor Tam O' Shanter.[33] Indeed, as one traveler phrased it, the humble cottage had emerged as "a spot sacred to every Scotchman, and indeed to all men." In 1855, James Grant Wilson, Chicago literary editor and later Union general, met a native Scot on the train from Glasgow to Ayr. The man remarked, "I'm thinking ye'll be gangin' to Ayr to visit the birthplace o' Robert Burnes." Afterwards, the Scot marveled at the number of Americans who came to Scotland for just that purpose.[34]

Wilson enjoyed Burns country as long as he could. He sought out Burns's last surviving sibling, his sister Isabella Burns Begg, then eighty-four, and shared tea with her. Widowed early in life, Isabella had raised nine children and established a village school before turning her cottage into a virtual monument to her brother. Over the years, she greeted countless tourists from around the world. Ever gracious, she told Wilson how much she enjoyed entertaining American visitors. Wilson relished his chat with her and her daughter and buoyed their spirits by informing them how many American cities were planning 1859 centenary celebrations to honor Robert's birth. The women were delighted when he assured them of the high regard that Americans had for Burns's verses. On departing, he picked a few leaves of ivy from Mrs. Begg's cottage as a memento of his visit. Awed though Wilson may have been to meet Burns's sister, he was appalled at the condition of the Auld Kirk that played so prominent a role in "Tam O' Shanter." Souvenir hunters had so dismantled the church that locals had been forced to rebuild it, in part, because of the number of "boxes toddy and porridge spoons" said to have been carved from the original timbers. Although Wilson delighted at the Twa Brigs spanning the River Ayr, the rough-hewn statues of Tam O' Shanter and Souter Johnny, and the manicured landscape surrounding the elaborate Burns monument, he was equally dismayed by the actual birth cottage itself. True, the visitors' book contained a bevy of important names, but the spence, or sitting room, had become a functioning pub, and he found many regulars quite the worse for the wear. Wilson considered this a disgrace to the land of Burns and Wallace.[35] His romantic image simply did not jibe with the sordid reality of peasant Scotland.

On his official visit that same year, Nathaniel Hawthorne came to similar conclusions. Appointed consul to Liverpool, England, by his old friend President Franklin Pierce, Hawthorne and his wife took a lengthy railway journey to visit several of the Burns haunts in 1857. New England Puritan as he was, Hawthorne viewed the squalid and cramped Ayrshire dwellings with dismay. He described the birthplace as "an exceedingly unsuitable place for a pastoral and rural poet to live or die in."[36]

If he found the Burns dwellings squalid, however, Hawthorne was truly captivated by the Ayrshire countryside. He gathered up a handful of daisies from the field where Burns had accidentally plowed one down, noting with undisguised pleasure how many of his American contemporaries would envy the pressed blossoms. Eventually, Hawthorne reworked his extensive notebook observations—deleting some of his harsher initial comments—for an October 1860 essay in the *Atlantic Monthly* on Burns Country.[37] Both Wilson and Hawthorne were stunned by the yawning gap between the inspiring lyrics of the "poet of democracy" and the squalid peasant conditions in which he had actually lived.

The pilgrimages continued all through the century. In 1867, Mary Todd Lincoln sought out Burns's birthplace, and four years later, former Confederate President Jefferson Davis spent an evening chatting with Burns's two surviving nieces. In a later speech in Memphis, Tennessee, Davis (who was of Welsh ancestry) praised "Tam O' Shanter" and boldly stated that if he had not been born an American, he would have chosen to become a Scotsman. As writer Thomas C. MacMillan observed in 1919, "His countrymen are well aware that the 'cottage where our Robbie Burns was born' is the shrine to which more American pilgrims annually travel, and is more popular, than even the home of the 'divine William' at Stratford-on-Avon."[38]

From the early 1800s to the end of the century, Americans from virtually every spectrum of society went out of their way to celebrate the genius of Robert Burns. *New York Tribune* editor Horace Greeley praised the poet's inspirational message and claimed that he seldom missed a Burns celebration. Brooklyn Congregational minister and famed orator Henry Ward Beecher suggested that children who were raised on Burns's lyrics would never elect tyrants to the legislature. Radical Denver Congregational pastor Myron W. Reed noted in 1893, "I have hope for the human race so long as they celebrate the birthday of Robert Burns. I hate to be cruel but think of celebrating the birthday of [railroad magnate George Mortimer] Pullman."[39]

Burns's appeal seemed to transcend traditional political and religious bounds. The foremost Freethinker of the land, Robert G. Ingersoll, who would have agreed with clerics Beecher and Reed on probably nothing else, joined them in praising the poet. He lauded Burns for destroying the cruel theology of Calvinism and for his democratic leanings. Ingersoll also wrote an official tribute in verse to the poet that is today prominently displayed in the Burns cottage in Ayrshire. Similarly, Democrat William Jennings Bryan and Republican William Howard Taft—rivals in the 1908 presidential election—each separately praised Burns's poetry. Single-tax advocate Henry George did so, as well as Scottish-born capitalist Andrew Carnegie. Freethinker and cleric, Democrat and Republican, socialist and entrepreneur—somehow everyone could find a way to celebrate the lyrics of Robert Burns. Many pre–Civil War magazine articles on him are simply apologies for his alleged shortcomings. Indeed, one searches in vain for any serious criticism of the Scottish poet.[40]

The Literary Establishment

As might be expected, the fledgling American literary establishment held Burns in the highest esteem. In the fall of 1832, young Connecticut poet Fitz Greene Halleck visited Burns country and plucked a rose from near the Alloway Kirk. This provided the inspiration for the first, and until 1859 probably the best, American poetic tribute to the Bard. In somewhat stilted quatrains, Halleck encapsulated his nation's selective reading of the Scots poet: Burns's verses reflected both Scotland's glory and her shame; he spoke in the language of the heart, as well as to the causes of patriotism, hope, and love; "Tam O' Shanter" proved his "master-lay," but "Auld Lang Syne" remained a close second; he extolled the virtues of democracy and individual integrity and simultaneously scorned rank, wealth, and hypocrisy. This view, in a nutshell, became the most common American reading, which stretched to include both north and south for at least three generations. Union officers read Burns for pleasure, and famed Confederate writer Mary B. Chestnut quoted "Tam O' Shanter" in her diaries. Civil War observer William Allan reported that he heard both Union and Confederate armies singing some of Burns's "Scotch songs."[41]

Critic Franklyn Bliss Snyder has perused the major American literary journals between 1835 and 1860 and found that they displayed considerable interest in Burns. The New York *Knickerbocker* and Philadelphia *Public Leader* carried extensive essays on him, as did the *Southern Literary Messenger*, *The Living Age*, *The National Magazine*, and the *Atlantic Monthly*. Virtually every editor, publisher, and major writer linked with the emerging American literary world had something to say on him. A few grumbled privately that Burns's use of Doric Scots restricted his appeal, but Ralph Waldo Emerson disagreed. He praised the vernacular poetry as "the only example in history of a language made classic by the genius of a single man."[42]

Most American poets were equally laudatory. Massachusetts Quaker John Greenleaf Whittier was introduced to Burns's poems at an early age, when he heard a Scottish visitor recite them in dialect. In his autobiography, he claimed that this experience encouraged him to write his own verse. In Burns's honor, Whittier wrote at least one poem in the Doric dialect. In 1840, he penned another tribute entitled "Burns: On Receiving a Sprig of Heather in Blossom." Two verses read:

> With clearer eyes I saw the worth
> Of life among the lowly;
> The bible at his Cotter's hearth
> Had made my own more holy.

> Through all his tuneful art, how strong
> The human feeling gushes!
> The very moonlight of his song
> Is warm with smiles and blushes!

It was Whittier who termed Burns the "truest and sweetest of all writers who had sung of home, love and humanity." In large measure, Burns's verse became the category by which American literature was judged. Washington Irving's short story "Rip Van Winkle" was termed "The Dutch Tam O' Shanter," and Whittier's classic poem "Snowbound" was called the American "Cotter's Saturday Night." Whittier was even described as the "American Burns."[43]

Massachusetts poet James Russell Lowell similarly revered Burns. He termed Burns the poet who best understood the heart of humankind and in 1837 wrote a lengthy verse "To G. B. Loring" in the Burns style and rhyme scheme, complete with Doric language. Lowell also drew on Burns's "The Twa Brigs" for the Mason and Slidell section in *The Biglow Papers* (the Union's illegal capture of two Confederate diplomats from the British ship *Trout*). When a friend gave Lowell one of Burns's sleeve buttons, he cherished the gift for a lifetime.[44]

Henry Wadsworth Longfellow, perhaps the most noted poet of his age, concurred. He wrote a verse in honor of the centenary of Burns's birth and missed the 1859 celebration only because of illness. His tribute to Burns follows.

I see, amid the fields of Ayr
A ploughman, who, in foul or fair
Sings at his task
So clear, we know not if it is
The laverocks song we hear, or his
Nor care to ask."[45]

From the late nineteenth century forward, however, critics have celebrated Walt Whitman as the chief bard of American democracy. His
classic "When Lilacs Last in the Dooryard Bloom'd" masterfully merges
Lincoln's life and death with the hopes of an evolving democratic nation,
all infused by the qualities of universal love. Perhaps out of jealously,
Whitman often criticized Burns. Citing Burns's lack of spirituality, he
stated that Burns was not equal to Shakespeare nor even to Tennyson or
Emerson. Still, from 1875 to 1886, Whitman thrice reprinted his essay on
Burns, and he softened his comments with each publication.[46]

On the night of April 14, 1887, the aged poet filled New York's Madison
Square Theatre with a lecture on his personal acquaintance with Abraham
Lincoln. At the back of his manuscript, he included copies of several poems
that the overflow audience might possibly call upon him to recite after his
performance. These included his other well-known poem on Lincoln, "O
Captain! My Captain!" but Whitman also added a copy of Burns's "John
Anderson, My Jo." With his reputation secure, Whitman seems to have
mellowed. Once he celebrated Burns's earthy love of life, noting, "Even
his platitudes have a special dash to them." Frontier humorist Josh Billings, who wrote in a Doric dialect all his own, summed up much of this
sentiment, "I consider he [Burns] was the *most* poet that ever lived."[47]

The absence of any serious American criticism of Burns can easily be
explained. In Scotland, the chief critics came less from literary figures than
from Presbyterian ministers and advocates of temperance. Their critique
lay as much with the poet's dissolute style of life as with his words. At the
centenary of Burns's birth, one Scottish cleric had to publicly deny that
he had called him "a drunken poet."[48]

But the Presbyterian clergy never played the same role in American
civic life as they did in Scotland. Although the various forms of American
Presbyterianism retained a strong Scottish "flavor," neither the Northern,
Southern, Cumberland, New School, nor Old School branch could ever
truly be termed a Scottish "ethnic church." When the Old School *Biblical
Repository and Princeton Review* reviewed Samuel Tyler's extensive biog-

raphy of Burns, they politely disagreed with many points, but they also noted that this simply was not their baliwick.[49]

Without any clerical or temperance opposition to halt the tide, American praise for Burns soon flowed over the top. Margaret Fuller claimed that no one stood nearer to God and the angels since Adam. Writer William Frye observed that the name of Robert Burns had become dearer to many Americans than any other except for Jesus.[50]

Celebration of the Anniversaries of His Birth

From the 1850s forward, the January Burns's dinners began to include increased political commentary. Speakers at the 1856 New York City gathering noted that the Know-Nothing Party could never fault the Scots for celebrating the birth of their peasant poet, for he was at heart a republican. The celebration the next year highlighted the fact that outside of Scotland proper, no country gave Burns greater homage than America. A speaker in 1858 called the United States—the land of his adoption—as "chosen by Providence to carry the ark of human liberty." Three years later, on the cusp of the dissolution of the Union, the main New York Burns Club speaker linked the Scot's poem to George Washington to his undoubted support for the Union for which Washington had fought—"Loud applause long continued."[51]

The culmination of these sentiments may be seen in America's participation in the worldwide commemoration of the centenary of Burns's birth on Tuesday, January 25, 1859. Although Burns's Day dinner celebrations had stretched back to 1801, the one hundredth anniversary naturally called for an especially vigorous celebration. Hundreds of venues in Scotland, sixteen in England, and two in Ireland hosted gatherings that Tuesday. Scottish writers gleefully pointed out that no other figure in British history had been so honored. No one had celebrated the centenary of Francis Bacon, John Milton, Sir Isaac Newton, or even Shakespeare, they observed. The Burns commemoration, however, "was substantially a most profound and true expression of such love and sympathy as no other poet of any time or country did ever evoke." Unlike William Wordsworth and Sir Walter Scott, Burns was not a poet in thrall to the aristocracy, said the *Scotsman*. Instead, he belonged to the people.[52] From France, politician Henry Lord Brougham wrote an extensive letter—read aloud in Edinburgh and later printed as pamphlet—that praised the educational system of Scottish parishes that had produced such a man. Perhaps Burns's chief importance, said Brougham, lay in his showcasing "the pure and classical language of

Scotland," which should never be regarded as a mere "provincial dialect."[53] As expected, the chief sour notes came from Scottish clerical circles. That centenary year, a pamphlet suggested that Burns's "polluting sentiments and licentious life" made him an unlikely hero for the nation. His profanity, impurities, and ridicule of scripture and the clergy—"The Bible was very much his text-book"—as well as his overall life made it impossible for Christians to join in the festivities, said the pamphleteer. The anonymous writer concluded with a warning to Scottish parents: "Beware lest by the homage you pay to Burns, you encourage [your children] to imbibe his sentiments and imitate his example." A decade later, the Reverend Fergus Ferguson, pastor of the East United Presbyterian Church, Dalkeith, raised the same question of the propriety of Christians commemorating Burns's birthday.[54] This issue would not die for over a century.

At the Dundee Burns Day dinner, Reverend George Gilfillan took the opposite tack. Noting that he did not stand alone among the clergy of Scotland in doing homage, he emphasized the poet's true faith: a religion of charity, love, and hope.[55] Reverend Robert Blackley Drummond, minister of St. Mark's Chapel in Edinburgh, delivered a similar lecture of defense on the next Sunday (later printed as a pamphlet).[56] Clearly, there was mixed feeling regarding the suitability of Burns as the ultimate national hero. Writing from Edinburgh in 1859, a reporter observed that no feature of the United States character impressed Scots more than the deep admiration that Americans displayed for the Scots' national bard.[57]

Naturally, the majority of U.S. antebellum Burns's Day dinners appealed chiefly to those of Scottish ancestry. But in 1859, the Scottish community deliberately reached out to all nationalities to help celebrate the centenary.[58] At least sixty-one U.S. cities joined their counterparts across the globe to toast the memory of the Bard. Albany, New York, Baltimore, Boston, Brooklyn, Buffalo, Chicago, Cincinnati, Cleveland, Detroit, Milwaukee, Pittsburgh, Rockford, Illinois, Sacramento, Springfield, Illinois, St. Louis, Troy, New York, and Washington, D.C., were just some of the U.S. communities that hosted large gatherings in his honor. Those who possessed Burnsian artifacts—such as, the Albany club, which boasted a holograph copy of "Auld Lang Syne," and a Boston publisher who owned an original love letter to Clarinda—proudly displayed their treasures to public view. In Boston, the diners shared a haggis that had actually been made in Burns's birthplace cottage. The speeches delivered in Milwaukee, St. Louis, Boston, New York, and Washington were all later published as pamphlets. The only sad note—acknowledged by a number of speakers—was that Burns's sister,

Isabella Begg, had not lived to witness the worldwide celebration.[59] (Burns's surviving illegitimate daughter, Annie Park Simpson, was conveniently ignored in these festivities.)

The *New York Times*—not yet the paper of record that it would later become—covered the celebration on both sides of the Atlantic Ocean. The editors denounced a minor poet's criticism of the Boston Burns gathering and devoted much space to the various national celebrations.[60] The newspaper dispatched a special correspondent to Dumfries to follow the Scottish aspect of the story. The unnamed correspondent, who had obviously never been to Scotland before, found himself gobsmacked (Celtic, "absolutely fascinated") by both the scenery and the ancient history of the region. He marveled at the all-out Dumfries display, one that included prancing horses, bagpipes, marching bands, triumphal arches, and endless evergreen boughs. As he noted, "The commemoration here seems no idle ceremony but, a heartfelt homage of love, in which all classes unite, from the highest to the humblest."[61]

In the States, senators, mayors, governors, and local dignitaries all graced the various head tables. The New York gathering invited President James Buchanan to attend, but he turned them down because of the press of public duties. He managed to send a message: "Poor Burns. I have always deplored his sad fate. He has ever been a favorite of mine. The child of genius and of misfortune, he is read everywhere and by all classes throughout the extent of our country, and his natural pathos has reached all hearts."[62] The Washington, D.C., Burns club also invited Buchanan to attend and received a similar reply.[63]

The Burns Club of New York City invited Reverend Beecher to speak, and the crowd filled the twenty-five-hundred-seat Cooper Institute—the same locale where Lincoln would charm his first eastern audience a year later—to overflowing. In his oration, Beecher noted that half the civilized world, plus the entire community of belle lettres, had come together that evening to celebrate a farmer's son who had taken the message of Scotland "into the world." Noting that Burns had almost emigrated to the West Indies, he scoffed at the idea that the bard could have followed a gang of slaves, whip in hand, while chanting "A man's a man for a' that" at which the audience applauded. Beecher closed with the observation, "As for his faults, let them be forgotten."[64]

The most elaborate of these 1859 gatherings occurred in Boston, the acknowledged literary center of the republic. Poets Oliver Wendell Holmes, Lowell, and Whittier all composed verses of honor for the occasion.

Because Whittier was unable to attend, Emerson read his poem, which contained an echo of Beecher's comment: "Today be every fault forgiven." Holmes observed that Burns should have lived in America, for his words reflected the theme of Bunker Hill, equality as the goal of the Revolution. Later, Emerson delivered his own brief address that brought the audience to its feet with loud applause. Burns, Emerson said, knew how to "take from fairs and gypsies and blacksmiths and drovers the speech of the market and clothe it with melody." He had become the poet of the American rising middle classes, reflecting their resentment against privileged minorities, a sentiment that Emerson saw as changing the face of the globe: "The people who care nothing for literature and poetry care for Burns . . . . Every boy's and girl's head carries snatches of his songs, and they say them by heart, and, what is strangest of all, never learned them from a book, but from mouth to mouth."[65]

The popularity of such statements has led literary critic Carol McGuirk to conclude that early-nineteenth-century Americans completely misunderstood the man whose work they celebrated. Unaware of his peasant background or the widespread rage of the underclass that he represented, most American readers, she suggests, transformed him into a poet of middle-class egalitarianism. Through his poetry and especially the songs, which carried an even wider impact, Americans constructed an idealized version of Burns, Scotland, and Scottish culture that proved a far cry from the actual world of eighteenth-century Ayrshire.[66]

An examination of the toasts and orations given in the States that Tuesday evening in 1859 reveals a common theme that might be described as "democratic inclusiveness." British flags were everywhere intertwined with American ones, and northern gatherings accorded Canadian dignitaries high honors as well. Many a glass was raised to the Queen and "the land we left," as well as to the president and "the land we live in."[67] Large southern cities joined their northern counterparts with enthusiasm. Charleston, South Carolina, toasted the worthies of Scotland and President Buchanan, as did the Burns gathering in New Orleans. In each case, speakers commented on the Scottish origin of the name Buchanan. "The South is gone as enthusiastic for Burns as the North," noted one orator.[68] And from far away San Francisco came the enigmatic message "We in distant California glory in Burns. Let us do as he did."[69]

In 1859, American orators found their own meaning in Burns. They showed no interest in using his verses to critique English writers. They never praised his celebration of the Lowland Scots language or warned

Christians to avoid his poetry. When they did refer to his short, tragic life, it was in the most sympathetic terms. Speakers everywhere noted that Burns's words perfectly described American ideals and that, in turn, these ideals were truly universal. A New York commentator observed, "We [the United States] have been too busy acting Epics to find time for writing them," and thus it was good that Burns existed to fill the gap.[70] A Washington, D.C., speaker noted how Burns's lyrics helped cultivate the American common man's pride and self-respect. His famous lines "The rank is but the guinea's stamp, / The man's the gowd for a' that" could never be confined to any nation. A New York cleric agreed: "'A man's a man for a' that' is the Declaration of Independence set to music." And on this night, he continued, it was "sung round the world."[71]

The Burns centenary had great appeal to Abraham Lincoln. We know that Lincoln attended the celebration in Springfield at the Concert Hall, where he heard numerous Burns songs and a recitation of his poetry. He also offered a brief toast to the Bard but precisely what he said has not survived. These Burns day celebrations on January 25, 1859, marked a high point of national unity for the rest of the century. The political tensions over slavery were momentarily forgotten as southern Burns clubs exchanged friendly greetings with their northern counterparts, and border cities heard equally from northern and southern orators. Moreover, a Buchanan sat in the White House to oversee the whole affair.

After the disruption of the Civil War, some Scottish Americans hoped the previous links might be quickly restored. In 1866, the president of the St. Andrew's Society of Charleston, South Carolina, which claimed to be the oldest in the nation, sent a letter of friendly greetings to its New York counterpart. The New York president replied in kind. One reporter hailed this exchange as, perhaps, "the best means for reconstructing the Union," but, of course, these pleasantries did not do much to bring it together again.[72]

Thus, for the first six decades of the nineteenth century, Robert Burns's lyrics became almost as American as they were Scottish. Indeed, it would be hard to find a writer who more clearly articulated the hoped-for social goals of the early American republic.[73] And, as the next chapter shows, these lyrics and rhythms had a formative influence on the life of young Abraham Lincoln.

3

The Lincoln–Burns Connection

In the fall of 1859, an old friend J. W. Fell of Springfield, Illinois, asked Abraham Lincoln for a brief biography to use in promoting his presidential aspirations. On December 20, 1859, Lincoln wrote the following:

I was born February 12, 1809, in Hardin Co., Ky. My parents were both born in Virginia, of undistinguished families—second families, perhaps I should say. My mother, who died in my tenth year, was of a family of the name of Hanks, some of whom now reside in Adams Co. and others in Mason Co., Ill. My paternal grandfather, Abraham Lincoln, emigrated from Rockingham Co., Va., to Kentucky, about 1781 or 1782 where a year or two later he was killed by the Indians, not in battle, but by stealth, when he was laboring to open a farm in the forest. His ancestors, who were Quakers, went to Virginia from Berks Co., Pa. An effort to identify them with the New England family of the same name ended in nothing more definite than a similarity of Christian names in both families, such as Enoch, Levi, Mordecai, Solomon, Abraham, and the like.

My father, at the death of his father, was but six years of age, and grew up literally without any education. He removed from Kentucky to what is now Spencer Co., Ind., in my eighth year. We reached our new home about the time the State came into the Union. It was a wild region, with many bears and other wild animals still in the woods. There I grew up. There were some schools, so called, but no qualification was ever required of a teacher beyond 'readin, writin' and cipherin,' to the rule of three. If a straggler, supposed to understand Latin, happened to sojourn in the neighborhood, he was looked upon as a wizard. There was absolutely nothing to excite ambition for education. Of course, when I came of age I did not know much. Still, somehow, I could read, write, and cipher to the rule of three, but that was all. I have not been to school since. The little advance I now have upon the store of education I have picked up from time to time under the pressure of necessity.

I was raised to farm work, at which I continued till I was twenty-two. At twenty-one I came to Illinois, and passed the first year in Macon County. Then I got to New Salem, at that time in Sangamon, now Menard County, where I remained a year as a sort of clerk in a store. Then came the Black Hawk War, and I was elected a captain of volunteers—a success which gave me more pleasure than I have had since. I went into the campaign, was elected, ran for the Legislature the same year (1832), and was beaten—the only time I have ever been beaten by the people.

The next and three succeeding biennial elections I was elected to the Legislature. I was not a candidate afterward. During the legislative period I had studied law, and removed to Springfield to practice it. In 1846 I was elected to the Lower House of Congress. Was not a candidate for re-election. From 1849 to 1854, both inclusive, practiced law more assiduously than ever before. Always a Whig in politics, and generally on the Whig electoral ticket, making active canvasses. I was losing interest in politics when the repeal of the Missouri Compromise aroused me again. What I have done since then is pretty well known.

If any personal description of me is thought desirable, it may be said I am in height six feet four inches, nearly; lean in flesh, weighing, on an average, one hundred and eighty pounds, dark complexion, with coarse black hair and gray eyes—no other marks or brands recollected.

Yours very truly,

A. Lincoln[1]

Here, succinctly, is the life of the man about whom more words have been written than any other person in history, save Jesus Christ. At the dawn of the twenty-first century, Lincoln still stands as the central figure of the American past. In December 2006, the editors of the *Atlantic* ranked him first in their list of "the 100 most influential Americans of all time."

During his Indiana and Illinois years, the young Lincoln, who was gifted with a prodigious memory, learned many of Burns's poems by heart.[2] The appeal was obvious. Both were sons of farmers, wrestled with the Reformed (Calvinist) version of human destiny, had great faith in reason, which was tempered by superstition, were often frustrated in love, and professed a profound belief in equality. Because many of Burns's poems described life in a poor farming community, Lincoln would have had no difficulty recognizing the themes. Burns also excelled as a master of satire, and Lincoln surely drew on these examples for his own satirical ventures. Finally, the transcendental message and driving rhyme patterns of the ploughman's poetry—committed to memory when Lincoln was very young—likely helped lay the groundwork for the lyrical power that one hears in Lincoln's greatest speeches from the 1850s forward.[3]

Where Did Lincoln First Meet Burns's Poetry?

There is no agreement as to precisely where and when the young Abraham Lincoln first encountered the poetry of Robert Burns. During his Kentucky youth, he surely would have heard versions of Burns's songs, and after the family crossed the Ohio River for Indiana in 1816, he may have read an isolated poem printed in a local newspaper. According to Noah Brooks, who knew Lincoln from 1856 forward, it was while living in Indiana that Lincoln borrowed a book of Burns's poetry, "a thick and chunky volume," as Lincoln later termed it, "bound in leather and printed in very small type." That description is not precise enough to determine exactly which edition he read, but an early Baltimore publication *The Works of Robert Burns* (1816) fits all the criteria. As there was no international copyright law, publishers F. Lucas Jr. and J. Cushing borrowed sections from Dr. John C. Currie's biography and R. H. Cromek's *Reliques of Robert Burns* and added miscellaneous correspondence, numerous songs, and a helpful glossary. Bound in leather, the volume reached 448 pages. Brooks goes on to say that Lincoln mastered "almost all its contents," clearly an exaggeration for Burns wrote over five hundred poems and songs.[4]

In the famed *Lincoln Memorial Album* (1883), Isaac N. Arnold, a former Chicago U.S. representative, similarly argued that Lincoln borrowed a stray volume of Burns from his pioneer Indiana neighbors. Historian M. L. Houser believes that the most likely person would have been either James Gentry or John A. Brackenbridge of Boonville. Arnold goes on to say that before Lincoln was nineteen, he read the Bible, Robert Burns, Aesop's Fables, *Pilgrim's Progress*, and two lives of George Washington.[5] All this would suggest that the young Lincoln had more than a passing familiarity with Burns's poetry well before the family decided to move to Illinois in 1830.

Lincoln's cousin Dennis Hanks once suggested that after Lincoln first read Burns, he started to write poetry himself. A number of Spencer County, Indiana, settlers later attested to young Lincoln's love of writing verse. When his sister, Sarah, married Aaron Grigsby in 1826, for example, he composed a lengthy piece of doggerel that the family sang to the gathering.[6]

Although Burns and Lincoln later gained fame as prodigious readers, each grew to maturity with one foot firmly planted in the British-American oral tradition. Even though Scottish peasant society proved literate above the norm, the taproot of the oral tradition rested just below the surface of Ayrshire life. So, too, with the Ohio River Valley. Lincoln's father could barely sign his name, and while tradition states that Lincoln's mother, Nancy Hanks, could read, there is no evidence that she could write. His close relatives John Hanks and John Johnston remained barely literate as well.

Those raised amidst oral cultures realize full well the power of words. The ancient Hebrews, for example, believed that God created the world through language and used language to reveal his design to humankind.[7] Other ancient societies spoke of "wordslaying." In the Finnish national epic, the *Kalevala*, an elderly bard *sings* a potential rival into a marsh. Similarly, an early Irish poet calmed a turbulent sea by invoking images of a pure idyllic Ireland. Medieval Arab poets actually created verses to be chanted by the soldiers as they rode into battle.[8] Even today, certain Great Plains Native Americans term the singing of Christian hymns as "throwing power" and "catching power."

The key to this oral world extends well beyond the simple relating of stories and anecdotes. Much of the impact comes through the element of *performance*. The moment the words leave a speaker's lips, they assume power, and the power rests primarily with the telling. It is a challenge to comprehend these stories out of context, and succeeding generations have often been sorely perplexed. (Most contemporaries, for example, struggle mightily to grasp the humor in the various compilations of Lincoln jokes. Students find them virtually unintelligible.) Although many of these stories appear simple, they are often quite profound. And they stick in the memory like burrs. One example: after hearing a lengthy discourse on slavery and emancipation from his friend Cassius M. Clay of Kentucky, Lincoln summed up the monologue, "Clay, I always thought that the man who made the corn should eat the corn."[9]

As historian Walter J. Ong argues, oral cultures all rely heavily on memory. These societies actively encourage memorization because books are scarce and the tracking down of precise references is often difficult. Those who grow to maturity in such surroundings frequently read books aloud, even when they are alone, as this helps embed thoughts in the memory. (This Lincoln did throughout his life.) Moreover, oral cultures place high value on stories and songs and an even higher value on a variety of mnemonic patterns and tricks to aid in the recall of these stories and songs. Oral cultures also draw heavily on tales, proverbs, wise sayings, ridicule, satires, jests, and especially words in music. Even though the actual thought of such cultures may not rank as formal "poetry," much of it tends to be rhythmic at the core. These rhythms aid in recall and help orally trained people to speak in "mnemonically tooled grooves."[10] Oral cultures tend to answer a question with another question so as to never be completely off guard. And one usually makes a major point by relating a story.

Although oral cultures vary, many seem to be strongly antagonistic. Proverbs, riddles, satire, and various tales can function as a form of verbal combat as well as entertainment. (Can you top this?) Both the Irish and Scots have a lengthy tradition of flyting: intense verbal jousting—often laced with vulgarity—that is similar to the dozens that one finds among contemporary inner-city African American youth. And oral cultures always accord high marks to satire.

The skilled use of satire takes this verbal jousting to its ultimate level— one step short of a fist fight. All words can sting, and hard ridicule, such as, mimicry, irony, and sarcasm, stings most painfully. When used by an expert, it can reduce an opponent to jelly. These exchanges strike with particular vengeance because, unlike a formal debate, satire cannot really be "answered." The words often mean just the opposite of what they say. Thus, a satirical attack calls forth a satirical response, which demands far more effort than simply defending one's position via logical argument.

In essence, this shared oral culture provided the bedrock for both Burns's and Lincoln's worlds. Thanks to energetic research, we know precisely what books Lincoln *read* while he was growing up. (President Bill Clinton kept on a White House shelf a collection of original editions of all the books that Lincoln read as a youth.)[11] But equally intriguing and impossible to recover is what he *heard*. Yet, the young Lincoln obviously heard a great deal more than he read. He would have been surrounded by hymns, political ditties, church songfests, both Calvinist and Arminian frontier preachers, folktales, read-aloud poetry, bawdy songs, dramatic recitations, satirical stories, and endless political discussions. There were few other forms of entertainment. Moreover, the worlds of print and oral culture on the Ohio Valley frontier often overlapped. Although newspapers were available, books were so scarce that people often read aloud to each other, which ensured that families heard the same words hundreds of times. During the weeks of the deep snow of 1830–31, when the Lincoln clan was largely confined to their newly erected Illinois log cabin, they probably read aloud to one another to pass the time. And the books most likely read from would have been the only ones available, such as, Robert Burns and the King James Version of Scripture.

Although they were composed in different time periods, the three classic texts of Lincoln's youth—the King James Version of the Bible, Shakespeare, and Burns—shared one thing in common: they were all meant to be *heard*. The Hebrew Bible, of course, was always intended to be read aloud.[12] Likewise, the first page of the King James Version states, "His Majesty's special commission, approved to be *read* in churches" (italics mine). Similarly, Shakespeare's plays were intended to be listened to rather than read. Shakespeare's contemporaries spoke of going to "hear" a play rather than "see" it. Shakespeare's favorite verse form—the iambic pentameter—lies very close to the rhythms of ordinary speech. Likewise, Burns's poetry was meant to be heard, even performed. There is abundant testimony that whenever Lincoln recited Burns, he usually acted out the story.

But here we enter a very gray area. Because of Lincoln's place in national mythology, many traditional Lincoln scholars have been somewhat leery of accepting the oral culture dimension of his youth.[13] Until recently, only a few historians ventured into this world. Reverend William E. Barton, who was deeply immersed in Kentucky and Indiana frontier life during the 1880s, suggested that the songs that Nancy Hanks sang to her children would have included "Barby Allen," "Fair Eleanor," "Jesus Is a Rock in a Weary Land," "Wicked Polly," and "Weevily Wheat" (in which the "Charlie" of the song is Bonnie Prince Charlie). Others have surmised that Lincoln would have also been exposed to "Way Down in the Paw Paw Patch," "Pop Goes the Weasel," "Old Sister Phoebe," "The Farmer Sows His Seed," "Hail Columbia Happy Land," "Rock of Ages," "There Is a Fountain Filled with Blood," and "Old Dan Tucker."[14] The simple repetitions, with modifications, plus the repeated refrains allowed these songs to be easily memorized.[15]

In the early twentieth century, English folklorist Cecil Sharp toured the Appalachian Mountains in search of ancient British folk melodies. There he met a people for whom singing was almost as common as speaking: "They knew their Bible intimately" and "subscribed to an austere creed, charged with Calvinism and the unrelenting doctrines of determinism or fatalism."[16] The same could be said for the Ohio River Valley a century earlier.

Because Burns wrote or modified so many lyrics, Lincoln surely would have encountered the most popular of his songs: "Auld Lang Syne," "My

Love Is like a Red, Red Rose," "Oh Wert Thou in the Cauld Blast," "Charlie, He's My Darling" (again, the Bonnie Prince), "A Man's a Man," and "The Highland Laddie." It's virtually certain that he heard Burns's bawdy songs, as well. Any discussion of "the oral dimension of Lincoln's youth," however, tends to send many Lincoln experts off their chairs. As James S. Ewing observed in 1909, "I think there have been more lies told about Mr. Lincoln than about Santa Claus."[17] So much nonsense has been written about him that for years, traditional Lincoln scholars demanded multisourced evidence before they would accept anything. Only recently have historians begun to mine the "reminiscence" material to illuminate his early life.[18]

In 1877, Lincoln's older cousin Dennis F. Hanks recollected that when the family lived in southern Indiana, he served as Lincoln's "preceptor, learned him his letters, spell, read and write." In another interview, William Herndon, former law partner and biographer of Lincoln, asked Hanks how he and Lincoln had learned so much amidst those bleak surroundings. Said Hanks, "We learned by sight, scent, and hearing. We heard all that was said, and talked over and over the questions heard; wore them slick, greasy, and threadbare. Went to political and other speeches and gatherings, as you do now: we would hear all sides and opinions, talk them over, discuss them, agreeing or disagreeing."[19] The Anglo-American oral world clearly stretched a long way.

Lincoln was steeped in this oral culture of the Kentucky and Indiana frontiers. His first schooling was a "blab" school, where all the children recited simultaneously. Gifted with marvelous memory, he could repeat sermons, speeches, and even newspaper articles almost verbatim. At his home in Springfield, he often annoyed Mary Todd by lying on the floor reading newspapers aloud. He also read poetry aloud, and his favorite form of entertainment remained the theater. But oral cultures contain a hard side as well. Robert Burns's contemporaries often spoke of his "keenness of satire." An aristocratic friend once took him aside to caution him against this tendency but to no avail. Even his peasant friends feared to cross him "lest he should pickle and preserve them in sarcastic song."[20] Burns had no master in this realm. A number of his political satires stress the rights of the common people to call their leaders to account if they failed in their assigned duties.

But political issues fade quickly, political satire along with them. Religious satire, however, transcends the years and retains a universal dimension; and here Burns reigns as the ultimate master. As Liam McIlvanney has shown, Burns attacked the spiritual vanity and arrogance of churchgoers overly assured of their salvation. Arguing from a moderate Calvinist rather than a hard Freethinker position, Burns scorned the "Unco Guid" (overly righteous) claim that they could decisively judge others by their behavior alone.[21] Ultimate judgments, Burns argued, could only be made by God. The last two verses of "Address to the Unco Guid, or the Rigidly Righteous" read:

> Then gently scan your brother Man,
> Still gentler sister Woman;
> Tho' they may gang a kennin wrang,
> To step aside is human:
> One point must still be greatly dark,
> The moving *Why* they do it;
> And just as lamely can ye mark;
> How far perhaps they rue it.
> Who made the heart, 'tis *He* alone
> Decidedly can try us,
> He knows each chord its various tone,
> Each spring its various bias:
> Then at the balance let's be mute,
> We never can adjust it;
> What's *done* we partly may compute,
> But know not what's *resisted*.

In verse 27 of "The Holy Fair," which lampoons religious revivals, one reads about the power of shared human passion that affects saint and sinner alike.

> O' sinners and o' lasses!
> Their homes o' stane, gin night, are gane
> As saft as onie flesh is:
> There's some are fou o' love divine;
> There's some are fou o' brandy;
> An' monie jobs that day begin,
> May end in houghmagandie [fornication]
> Some ither day.

Finally, Burns's poems and songs conveyed yet another dimension that would later characterize Lincoln's best writing—a profound simplicity of language. All the well-known orators of Burns's and Lincoln's eras went on at great length. Even the greatest—William Pitt, Henry Clay, and Daniel Webster—used ten words when one might do. But Burns possessed the gift of reducing a complex position to a couplet. As students of Lincoln's prose have noted, this simplicity and clarity of argument characterize his best speeches as well.

The Legacy of Rhythm

Although Lincoln appears to have borrowed *themes* rather than precise phrases from Burns, he seems to have also borrowed something else: a heightened sense of poetic cadence. Both in his poetry and songs, Burns utilized a variety of stanza forms and rhyme schemes. For example, "The Cotter's Saturday Night" and "Tam O' Shanter" reflect very different patterns of rhythm. But the poet drew most heavily on what has been termed the "Habbie" or the "Habbie Noble." This verse form is especially effective in creating irony, forging epigrams, and heightening poetic tension. It is the rhyme scheme most associated with Burns. It has an A-A-A-B-A-B rhyme, with four beats to the A measures and two to the B.[22] Three examples follow, all from poems that Lincoln especially admired. "To a Mouse":

Wee, sleekit, cowrin, tim'rous beastie,	A—4 beats
O, what panic's in thy breastie!	A—4 beats
Thou need na start awa sae hasty	A—4 beats
Wi' bickering brattle!	B—2 beats
I wad be laith to rin an' chase thee,	A—4 beats
Wi' murdering pattle!	B—2 beats

"To a Louse, On Seeing One on a Lady's Bonnet at Church" (stanza 2):

Ye ugly, creepin blastit wonner,
Detested, shunn'd by saunt an' sinner,
How daur ye set your fit upon her—
Sae fine a lady!
Gae somewhere else, and seek your dinner
On some poor body.

"Holy Willie's Prayer":

O Thou that in heaven does dwell!
Wha, as it pleases best Thysel,
Sends ane to heaven and ten to Hell,
A' for Thy glory!
And no for onie guid or ill
They've done before Thee!

The pulsing beat of the Habbie Noble drives home the poet's message with relentless force. Thus, Burns embedded his ideas of democracy, social equality, justice, attacks on hypocrisy, and appeals for forgiveness in the most pulsating poetic meter of the day. One hesitates to compare on the level of greatness, but few sections of either the King James Version or Shakespeare resound with the same driving rhythm of Burns's Habbie Noble verses. It was the most powerful beat around. As all who admire poetry realize, the true power of verse rests with the unique blend of sound and lyric. Douglas Wilson's magisterial assessment of Lincoln's power over words frequently notes how often he let himself be guided by the *sound* of what he was writing. Although it cannot be precisely proven, it seems highly probable that Lincoln's admiration for Burns's rhyme schemes deepened his own sense of cadence.

Lincoln's Use of Satire

Several of Burns's best-known poems virtually raised social satire to the level of high art, and Lincoln obviously drank deeply from this satirical well. Herndon describes him as "merciless in satire" during his early years.[23] This theme may be clearly seen in the Crawford, Grigsby, Forquer, Thomas, and Shields affairs (discussed shortly), encounters that form part of the less-than-heroic Lincoln (or, from another perspective, a more human, frontier Lincoln). These incidents also reveal his thorough grounding in the hard side of Anglo-American oral culture. They also suggest a deep familiarity with the satires of Robert Burns.

Lincoln's southern Indiana friend Josiah Crawford, from whom he once borrowed a *Life of Washington* and had to pull fodder for three days because the rain ruined it, sported a gigantic nose. It was misshapen, filled with pimples and blue. During the 1820s, Lincoln composed a crude piece of doggerel on Crawford's appendage that wounded him deeply and gave the nose "a fame as wide as to the Wabash and the Ohio."[24] The lyrics have not survived.

The Grigsby incident occurred in 1828, shortly after the nineteen-year-old Lincoln had lost his sister, Sarah, whose husband, Aaron Grigsby, was a member of the most prominent family in Gentryville, Indiana. It appears as if Lincoln blamed Aaron for his sister's death in childbirth, and hard feelings arose between the families. When two other Grigsby brothers married two sisters, Lincoln was not invited to the infare to celebrate their unions. So, he devised a rude scheme to place the brides in the wrong bedrooms and later wrote a quasi-biblical account he called "The

Chronicles of Reuben" and a brief satirical poem to further embarrass the Grigsby family. This poem contains these lines.

> But Betsy, she said,
> You cursed bald head
> My suitor you never can be,
> Besides your ill shape
> Proclaims you an ape
> And that never can answer for me

The goal, of course, was public ridicule. These and various other bawdy Lincoln satires circulated in oral form for over a generation. William Herndon first wrote some of them down when he visited Indiana in the late 1860s in search of Lincoln stories. But because the originals do not exist in Lincoln's own handwriting, the editors of his *Collected Works* have elected not to include them in the official compilation.[25]

Lincoln drew on public ridicule again in 1836, when he was a candidate for reelection to the Illinois House of Representatives. The story comes from his friend Joshua Speed, who had just moved from Kentucky, a state long famous for great orators. Lincoln's opponent was Democrat George Forquer, who told the crowd that he would have to take Lincoln "down a peg" and proceeded to give what Speed termed a "slasher-gaff" speech that was filled with ridicule and sarcasm. Lincoln heard his opponent out and mounted the platform to reply. Stump speaking in those days was purely spontaneous. There were no podiums to hold any "paper-canned thoughts in manuscript," as one observer phrased it. Instead, each speaker had only his wits to rely on. Carefully, Lincoln began his response. (To understand the reply, one must know that Forquer had recently switched from the Whig to the Democratic Party and had subsequently been appointed register of the Land Office. His house also boasted the only lightning rod in the county, which Lincoln had seen for the first time the day before.) Said Lincoln, "The gentleman commenced his speech by saying that this young man will have to be taken down, and that he was sorry that the task devolved upon him. I am not so young in years as I am in the tricks and trades of a politician; but, live long, or die young, I would rather die now, than, like the gentleman, change my politics, and simultaneously with the change receive an office worth $3,000 per year, and then have to erect a lightning-rod over my house to protect a guilty conscience from an offended God."[26]

Four years later, Lincoln drew from the same fount to destroy Judge Jesse B. Thomas, a Democratic opponent who had previously attacked him in an earlier speech. From the podium, Lincoln resorted to satire and mimicry so severe that it reduced poor Thomas to tears. The audience howled with glee, but Lincoln felt remorse and later sought out Thomas to apologize for his cruel use of words. For years, however, this incident was locally recalled as "the skinning of Thomas."[27]

Lincoln also drew on the fount of public satire in August of 1842 in Springfield. Newspapers of the day frequently published anonymous articles, and the *Sangamo Journal* did so that month with four letters signed "Rebecca" and one poem signed "Cathleen."[28] These missives viciously ridiculed James Shields, then the auditor of the State of Illinois. Lincoln wrote the most devastating of the "Rebecca" letters, but Mary Todd and a friend, Julia Jayne, wrote at least one of the others; still, when pressed, Lincoln graciously assumed all responsibility. These satires worked on the same gritty level as the Crawford or Grigsby poems. They accused Shields of theft, sexual adventurism, body odor, and arrogance: "Dear girls, *it is distressing,* but I cannot marry you all. Too well I know how much you suffer; but do, *do* remember it is not my fault that I am *so* handsome and *so* interesting."[29] A Catholic immigrant from Northern Ireland—and thus someone well aware of the unwritten rules of flyting—Shields demanded justice, and only the timely intervention of friends avoided a formal duel.

If his verbal assault on Thomas filled Lincoln with remorse, his attack on Shields festered as a sore point for years. He and Mary agreed never to mention it again. He once complained to Herndon that if all the good things he had ever done were remembered as long as his scrape with Shields, he would never be forgotten.[30] In an 1885 reminiscence, humorist David R. Locke recalled Lincoln's incredible skill with words: "He was a master of satire, which was at times as blunt as a meat-ax, and at others as keen as a razor; but it was always kindly except when some horrible injustice was its inspiration, and then it was terrible."[31] From the Shields affair forward, Lincoln became much more circumspect in his use of political satire. Henry C. Whitney, who rode with him on the Illinois Circuit, noted that only "in the privacy of a judicial circle (but very rarely) [would he] . . . impale an object disagreeable to him on a sarcastic lance quite as effectually, and in better style than in his youthful days."[32]

In his later years, Lincoln relied on logical argument far more than satire, although satire persisted in a few instances: various anonymous articles, in a speech protesting a Zachary Taylor veto, in a speech to the Scott Club of Springfield, and occasionally in the debates with Stephen Douglas. But there is no satire whatsoever in his major statements from the White House. Still, his early wielding of the most lethal weapon of oral culture reflects a world he shared with—and almost certainly partially borrowed from—Scotland's most famous poet.[33]

New Salem and Jack Kelso

On February 12, 1830, Abraham Lincoln turned twenty-one and thus was no longer required by law to turn over his wages to his father. So, after driving an ox wagon to Illinois to help his parents settle in Macon County, he decided to strike out on his own. The next spring, shortly after "the winter of the deep snow"—when snowpack lay four feet on the level for about six weeks—Lincoln left the family cabin and moved to the hamlet of New Salem, where he would spend the next six years of his life. It was there he met the enigmatic John (Jack) Kelso, who, persistent legend has it, was the person who introduced him to the works of William Shakespeare and (re?)introduced him to the poetry of Robert Burns.

Relatively little is known about Kelso and his wife, Hanna. After New Salem collapsed in the late 1830s, they moved to Missouri where they virtually disappeared from the historical record. Herndon never tracked them down in his relentless search for people who had known Lincoln in his early days. Consequently, a good deal of mystery surrounds Kelso and his role in shaping the young Lincoln. *Kelso* is a Scottish Borders name. The compact town of Kelso lies at the confluence of the Tweed and Teviot rivers, about five miles from the English border. Some believe that Jack was born in either Virginia or Kentucky but he and his parents may well have emigrated from the Borders region, which would have given him a first-hand knowledge of the Scots language. Jack and Hanna had no children, and no photos have survived, but a grand nephew, who knew Jack in his sixties, described him as follows: "He had a florid complexion, with white, bushy hair, he was about 5'10" tall and inclined to be stout, weighing about 200 lbs."[34]

Jack and Hanna Kelso arrived in New Salem in tandem with Joshua and Nancy Miller (the women were sisters) during the summer of 1832. Because Miller was a blacksmith, his skills were much in demand, and he soon established a small forge in the center of town. The couple lived in a double residence linked by an open area, probably used for eating, situated on the west end of the Petersburg-Springfield road. Lincoln scholars have reached no agreement regarding Jack Kelso. William E. Barton termed him "a peculiar, unpractical genius" while Carl Sandburg and M. L. Houser called him a "loveable vagabond." David Donald dismissed him as fat and lazy, while William E. Gienapp described him as a "village idler." Helen Nicolay depicted him as the "disreputable town drunkard."[35]

Historical archaeologist Mary Turner is far more sympathetic. She maintains that Kelso had "personality." Although his brother-in-law ran the New Salem blacksmith's shop, none of Herndon's informants, as compiled by historians Douglas L. Wilson and Rodney O. Davis, ever mentioned Miller. But numerous contemporaries recalled Jack Kelso.[36] Turner also argues that Kelso was less an "idler" than a throwback to an earlier generation of frontiersmen who had been able to live off the land. Kelso had numerous talents along this line. He knew how to stalk the deer that migrated in herds as large as thirty-six to drink at dusk in the Sangamon River, and he sold smoked venison to nearby Petersburg. He gathered wild red and yellow plums and helped Hanna preserve them in local honey. He had a secret way of spitting on his hook while baiting it, and his fishing skills became the envy of the town. He often sold black perch to Petersburg as well. In addition, Jack Kelso was a good citizen. He served on various town assignments, joined the debating society, and became the central figure in a celebrated court case involving a stolen hog. In short, Turner argues, Jack Kelso was a representative frontiersman of his time.[37]

Unlike many of his neighbors, however, Kelso proved exceptionally literate. One of his contemporaries described him as "deeply and thoroughly read in Burns and Shakespeare."[38] As a consequence, he was considered very well educated for his day.[39] Exactly where he acquired this knowledge is uncertain. One legend suggests that he had worked as a Scottish schoolmaster before sailing from a port north of Glasgow.[40] Another credits him with owning a library of twenty-seven volumes, surely the largest in the village. None of these tales can be verified.

Kelso's career after the family left New Salem is equally vague. In the early 1840s, the Millers and Kelsos moved west to Macon County, Missouri, and, in 1850, to Achinson County, in the northeastern corner of that state. Miller family legend maintains that in the election of 1860, Miller, Miller's son, and Kelso were the only Lincoln supporters in the entire county and that they endured much criticism from their neighbors because of this. Another version states that Kelso walked three miles to vote for Lincoln in 1864 and then died from a sudden heart attack upon return. (This is unlikely because he signed a deed in 1866, the last record of him.) The Kelso farm initially bordered the Missouri River, but over time, the river shifted and gradually inundated the land. It is perhaps fitting that the old Kelso farm site is now the Langdon Bend public fishing area.[41]

From 1831 to 1837, Lincoln called New Salem home. In a town of about a hundred people and twenty-five buildings, he knew Jack Kelso well, especially as they boarded together for a period. Contemporaries recalled that he and Kelso often fished together, even though Lincoln generally considered fishing a waste of time. Although Lincoln enjoyed considerable capacity for both rhythm and rhyme, his poetic tastes had hitherto been restricted to nonsense jingles and satirical doggerel. Jack Kelso changed all this. Although it is doubtful that Kelso *introduced* Lincoln to Burns, it is highly likely that he was the man who encouraged him to read and memorize large portions of Shakespeare and Burns. Thus, Kelso has been firmly entrenched in the myth/history that surrounds Lincoln's early life. Later, Illinois poet Edgar Lee Masters wrote a poem about Kelso.[42]

Lincoln's Links with Burns

If, indeed, Jack Kelso reacquainted Lincoln with the poetry of Burns, he did an excellent job, for Lincoln's love of Burns's verse proved no youthful infatuation. Instead, it became an essential part of his makeup. A number of Herndon's New Salem informants testified to that. Lincoln "knew all of Burns by heart," recalled Charles Maltby. "Burns and Byron were his favorite books," said W. G. Greene. "Burns seemed to be his favorite," said N. W. Branson. Lincoln read, "Considerable of Burns' poem[s]," recollected Abner Y. Ellis, and so on. He later "forsook Byron—never Shakespeare and Burns," said Speed.[43]

During his time as a clerk in Denton Offutt's store in New Salem, Maltby recalled, Lincoln would relax by reading Burns aloud with great hilarity. Milton Hay, who served as a clerk in Lincoln's Springfield law office, told a reporter that Lincoln "could quote Burns by the hour. I have been with him in that little office and heard him recite with the greatest admiration and zest Burns' ballads and quaint things." Hay recalled that Lincoln had memorized all of "Tam O' Shanter" and "Holy Willie's Prayer," plus most of "The Cotter's Saturday Night." To this Maltby added "Address to the Deil," "Highland Mary," "Bonnie Jean," and "Dr. Hornbook."[44]

Lincoln's familiarity with Burns may be further inferred by his handwritten corrections—or rather, the lack thereof—on the pages of his 1860 presidential biography written by William Dean Howells. Just before publication, Howells mailed a copy to Lincoln in Springfield for his final assessment. Lincoln made several changes to the manuscript, but he let pass without comment the following sentence: "When practicing law before his election to Congress, a copy of Burns was his inseparable companion on the circuit; and this he pursued so constantly, that it is said he now has by heart every line of his favorite poet." Visitors to the Lincoln home in Springfield during the 1850s might well be entertained by one of his son's formal recitations of Burns. Whenever a few people were gathered in the White House during an evening, Lincoln would frequently read aloud to them from Shakespeare or Burns. The Scots dialect, which seemed alien to many, did not appear to bother Lincoln, as contemporaries maintained that he could duplicate much of the Scottish pronunciation.

Lincoln's admiration for Burns never wavered. According to James Grant Wilson, editor of the *Record*, Chicago's first literary magazine, and an early Republican supporter, Lincoln once stopped by to see him in 1860. He noticed busts of Shakespeare and Burns in Wilson's office, and when Wilson told him he had purchased them in Stratford-on-Avon and Ayr, he was dutifully impressed. Said Lincoln, "They are my two favorite authors, and I must manage to see their birthplaces some day if I can contrive to cross the Atlantic."[45] Later, Wilson wrote Lincoln to inform him that he had spent an entire day in Prestwick, near Ayr, speaking with Burns's youngest sister, Isabella Burns Begg, then eighty. Wilson enclosed a small book of verse by Fitz Greene Halleck, which included Halleck's tribute to Burns, "Burns—To a Rose, Brought from near Alloway Kirk, in Ayrshire, in the Autumn of 1822." Lincoln dashed off a brief note of thanks for the book, expressing his admiration that Wilson had known Burns's sister.

During Lincoln's years in the White House, the Philadelphia and Washington, D.C., Burns Clubs staged annual celebrations every January of the poet's birth. In 1864, the Philadelphia club saluted the president's health and informed him of the toast and the formal acknowledgment of it. The Washington, D.C., club invited Lincoln to join them in 1864, and while there is a persistent rumor that Lincoln attended at least one of these gatherings, that has never been substantiated. Because Scotsman Alexander Williamson, who tutored Tad and Willie Lincoln, also served as secretary of the Washington club, he had special access to the president. On January 24, 1865, he asked Lincoln for a "recognition of the genius of Scotland's bard, by either a toast, a sentiment, or in any other way you may deem proper" (not precisely an invitation to attend the gathering, as is usually supposed). Lincoln penned a hasty note that was dutifully read at the celebration: "I cannot frame a toast to Burns. I can say nothing worthy of his generous heart and transcendent genius. Thinking of what he has said, I cannot say anything worth saying."[46] Lincoln's final reference to Burns came just days before his death. John Hay, Lincoln's secretary in Washington, recollected that when he and Lincoln sailed down the Potomac in early April 1865, Lincoln recited from several Burns's poems. He closed with the last verse of "Lament for James, Earl of Glencairn."

> The bridegroom may forget the bride
> Was made his wedded wife yestreen.
> The Monarch may forget the crown
> That on his head an hour has been
> The mither may forget the bairn
> That smiles sae sweetly on her knee,
> But I'll remember thee Glencairn
> And all that thou hast done for me.

Turning to Hay, Lincoln said that Burns never touched sentiment without carrying it to its ultimate expression and leaving nothing further to be said.[47]

The National Park Service has officially recognized the Lincoln-Burns connection. In 1988 when they refurbished the Lincoln family home in Springfield, they relied heavily on a woodcut of the family parlor—taken from a now-lost original photo—that revealed the presence of several heroic busts in the room. Because it was not possible to determine precisely whom the busts depicted, the Park Service chose three: Shakespeare, Charles Dickens, and Burns. Tucked into the northeast corner of the Lincoln parlor and one of the first objects that the four hundred thousand annual tourists to the Lincoln home see is a heroic bust of Robert Burns.

Why the Appeal?

What was there about Burns poetry that so captivated the young Lincoln? And why did the appeal remain throughout his lifetime? From the perspective of the twenty-first century, it is intriguing how the two men's lives paralleled one another. Each was born into a humble family, worked as a farm laborer, briefly tried surveying, regularly battled depression, and felt himself uncomfortable when moving among the upper-class women of his day. In addition, each shared an innate sense that he had been destined by Providence for better things in life (perhaps a reflection of a shared Calvinist background). As Lincoln told Speed during the bleak winter of 1841, "But I have an irrepressible desire to live till I can be assured that the world is a little better for my having lived in it."[48] A Burns letter to Mrs. Scott of Wauchope, Scotland, expresses the same sense of destiny.

That I for puir Auld Scotland's sake
Some usefu' plan or
book could make,
Or sing a sang at
least.

Clearly, Lincoln found in Burns a kindred spirit in both upbringing and intellectual concerns. This shared outlook is especially visible in three areas: knowledge of farming, a common Reformed Christianity, and a faith in reason, equality, and the intrinsic worth of the ordinary individual.

Farming

Burns's father William Burness has frankly been described as a "Scotch peasant." No author has so designated Abraham's parents, Thomas and Nancy Hanks Lincoln, but that was surely what they were. In terms of agrarian lifestyle, persistent poverty, and sparse material possessions, the Lincolns (initially pronounced "Link-horn") operated well within the framework of a peasant society. The "auld clay biggin" that William Burness built for his wife, Agnes Broun, contained about as much interior space as the Kentucky cabin where Lincoln was born or the Indiana cabin to which Thomas Lincoln brought his second wife, Sarah Bush Johnston, although the American homes lacked the byres for the animals. The sleeping loft that Robert shared with his brother resembled the sleeping quarters that Abraham shared with his stepbrother John Johnston and cousin Dennis Hanks. When one rolled over, all had to move at the same time.

Given the modest size of their homes, plus the relatively moderate climates of southwest Scotland and the Ohio River Valley, both Burns and Lincoln must have spent most of their youth out of doors. Persistent farm work would have kept them there as well. A modern Burnsian scholar has tabulated twenty-eight hundred references to nature in Burns's works.[49] Although Lincoln left farming as soon as he could, never bothering to establish even a "hobby farm," he still retained an interest in agriculture all his days. In 1859, he gave a speech in Wisconsin on that theme, emphasizing the importance of agricultural fairs. Historian Wayne Temple has noted how frequently he drew on agricultural imagery to make his major points. Fellow lawyer Henry Clay Whitney recalled that whenever they stopped at a farmhouse for dinner, Lincoln would examine some farming implement or tool and make a comment on it.[50] At the 1864 Hampton Roads Conference with Confederate leaders, he described Alexander H. Stephens, the diminutive vice president of the Confederacy, as "the biggest shuck and the littlest ear that ever you did see."[51] When he finished delivering his Gettysburg Address, he turned to his friend Ward Hill Lamon and said ruefully, "Lamon, that speech won't scour." (When a plow cuts through the soil cleanly, without sticking to the plowshare and moldboard, it is said to "scour.")[52]

Farm life is seasonal, and there could not have been much difference between William Burness's planting and harvesting oats, vegetables, and kale and Thomas Lincoln's planting and harvesting potatoes, wheat, alfalfa, and vegetables. (Indeed, Lincoln's first childhood memory was that of planting pumpkin seeds on the Kentucky farm, seeds that a spring shower later flooded out.) Unlike the Burness family, of course, Thomas Lincoln relied heavily on maize. Indeed, maize, alone among the major grains, allowed American frontier farm families to survive, for it could be sown in patches among the stumps of an only partially cleared field. The pioneer phrase "corn dodgers [corn meal] and common doings" came to mean ordinary table fare. As British traveler John Woods, who spent 1820 to 1822 in Illinois, noted, "The American live mostly on corn-bread; the English eat little of it." But even if the crops differed slightly, the plows, scythes, hoes, and sickles used by Robert and Abraham would have been much the same. In terms of agricultural education, William Burness clearly surpassed Thomas Lincoln. William was a professional gardener, while Thomas never ranked above the "middlin" level of agriculture. Several contemporaries ranked him as a carpenter first and only secondarily a farmer. Both Burns and Lincoln must have spent countless hours engaged in similar tasks: plowing, planting, hoeing, threshing, gathering wild fruits and berries, swatting insects, collecting honey, gathering eggs, butchering hogs, cattle, chickens, and sheep, caring for horses, driving oxen, piling rock (Burns), or splitting rails (Lincoln) for fences. As Lincoln's 1859 letter to J. W. Fell wryly notes, "I was raised to farm work, at which I continued till I was twenty-two." When Burns described the weekend relaxation of a peasant farm family in "The Cotter's Saturday Night" (a Lincoln favorite), Lincoln could surely identify with every line.

What most separates their two worlds is the American Revolution. Peasant though they may have been in work and lifestyle, Thomas, Nancy Hanks, and Sarah Lincoln did not share a peasant worldview. There were no titled nobles or great country houses nearby. No majestic city of Edinburgh, with its Castle, Holyrood Palace, St. Giles Cathedral, and emerging New Town lay within two-days' ride to remind the Lincolns of their lowly station in life. Frontier Louisville or Cincinnati hardly matched Old Town

Edinburgh and the Edinburgh Castle. Impressive though they might have been, Kentucky's finest homes—usually built of wood—could not hold a candle to the towering stone houses of Glasgow, Perth, and Aberdeen. As British émigré John Woods noted of frontier Illinois, "But this is not the country for fine gentlemen or those who live in a grand style."[53]

Although the American Revolution never quite achieved its goal of promised social equality, it did institute a process that began to ease the most rigid of these social distinctions. Thus, the senior Lincolns and their neighbors never thought of themselves as "peasants." In his visit to America in 1837, French aristocrat Alexis de Tocqueville noted this: "Americans never use the word *peasant*, because they have no idea of the class which that term denotes; the ignorance of more remote ages, the simplicity of rural life; and the rusticity of the villager have not been preserved among them; and they are alike unacquainted with the virtues, the vices, the coarse habits, and the simple graces of an early stage of civilization."[54] Perhaps one is not really a peasant if one does not think so.

Religion

The second area of overlap involved the Reformed faith and the social role played by the churches in each culture. Here the American Revolution, culminating in the Constitution with its famed separation of church and state, serves as a central pivot. Although Burns and Lincoln each wrestled with theological/ultimate issues, their religious worlds had very different boundaries. Burns's church or kirk was "established," that is, a national church that retained a variety of legal functions. The American Revolution changed all that for both Kentucky and the Old Northwest, where there could be no "established" faith; instead, each religious denomination had to *persuade* people to join voluntarily.

Burns's world included a number of well-meaning but stodgy ministers, such as, long-term parish cleric "Daddy" Auld, but it also abounded with a variety of learned theologians. Unlike the French Revolution, the Scottish Enlightenment always retained a major place for the educated cleric, such as Reverend Hugh Blair, as spokesperson of new ideas. Burns was also friends with the prominent Catholic Bishop John Geddes. Lincoln, however, grew to maturity among frontier revivalists—many of whom lacked the bare rudiments of learning. He was known to repeat their sermons as a form of ridicule. He probably never confronted a learned cleric until he met Scotsman James Smith, pastor of the Springfield First Presbyterian Church. Yet, similar theological concerns swept through both worlds.

Late eighteenth-century Ayrshire and the early nineteenth-century Ohio River Valley abounded with discussions of reason versus revelation, salvation, damnation, free will, the nature of Grace, God's role in history, the accuracy of the Bible, Calvinism, Arminianism, the afterlife, prophecy, and proper moral behavior.

Discovering the faith of either Burns or Lincoln has proven a challenge. Both Maurice Lindsay and Thomas Crawford have termed Burns a "wistful agnostic." The description at the Burns Center in Dumfries, Scotland, frankly lists him as an "atheist."[55] His landlady, however, considered Burns "but a rough and roun' Christian."[56] Scottish writer Alan Bold describes him as "a moderate and humane" Presbyterian, and Liam McIlvanney insists that his kirk satires derived from a Reformed Christian base rather than one of pure rationalism.[57]

The evidence is contradictory. Burns attended church, both in Ayrshire and Dumfries, however reluctantly, and took his prescribed part in family devotions. After his father's death, because he was the eldest son, Robert led these ceremonies, conducting family worship every night during his residence at Mossgeil. One finds a sympathetic view of religion in his "Selkirk Grace" and especially in "The Cotter's Saturday Night" (a poem that Lincoln admired).

But then there is the other side: the scorn of Unco Guid, "Holy Fair," and "Holy Willie's Prayer." There is also the lighter spoof of religion in "The Kirk's Alarm," which begins, "Orthodox, orthodox, wha believe in John Knox." In a letter to Rachel Dunlop on August 2, 1788, Burns wrote that he was in "perpetual warfare" with the doctrine of original sin. Although he never stated it as such, he was far more in "perpetual warfare" with the church's attempt to control peasant sexual behavior, its moral control rather than its theological point(s) of view. Burns probably had one foot in the deist camp, but the other rested firmly in the historic Christian/Scottish Enlightenment view of universality (the idea came in two versions). Burns extended God's benevolence to both mouse and daisy. In "Address to the Deil," he even hoped that Old Nick himself might someday achieve salvation.

Although legend states that Lincoln served as a teen-aged sexton for the Pigeon Creek Baptist Church in Spencer County, he soon became enthralled by the deist writings of Thomas Paine and the Comte de Volney. By the time he moved to New Salem, he was clearly a frontier Freethinker. Herndon always considered Lincoln an infidel, as Herndon termed himself. Contemporaries recalled how much Lincoln relished Burns's religious satires and his critique of the reigning religious establishment. These verses certainly would have resonated with a man who always felt himself an outsider to organized religion. Indeed, New Salem Freethinker James H. Matheny declared that Burns's "Address to the Unco Guid, or Rigidly Righteous" and "Holy Willie's Prayer" were "Lincoln's religion" during the time he knew him at New Salem.[58]

The claim that Burns's religious satires played a role in enticing Lincoln into the rationalist camp continued for years. In 1872, an observer argued in the *Scotsman* that Lincoln's reading of "Holy Willie's Prayer" had served just that purpose. But four days later, "An Old Subscriber" challenged this interpretation: "Holy Willie's Prayer" did not reflect Burns's personal views. Rather, the poem served as a biting satire on religious hypocrisy in general. The "Old Subscriber" doubted that Lincoln could have missed this obvious aspect of the poem.[59]

Simultaneously with its emphasis on reason, however, Burns's lyrics would also have intersected Lincoln's world in his bemused treatment of the supernatural. Just as Burns's eighteenth-century kirk could never quite suppress the pagan subculture of Ayrshire, neither could the American Enlightenment suppress the persistent supernaturalism of the frontier Midwest.[60] Lincoln's youth abounded with healing herbs, the foreshadowing of dreams, spells to charm a rifle, and love potions. Dousing rods of witch hazel could find water, and healing by faith proved as effective as consulting local physicians. Everyone knew that fence-post trees had to be cut before noon and that potatoes and other vegetables should be planted under a bright moon. It was common knowledge that if a horse breathed on a child, the child would soon catch whooping cough, or if a person killed a snake and left it belly up, the rain would never cease. O. H. Browning recalled that Lincoln had a "tolerably strong vein of superstition in his nature" and generally all his life believed in presentiments.[61]

Presentiments—what we would now term "foreshadowing" of events—were similarly woven into the fabric of everyday life. His stepmother, Sarah Lincoln, later confessed that she knew in her heart that something evil would befall Abraham if he were elected president. Lincoln himself marveled at the probable foreshadowing of many of his dreams; he frequently suggested that he would be fortunate to survive the war. After the loss of their son Willie, he probably accompanied Mary to séances held in the White House. In spite of Lincoln's oft-professed faith in reason and logic, he frankly termed himself "superstitious."[62]

Lincoln's long-term familiarity with the supernatural would have echoed in his reading of Burns's "Halloween," in which the goodwife tries to divine the future. It would also have resonated in "Tam O' Shanter," (a Lincoln favorite) when a slightly tipsy Tam observes a witches' dance in the auld kirkyard and barely escapes with his life by fleeing across the River Doon (witches cannot cross water). But his faithful horse, Meg, lost her tail.

Nailing down Lincoln's religious faith has been even harder than describing that of Burns.[63] Casual readers are surprised to discover that historians have spilled more ink over Lincoln's religion than any other aspect of his life except his views on race and slavery. Freethinkers, Catholics, Unitarians, Spiritualists, Quakers, and Presbyterians (among others) have claimed him as their own. Biographer Douglas L. Wilson argues that Lincoln was deliberately duplicitous in this area, but this is hotly disputed.[64]

As with Burns, the evidence is ambiguous. While they lived in Kentucky, Lincoln's parents, Thomas and Nancy, were members of the Little Mount Separate Baptist Church, which accepted the Bible as its only guide. In Indiana in 1818, Thomas, daughter Sarah, and new wife Sarah united with the Pigeon Baptist Church, a Regular (Primitive)—sometimes called Hardshell—Baptist church, which was Calvinist in orientation. Unlike the Methodists, the Regular Baptists denied that man could do anything to save himself. God had made this decision before time began. Their creed—and they were one of the few Baptist groups to subscribe to a creed (the Philadelphia Confession)—overlapped in many areas with the Westminster confession of the Presbyterians.[65] Lincoln attended some (we don't know how many) services there.

Lincoln never joined any denomination. As he phrased it,

> I have never united myself to any church, because I have found difficulty in giving my assent, without mental reservation, to the long, complicated statements of Christian doctrine which characterize their articles of belief and confessions of faith. When any church will inscribe over its altars, as its sole qualification for membership, the Saviour's condensed statement of the substance of both law and gospel, "Thou shalt love the Lord thy God with all thy heart, and with all thy soul, and with all thy mind, and thy neighbor as thyself," that church will I join with all my heart and all my soul.[66]

Like Burns, Lincoln often treated the reigning religious establishment in a hands-off fashion. Still, he was married in an Episcopal ceremony, owned a pew at the Springfield First Presbyterian Church, attended the

New York Avenue Presbyterian Church in Washington, and hoped to visit the Holy Land after the war. Mary Todd admitted that he was not "technically" a Christian, but his friend Jesse W. Fell noted, "His principles and practices, and the spirit of his whole life, were of the kind we universally agree to call Christian." His old friend Judge David Davis bluntly said that nobody knew anything about his faith, a sentiment echoed by the funeral sermon given by Methodist Bishop Mathew Simpson at the Oak Creek Cemetery in Springfield.[67] Lincoln observed in 1863, "I have often wished that I was a more devout man than I am" but noted also that "amid the greatest difficulties of my Administration, when I could not see any other resort, I would place my whole reliance in God, knowing that all would go well, and that He would decide for the right."[68] Biographer J. G. Randall once said that to discover Lincoln's philosophical/theological views, historians have had to weave between Herndon's excessive emphasis on his alleged religious infidelity and the overly pious claims by a number of clerical writers.[69] It has not been an easy task.

Many students of Burns's life argue that he rejected the Calvinism of the Church of Scotland for an aggressive pursuit of physical pleasure. Indeed, rationalists such as Robert G. Ingersoll and Andrew Carnegie celebrated Burns, in part, because of his attacks on Calvinistic determinism. Contemporary Scottish theologians admit that Burns was "haunted" rather than helped by his inherited Calvinist/Presbyterian faith. Yet, his collected letters show how frequently he wrestled with these questions.[70]

Lincoln responded in a very different fashion. Unlike Burns, he never really escaped his initial immersion in frontier Calvinism. One could argue that Lincoln's understanding of Calvinism proved strangely liberating. In a sense, he felt that Providence was utilizing him for a distinct purpose, which eventually evolved into not just the saving of the Union but also the emancipation of the slaves. The two organized religious groups to which Lincoln was most closely connected—the Regular (Primitive) Baptists of Indiana and the Old School Presbyterians of Springfield and Washington—both held to a moderate Calvinist position, what Lincoln once termed the "doctrine of necessity."

Late eighteenth- to early nineteenth-century Calvinism came with a variety of subtle emphases that shifted over time. But the core of the Reformed position—strangely ignored in most discussions—revolved around the statements contained in the Westminster Confession of Faith. This venerable document, approved by the Scottish General Assembly in 1647, was adhered to by the Church of Scotland and by all the larger branches of American Presbyterianism. The seventeenth-century Puritans of New England also adopted it—with some changes to allow for differences in church government—and the Regular Baptists did so, in essence.[71] The first article of the Westminster confession reads as follows: "The whole counsel of God concerning all things necessary for His own glory, man's salvation, faith and life, is either expressly set down in Scripture, or by good and necessary consequence may be deduced from Scripture." A few lines later is, "Those things which are necessary to be known, believed, and observed for salvation, are so clearly propounded, and opened in some place of Scripture or other, that not only the learned but the unlearned, in a due use of the ordinary means, may attain unto a sufficient understanding of them." And a few lines further on: "God from all eternity, did, by the most wise and holy counsel of His own free will, freely and unchangeably ordain whatsoever comes to pass."[72] In other words, the Westminster Confession declared that history is not simply a random, haphazard series of events. Rather, God has a specific plan for each person, each nation, and for the world. God fully comprehends the *end* of each event at its beginning. Thus, history is unfolding precisely according to divine purpose. The belief that the truths of Scripture were open to both the wise and foolish, that the words should be interpreted not necessarily literally but logically ("deduced from"), and that God was using every human action for His own purposes proved much a part of both Burns's and Lincoln's views of the world. In a strange way, this position can be a liberating one.

Lincoln remained a man of great sensitivity. Yet, when he arrived in Washington in 1861, he had to preside over the worst war of the century, one where over six hundred thousand men lost their lives. Was he, he must have asked, somehow responsible for this carnage? Could he have been swept by guilt for the part that he had played in the onset of the Civil War? Bearing guilt of this nature would be impossible for any national leader. It would paralyze action. No one could live with it for long. Thus, Lincoln began to draw again on the modified version of things-happen-because-they-must that he met from the early Reformed Churches. It is possible that this residual determinism was what drew him back while he was in the White House to Shakespeare. Shakespeare's insights on the ambiguity of human nature and the consequences that follow to innocent and guilty alike from stark ambition must have equally struck home. Lincoln once remarked to John Hay that honest statecraft involved using individual meanness to produce a public good. Lincoln's reliance on this perspective—call it Calvinism, fatalism, the doctrine of necessity, or what have you—meant that ultimately God, not Lincoln, was responsible for the conflict. If so, then God would devise a way to bring something positive from it. As the president wrote to Quaker supporter Eliza P. Gurney in 1862, "Being a humble instrument in the hands of our Heavenly Father, as I am, and as we all are, . . . I have sought his aid—but if after endeavoring to do my best in the light which he affords me, I find my efforts fail, I must believe that for some purpose unknown to me, life wills it otherwise."[73]

In accepting this sense of an overriding destiny, we hear distinct echoes of Burns's "To a Mouse," that

> The best laid schemes o' Mice an' Men
> Gang aft agley

as well as Shakespeare's comment in *Hamlet* that

> There is a divinity that
> shapes our ends,
> Rough-hew them how
> we will.[74]

From this perspective, *everyone* has a role to play in God's ultimate plan for the world.

As historians Ronald C. White Jr. and Allen C. Guelzo recently noted, this sense may be clearly seen in Lincoln's private, September 2, 1862, musings that his secretary John Hay later designated "Meditation on the Divine Will." In dismay after the Union defeat at Second Bull Run, Lincoln wrote:

> The will of God prevails. In great contests each party claims to act in accordance with the will of God. Both *may* be, and one *must* be wrong. God can not be *for* and *against* the same thing at the same time. In the present civil war it is quite possible that God's purpose is something different from the purpose of either party—and yet the human instrumentalities, working just as they do, are of the best adaptation to effect His purpose. I am almost ready to say this is probably true—that God wills this contest, and wills that it shall not end yet. By his mere quiet power, on the minds of the now contestants, He could have either *saved* or *destroyed* the Union without a human contest. Yet the contest began. And having begun He could give the final victory to either side any day. Yet the contest proceeds.[75]

One could hardly find a better expression of the moderate Calvinist confrontation with the mystery of God. This theme is repeated in the far better known closing words of the Second Inaugural, when he similarly argued that God's ways were different from either North or South (discussed later in the current chapter).

Although Burns and Lincoln both held their respective Presbyterian churches at arm's length, their reliance on the King James Version of Scripture remained constant. As Reverend W. C. Bitting has argued, one cannot comprehend Burns's poems or letters (less so the songs) without deep familiarity with the Bible. So, too, with Lincoln. He quoted Scripture easily with no trace of unctuousness. His greatest speeches all resonate with a biblical subtext. Thus, for both men, it was the words of the Scripture, not statements by denominational assemblies, local churches, or individual pastors, that provided their understanding of the divine will. In this regard, they were peas from the same pod.[76]

Democracy

Burns's oft-quoted lines on equality and his contempt for social class would surely have resonated with the young Lincoln. Lincoln's political philosophy proved relatively simple, based as it was on the preamble to the Declaration of Independence: "We hold these truths to be self-evident, that all men are created equal." These lines he considered to be the "sheet anchor" of Republicanism. As he noted when he visited Independence Hall in Philadelphia in 1861, he had never held any political view that did not spring directly from the Declaration of Independence.[77] Similarly, in the 1859 centenary celebration, a cleric remarked that Burns's lyrics on equality were the Declaration of Independence "set to music." Much of Burns's poetry pointed to the fact that the haughty, scornful aristocracy and the honest rural poor all shared the same human virtues and foibles. The poem "The Twa Dogs" shows this to perfection, as Caesar, an "aristocratic," and Luath, a "peasant" dog, discover that they share a good deal in common.

Both Burns and Lincoln understood human nature. They could see through social class to appreciate the worth of the individual beneath. A famous Burns story goes like this: While riding outside Edinburgh with several aristocratic friends, Burns paused to chat with an ordinary farmer. When his friends ridiculed him for speaking with someone so poorly dressed, he replied, "I was talking to the man, not the clothes." A similar Lincoln anecdote (both probably apocryphal) has Lincoln breaking off conversation with a foreign ambassador at the White House to greet a roughhewn Illinois farmer and his wife whom he had known from New

Salem. Another Lincoln comment is, "The Lord must have loved the common people for he made so many of them." When he met an Irish contingent shortly after his election, Lincoln jested that a recently arrived Irishman once observed, "In this country one man is as good as another; and for the matter of that, very often a good deal better."[78]

The Problem of Quotation (or Lack Thereof)

Given all these connections—Lincoln's well-documented love of Burns's lyrics, the numerous parallels in their lives, plus the widespread popularity of Burns among ordinary people, historians have been left with a dilemma. In all his writings, Lincoln quoted Burns only once. In a rather low-level "Second Reply to James Adams" in the October 28, 1837, *Sangamo Journal*, he said, "In the mean time, Adams himself is prowling about, and as Burns says of the devil, '*for prey, a' holes and corners tryin'*,' and in one instance, goes so far as to take an old acquaintance of mine several steps from a crowd, and apparently weighed down with the importance of his business gravely and solemnly asks him if 'he ever heard Lincoln say he was a deist.'"[79] The Burns quotation comes from "Address to the Deil."

As this ranks as Lincoln's only direct quotation, most of Burns's influence on his thought has to be inferred from *content* rather than actual language. For example, the central theme of Burns's satire "Address to the Unco Guid" (one of Lincoln's favorites) can be read as a plea for simple charity.[80] In powerful, driving verse, the poem says that people should temper their criticism of the behavior of others because ultimate judgment is best left to God. From the 1830s forward, this view of the world became the sheet anchor of Lincoln's life. New Salem resident James H. Matheny recalled a verse from an early, obscure Lincoln poem—written for a local poetry gathering—that reflected the same theme.

> Whatever Spiteful fools may say—
> Each jealous, ranting yelper—
> No woman ever played the whore
> Unless she had a man to help her.[81]

Lincoln's 1842 temperance address at the Second Presbyterian Church in Springfield draws on a similar point of view. Decrying the widespread condemnation of both the sellers and consumers of drams, Lincoln suggests that those who were not alcoholics have been spared largely from *lack of desire* rather than any moral superiority.[82]

Even after acknowledging Lincoln's reliance on Burnsian themes, however, we are still faced with the issue of the absence of direct quotation.

There is abundant evidence that Lincoln recited Burns in *private*—indeed, only days before his assassination, he did so to John Hay. But why did he not do so publicly? Most of the popular public speakers of the day quoted Burns in their various addresses. So why did Lincoln not drop "a man's a man for a' that" into any of his letters, stump speeches, or state papers?

To these questions—which probably can never be fully resolved—I would like to propose some tentative theories. First, powerful poems committed to memory during one's youth remain there for a lifetime. One can revisit the various lines at any time for they are always there. Lincoln's prodigious memory allowed him to resurrect Burns's verses at the drop of a hat throughout his entire career. Given this, it is obvious that Burns's poetry had an influence on Lincoln. But now the question is, what kind?

Here the Burns supporters have generally overstated their case. Historian Emanuel Hertz credits Lincoln's love of Burns as the inspiration for the Emancipation Proclamation. Minnesota lawyer A. C. McKnight argues that Burns gave Lincoln his sympathy for the less fortunate of life. Milton Hay opined that Burns's ballads provided "one of the sources of his wisdom and wit."[83]

These are overstatements. Actually, Burns's verses helped *reinforce* many of the ideas that Lincoln absorbed while growing up. The 1863 Emancipation Proclamation had its roots both in Lincoln's upbringing and in the successes and failures of the Union armies. Similarly, Lincoln's boyhood poverty in Kentucky and Indiana provided him with numerous opportunities to learn empathy for the poor on a first-hand basis. He hardly needed Burns for that. And growing up surrounded by frontier anecdotes and stories provided him with all the wit and humor he needed. Not until Mark Twain's *Tom Sawyer* and *Huckleberry Finn* would people begin to appreciate the power behind this form of American vernacular speech. Lincoln had no need to borrow from Burns's Doric Scots; he grew up with a distinctive frontier dialect much closer to home.[84]

A much more likely interpretation goes as follows: a frontier farm boy, conscious of his awkwardness and social inferiority, must have rejoiced to discover that the most revered poet of the day expressed his own views in powerful, rhythmic verse. This remains a constant for all young readers: how clever of (say) Herman Melville to have thought my exact thoughts. The most probable impact of Burns on the young Lincoln rests with the realization that his fledging views of equality and democracy were on the right track after all.

But the question still remains. Given the popularity of Burnsian phrases, especially in the atmosphere of the 1859 centennial celebration, why did not Lincoln quote a line or two in his debates with Stephen Douglas or his formal speeches or pronouncements? The events leading up to the Emancipation Proclamation of 1863 and the push in 1864 for the Thirteenth Amendment outlawing slavery would seem to have provided ideal opportunities. Other prominent antislavery speakers, such as, Henry Ward Beecher and Frederick Douglass, often quoted from Burns. Why was Lincoln silent? There seem to be two chief reasons for this situation. First, the road to emancipation proved as complex as any of the most convoluted Civil War battles. On this issue, Lincoln responded primarily as a lawyer, cautious and judicious in all he said and did. In the fall of 1861, he overruled General John C. Fremont's August proclamation that emancipated the slaves held by Confederate sympathizers in Missouri. In May 1862, he similarly overruled General David Hunter's emancipation proclamation freeing the slaves in Florida, Georgia, and South Carolina. "Slavery," he said, was an issue he "reserved to myself." Even though slavery was, to him, a moral wrong, his legalistic view of the Constitution meant that he initially felt he had no power to deal with it.[85]

Moreover, the preliminary Emancipation Proclamation of September 22, 1862, included the (at least theoretical) provision that the South might return to the Union with its basic institutions intact. Because Lincoln believed that only Congress or the states had the power to deal with the issue of slavery, his final proclamation of January 1, 1863, drew on his position as commander in chief to free slaves in only those states still in rebellion against the Union. The slaves in loyal Border States remained in bondage. In 1864, the Congregational Church of Patterson, New Jersey, urged him to issue a second Emancipation Proclamation "for all those whom your first Proclamation passed by."[86]

As has been frequently noted, the language of the Emancipation Proclamation is dry and legalistic, completely barren of Lincolnian eloquence. Still, whatever its language, the proclamation boldly announced to both nation and world that the end of slavery was imminent. Although it might lack eloquence, it never lacked purpose. And for over three generations, the Emancipation Proclamation remained the document on which Lincoln's reputation hinged. As Henry Clay Whitney noted in 1892, the Emancipation Proclamation proved as essential to the nation as the Declaration of Independence.[87] As historian Philip Shaw Paludan later phrased it, "The language of the great deed had to be a lawyer's language because Lincoln was taking legal action. He was placing the great ideal of freedom within the constitutional fabric—the only place that it could have life in a constitutional republic."[88] Be that as it may, the central phrase of "military necessity" sends few tingles up anyone's spine.[89] Burns's most famous phrase regarding equality—"A man's a man for a' that"—simply didn't fit here. It proved more expansive than the circumstances of either the preliminary or final Emancipation Proclamation allowed. To quote him would have sounded hollow.

Moreover, Lincoln was simultaneously attempting to avert a postwar Southern economic collapse—which, in fact, did occur—by proposing some form of federal compensation for masters who freed their slaves. Here he doubtless drew upon the British experience with West Indian slavery, where the slave owners received national funds in a scheme of gradual emancipation during the mid-1830s.

Lincoln's vision proved truly national. He argued that since both North and South had shared in the guilt of establishing the institution, each should pay for its removal. When he served as Congressman, Lincoln prepared a bill (never introduced) for compensated emancipation for the District of Columbia upon agreement of the voters. Paralleling the Congressional confiscation acts of August 6, 1861, and July 17, 1862, plus the 1862 Congressional abolishment of slavery in the District of Columbia (with compensation) and in the Territories, Lincoln constantly badgered the legislatures of the Border States to accept some form of federal compensation. He got nowhere. Even Delaware, with fewer than two thousand slaves, showed no interest. His beloved Kentucky similarly rejected the repeated offers.[90] The day after the Hampton Roads Conference with Confederate leaders, he astounded his cabinet by suggesting that $400 million be appropriated from the federal treasury for such a purpose. To a person, they rejected the idea, and he said no more about it. Lincoln could not rely on Burns's poetry in this situation either. "A man's a man" and *compensation* do not easily mesh.

The push for the Thirteenth Amendment in Congress found Lincoln in the same dilemma. This Republican measure to outlaw slavery was introduced in the Thirty-eighth Congress in December 1863, and while it passed the Senate on the first try, it failed to earn the necessary two-thirds vote in the House (94 to 64). Afterwards, it became a key issue in the 1864 Union Party platform. With his second victory, Lincoln used every tactic available to him to marshal the favorable lame duck House vote, which finally came on January 31, 1865 (119 to 56). Lincoln viewed his reelection in 1864 as reflecting popular public support for such a measure. The amendment still had to go to the states for final approval, but Lincoln did not live to see its passage. Additionally, while all this was under way, Lincoln was pursuing, although perhaps not very seriously, the idea of colonizing free Blacks to Africa. *A man's a man* and *colonization* similarly clang on the ears.

The Emancipation Proclamations, the compensation schemes, and the Thirteenth Amendment reveal Lincoln as the ultimate devotee of Constitutional law, as opposed to a person relying on Burns's broad, idealistic statements. Since the last amendment to the Constitution (the Twelfth) had been added in 1804, there had been no change in America's primary political document during his lifetime. In Lincoln's eyes, the Thirteenth Amendment would provide the ultimate *legal* means to ensure that there could be no attempts to reenslave any freedman after the fighting ended.[91] It seems obvious, then, that Lincoln never quoted Burns's idealistic statements on equality during this time because they were simply too broad to fit the gritty political realities of his day.

To Which Authors Did He Turn during These Crises?

Fellow lawyer and political supporter Leonard Swett once observed that Lincoln seldom asked anyone for advice. He would listen to others but he usually "arrived at conclusions from his own reflections, and when his opinion was once formed he never had any doubt but what was right."[92] Secretary of State William H. Seward agreed. As he wrote his wife, "There is but one vote in the cabinet and that is cast by the President. The President is the best of us all."[93] In the summer of 1863, John Hay wrote John Nicolay that "the Tycoon," as they termed Lincoln, ruled the cabinet with "tyrannous authority."[94] In his latest study of the president, historian David Herbert Donald argues that Lincoln had relatively few close friends on whom he could rely.[95] Handicapped by an unstable wife—a "stone of abrasion" throughout the White House years—Lincoln faced the worst political crisis in American history virtually alone.

Or did he? Although he kept abreast of current affairs via the newspapers, he also increasingly returned to his favorite authors to try to comprehend the bewildering political situation as it unfolded around him. And here it seems that he drew less on Robert Burns for public pronouncements than the King James Version of Scripture and the other author whom Scotsman Jack Kelso had introduced him to—Shakespeare.

It is not possible to determine how much Lincoln read, or reread, Scripture during his White House years, but the indications are that it was considerable. Numerous correspondents, including Quaker Eliza Gurney, recommended specific biblical passages to him. In 1864, he accepted an Oxford (King James Version) Bible from a delegation of African Americans from Baltimore; Scots tutor Alexander Williamson once recalled helping him find a biblical concordance on his shelf. An Army captain at the Soldiers' Home retreat often found him reading the Bible early in the morning. O. H. Browning, who spent occasional Sunday afternoons with Lincoln in the White House library, remembered that he usually read the Bible then. (The Lincolns held no family prayers and did not invoke blessings at mealtimes.) Noah Brooks recalled Lincoln saying, "I have been driven many times upon my knees by the overwhelming conviction that I had nowhere else to go. My own wisdom and that of all around me seemed insufficient for that day."[96] All one can say for certain is that Lincoln read Scripture extensively—some say daily—during his troubled White House years.

There is considerably more evidence as to the number of times he revisited Shakespeare during this period. Indeed, when the Lincolns moved to Washington in 1861, he had, really for the first time in his life, access to some of the most sophisticated theater of the country. Washington impresario Leonard Grover, who was well aware of the president's interests, invited him to attend a premier *Othello* performance in October 1863, promising him any box he wished. He also volunteered to produce *Hamlet*, *Richard III*, or *Macbeth* if the president should prefer one of them. Later, Grover recalled that Lincoln visited his theater over one hundred times during his administration.[97] This is a slight exaggeration, but historians have documented about fifty presidential visits to local theaters. In a three-week stretch during the winter of 1864, Lincoln heard five plays: *Richard III* (twice), *Julius Caesar*, *The Merchant of Venice*, and *Hamlet*.[98]

Lincoln attended Washington vaudeville shows at least twice and perhaps ten performances at Ford's Theater prior to that fateful Friday of April 14, 1865. Indeed, attending the theater became his major form of relaxation. (Grover claims Lincoln would even watch rehearsals.) Contemporary John W. Forney argued that Lincoln visited the theater less for the plays themselves than for the rest that it gave him. Although occasionally in his private box he chatted with actors, he showed no interest in visiting behind the scenes. To do so, he said, would spoil the magic for him. Lincoln also reached out to several Shakespearean actors during his tenure in Washington. He astounded the actor John McDonough by taking down a copy of *Henry IV* from his shelf and reading an extended passage from it. The next day he entertained yet another actor with a similar reading. Famed Shakespearean actor William Hackett visited Lincoln once and, to the president's embarrassment, tried to curry political favor from him. Lincoln also wrote Hackett of his love for *King Lear, Richard III, Henry VIII, Hamlet,* and *Macbeth.*[99] Historians have counted the president's presence at Washington performances of *Richard III, The Merchant of Venice, King Lear, Othello, The Merry Wives of Windsor,* and *Henry IV,* parts 1 and 2. After a performance of *The Merchant of Venice,* he remarked that "a farce or comedy is best played; a tragedy is best read at home."[100]

A number of memoirs testify to Lincoln's increased reading of Shakespeare during his White House years. His secretaries John Nicolay and John Hay noted that he would often read aloud to them, both in the White House and at the Soldiers' Home. Isaac N. Arnold recalled that while on a journey to visit an army post, Lincoln would often pull out a book and say, "What do you say now to a scene from *Hamlet* or *Macbeth?*"[101] When spending time at Fortress Monroe, Virginia, his favorite pastime seemed to come from reading Shakespeare, often aloud. David Homer Bates, manager of the War Department Telegraph Office, also recalled that Lincoln read from *Macbeth* and *The Merry Wives of Windsor* to the telegraph staff from a well-thumbed copy that he carried around with him.[102]

The most dramatic of his Shakespearean readings occurred on the last Sunday of his life, April 9, 1865, when, fresh from a triumphal visit to Richmond, he was sailing up the Potomac River on the steamer *River Queen.* A Black servant brought a copy of Shakespeare to Lincoln, who was sitting at a table, and Lincoln began to read from *Macbeth.*

> Duncan is in his grave; After life's fitful fever he sleeps well.
> Treason has done his worst; nor steel, nor poison,
> Malice domestic, foreign levy, nothing
> Can touch him further.[103]

So moved was he by this passage that he read it a second time, radical Republican Charles Sumner later recalled. After Lincoln's death, his family donated this set of six quarto volumes to the Harvard University Library.

What did Lincoln derive from Shakespeare in these moments of crises that he missed in the work of Robert Burns? The answer seems to be political complexity. Aside from a verse to honor George Washington's birthday and (perhaps) several anonymous poems extolling the French Revolution, Burns's words dealt little with actual political situations. In late eighteenth-century Scotland, only 4,000 out of about 1.25 million people were eligible to vote, and Burns was not among them. The majority of men in Great Britain did not receive the franchise until the Reform Acts of 1867 and 1884. Moreover, Burns held the politically sensitive government job of excise man, which meant he had to carefully watch his public statements. Thus, Burns always spoke of liberty and equality in the most general terms; never did he mention actual political intrigue, save in a church situation. His poems speak in democratic generalities and ultimate goals rather than actual political dilemmas.

But the tragedies of Shakespeare are riven with specific political intrigue. In a few lines preceding the famous "Duncan's in his grave" passage, which Lincoln may also have read at table on the *River Queen*, Macbeth says:

> We have scotched the snake, not killed it.
> She'll close, and be herself, whilst our poor malice
> Remains in danger of her former tooth.[104]

So many of the Shakespearean tragedies seemed to leap right from the headlines of the Civil War years, especially the history plays. For example, Richard II despairs over the sad fate of once-powerful rulers (John Hay said he often heard Lincoln recite this passage).

> For God's sake, let us sit upon the ground,
> And tell sad stories of the death of kings:
> How some have been depos'd, some slain in war,
> Some haunted by the ghosts they have deposed;
> Some poisoned by their wives, some sleeping kill'd;
> All murdered.[105]

King Henry VI finds himself caught in a continuing Civil War as the House of Lancaster battled the House of York. The evil Richard III brings great suffering to his nation, but England not only endures the calamity, it also progresses toward potential regeneration. Richard's famous soliloquy opens the play.

> Now is the winter of our discontent
> Made glorious summer by this sun of York,
> And all the clouds that loured upon our house
> In the deep bosom of the ocean buried.[106]

In a similar vein, Hamlet treats the terrible consequences that flow from indecision. In that play, Lincoln greatly admired Claudius's soliloquy, "O, my offence is rank."

Try what repentance can. What can it not?
Yet what can it, when one can not repent?
O wretched state, O bosom black as death,
O limed soul, that struggling to be free,
Art more engaged![107]

Finally, *King Lear*, one of Lincoln's favorite plays, deals with betrayal and suffering as a very condition of life itself.[108] James G. Randall has pondered this question with considerable wisdom: "Lincoln's attention to Shakespeare was evidence of more than a literary interest, though that interest was strong. There are overtones in the subject which are not always easy to catch but which bear upon the half expressed thoughts and emotions which flitted through Lincoln's mind. Shakespeare was preeminent in giving flitting expression to thoughts which are inadequately conveyed unless they have Shakespearean phrasing. When we deal with Lincoln and Shakespeare we are dealing with something that goes rather deep."[109]

Perhaps the foremost reason why Lincoln did not cite Robert Burns directly during his presidency is a simple, almost overlooked one. Excluding Scripture, Lincoln seldom quoted *anybody*. Professor Daniel K. Dodge, an early twentieth-century scholar who combed through Lincoln's collected prose, concluded that the president quoted from about thirty authors (not counting the Bible) and then only rarely. Of these, Lincoln referred most frequently to Shakespeare: *Hamlet, King Lear, Macbeth, The Merchant of Venice*, plus a reference to Falstaff, from *Henry IV*. He occasionally drew from Charles Dickens, Sir Walter Scott, Robert Herrick, and Alexander Pope. Once, when asked about his early life, he responded in the words of Thomas Gray's "Elegy Written in a Country Churchyard": "the short and simple annals of the poor." We have abundant testimony that Lincoln often quoted from Burns in his private conversations, but never did he do so in any formal addresses.[110]

The main font from which he drew for his speeches, of course, was the Authorized or King James Version of Scripture. In one assessment of twenty-five speeches, Bruce Barton discovered twenty-two biblical references, eight from the Old Testament and fourteen from the New Testament. Lincoln's "lost speech" at Bloomington, Illinois, as recalled by one hearer, included six biblical quotations. As historian Adam Nicholson has recently observed, the King James Version incorporated "a deliberate carrying of multiple meanings beneath the surface of a single text."[111] Lincoln absorbed this to perfection. The Second Inaugural Address reads like a statement from an Old Testament prophet. Without a deep familiarity with the Bible, he never could have written the Gettysburg Address either.

Lincoln's prose echoes the freighted richness of Scriptural themes on every turn. From the Hebrew poetry of the Old Testament, he drew his propensity for parallelism. In the Hebrew verse form, the second statement develops or amplifies the first. Compare, for example, the sentence structure of Psalm 117.

> O Praise the Lord
> All ye nations: praise him
> All ye people.
> For His merciful kindness
> is Great toward us:
> And the truth of the Lord endureth forever
> Praise ye the Lord

with Lincoln's similar use of parallels in his proclamation for the first National Thanksgiving: "No human counsel hath devised, nor hath any mortal hand worked these great things." Or in his October 26, 1862, letter to Eliza P. Gurney: "If I had my way, this war would never have been commenced; if I had been allowed my way, this war would have ended before this." Similarly, The Second Inaugural drew explicitly from at least four biblical passages.

> In the sweat of thy face shalt thou eat bread. (Genesis 3:19)
> Judge not, that ye be not judged. (Matthew 7:11)
> Woe unto the world because of offences: for it must needs be that offences come; but woe to that man by whom the offence cometh! (Matthew 18:7)
> The judgments of the Lord are true and righteous altogether. (Psalms 19:9)[112]

Lincoln would have been astonished to find himself termed a man of letters. But with these speeches, that was precisely what he had become. In 1866, his friend Isaac N. Arnold observed, "The words of Lincoln have done more in the last six years to mold and fashion the American Character than those of any other man."[113]

Lincoln's youthful attempts at poetry have been discreetly forgotten, but numerous historians have noted how his major public addresses all resounded with a powerful poetic cadence. Critic Owen Barfield has argued that because sound lies at the heart of true poetic meaning, the term *poetic diction* is wide enough to encompass both poetry and prose.[114] In

1901, R. V. Bieder commented that Lincoln's literary style revolved around a "pleasing cadence" that carried a burden of high hope as well as heroism. English biographer Lord Charnwood similarly observed that Lincoln's speeches sounded more like what one would hear in a tragic drama than from an ordinary politician.[115] A generation later, poet Marianne Moore frankly termed Lincoln's writings "poetry."[116] The analysis by contemporary historians Herbert Joseph Edwards and John Erskine illustrates this to perfection.[117] It is, indeed, possible to scan many of Lincoln's speeches as one might scan a poem. At the 1865 inaugural ball, the president asked Black abolitionist Frederick Douglass what he thought of his Second Inaugural Address. Douglass's reply: "a sacred effort." Later, Carl Schurz would term it a "sacred poem."[118] As early as April of 1865, a British observer commented on the "curious instance of involuntary rhyme" in the Second Inaugural Address:

> Fondly do we hope
> Fervently do we pray
> That this mighty scourge of war
> May speedily pass away:
> Yet if it be God's will
> That it continue until—

(Then the rhyme breaks off.)[119] In the famed 1895 special issue of the magazine *Independent*, Theodore L. Cuyler similarly reminded the nation again that parts of the Second Inaugural Address should be read as a quatrain:

> Fondly do we hope,
> Fervently do we pray,
> That this mighty scourge of war
> May speedily pass away[120]

In these classic speeches, Lincoln's mixture of poetry-in-prose served as the literary equivalent of perfect pitch.[121] The ideas simply could not be better expressed. Historian Douglas L. Wilson has characterized Lincoln's power of words as his "sword."[122] Historian James McPherson has similarly noted that Abraham Lincoln won the Civil War with words.[123] If that is so, Lincoln's lifelong admiration for the poetry of Robert Burns may well have played a role in the ultimate Union victory.

Stereo card of Burns's birth cottage, about two miles south of Ayr, Scotland, in about 1890, by then a place of pilgrimage for more than two generations. Author's collection.

Lincoln's log-cabin birthplace, enclosed in a Grecian temple (dedicated 1911), not far from Hodgenville, Kentucky. Administered by the National Park Service, the Abraham Lincoln Historic Site is visited by thousands of people every year. Photo by author.

George Washington Brownlow (1835–76), *Murdoch Instructing Burns.*
The original hangs in the Burns House in Dumfries, Scotland.

Courtesy of the Dumfries and Galloway Council, Dumfries Museum.

Young Lincoln studying by firelight. Chromolithograph published by Louis Prang and Company, after a late-nineteenth-century painting by Eastman Johnson. Courtesy of the Lincoln Museum, Fort Wayne, Indiana. No. 4433.

Robert Burns - Poet

An American steel engraving of Burns (1859), designed to tap the excitement surrounding the celebration of the centenary of his birth. From Henry Coppee, *A Gallery of Famous English and American Poets* (Philadelphia: E. H. Butler and Co., 1859). Author's collection.

"MacLincoln's Harrisburg Highland Fling," *Vanity Fair* cartoon ridiculing the president's alleged "disguised" entry into Washington in 1861.
Author's collection.

A Boy Scout wreath-laying ceremony at the Lincoln statue by John Rogers in Manchester, New Hampshire, probably February 12 (?1915). Courtesy of the Lincoln Museum, Fort Wayne, Indiana.

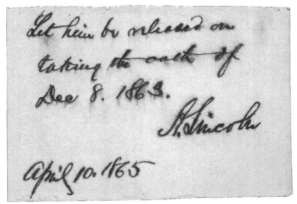

A Lincoln forgery by Joseph Cosey, who followed in the trail of Alexander Howland "Antique" Smith, premier forger of Burns materials. Cosey was detected only because he failed to master the proper upward slant on the signature "A. Lincoln." Author's collection.

Stamps honoring Burns and Lincoln. Many countries view Burns and Lincoln as international symbols of equality. In 1959, the Soviet Union became the first nation to place Burns's image on a stamp (*center three*). The United Kingdom followed in 1966 (*above left*) and in 1996 (*above right*). A number of nations such as the Federal Republic of Cameroon (*bottom*) have issued commemoratives in honor of Lincoln.

Photo by Kim Jew Studios from the collection of the author.

Statue of Burns in New York City's Central Park, the first erected outside
Scotland. At the dedication, one speaker observed that both Lincoln and
Burns were products of "the people" and that "America was trying to make
the ploughman's words true." *Harper's Weekly*, October 16, 1880.

Author's collection.

The first statue to Lincoln outside the United States, erected in Scotland in 1893. Located in the Old Calton Hill Burial Ground in Edinburgh, the site reigned as a must-see venue for American tourists for years.

Photo by author.

Theodor Horydczak, *Lincoln Memorial Statue with Children*, ca. 1950.
Scottish visitors, along with others, often view Daniel Chester French's
monumental statue in Washington, D.C., as the architectural heart of the
American republic. Courtesy of the Library of Congress, LC-H814-T-L05–085-B.

4

Scottish Émigrés and Scottish Ideas in Lincoln's World

The poetry of Robert Burns did not mark the sole Scottish impact on the life of Abraham Lincoln. Scottish immigrants and Scottish ideas were intertwined with his entire career. From his birth to his assassination, Lincoln never moved far from the long reach of Scots/Scotch-Irish cultural influences.

To paraphrase the writer Saki (A. A. Munro), Scotland produced far more history than could ever be consumed locally. Thus, migration emerged as a central pivot of the national experience, and by 1860 about a hundred thousand Scottish émigrés resided in the United States.[1] The truism that "Dukes don't emigrate" meant that the vast majority of "Scoto-Americans," as they were often termed, consisted of ordinary people.

The immigrants carried with them a variety of Scottish traditions: a culture of hard drinking, a heritage of proud military service, faith in widespread education, respect for Roman Catholic and Presbyterian churches, belief in individual achievement, pragmatism, versatility, and more than a little clannishness. During the first half of the nineteenth century, the Scots (as well as the even more numerous Scotch Irish) generally melded to become America's "invisible immigrants."[2] Scottish and Scotch-Irish names came to be seen as typically "American" names. Simultaneously, more than any other group, the Scotch-Irish settlers from Ulster "created" the first American frontier. In essence, they forged the social world that surrounded the lives of Thomas and Nancy Hanks Lincoln and their family. The name "Hanks" is probably a corruption of the Scottish name "Henry."

Native-born Scots and their descendants fought on both sides of the American Civil War. Clyde-built blockade-runners regularly brought illegal goods to the Confederacy, and at least twenty-six Scottish lithographers spent the war in Richmond helping to manufacture Confederate currency. One of the most famous Confederate nurses was Leith-born émigré Kate Cumming. On the other side, the most striking photographs of Lincoln were taken by Scottish émigré Alexander Gardner of the Mathew B. Brady studio, and the most powerful editor of Lincoln's era was Keith, Scot-land–born James Gordon Bennett of the *New York Herald.* The list could be extended.

Taken in the broadest sense, popular poetry mostly likely enjoyed a much larger role in late-eighteenth- to early-nineteenth-century Anglo-American life than it does today. For example, the British scientist Eras-mus Darwin (grandfather of Charles) wrote his *Botanic Garden* (1791) in rhyming couplets, and it became a best-selling scientific work. Early-nine-teenth-century American newspapers often inserted poems to fill in their columns, and lovers courted by slipping each other snippets of romantic verse. Political poetry remained commonplace as well, as poets extolled the exploits of various generals and politicians. Educator Alexander Wil-liamson wrote a poem in honor of General Ulysses S. Grant's leadership. When the *London Times* finally acknowledged Lincoln's greatness after his death, the newspaper's apology was in the form of a lengthy poem. The British magazine *Punch* similarly apologized in May of 1865 in the same form. Almost every American mother crooned Mother Goose lullabies to her children, and there were few people who could not recite a verse or two of "Barby Allen."

Because Lincoln grew to maturity in this environment, his well-known love of poetry was not that unusual. From the snippets he met in his four early school readers to the songs he heard at various frontier gatherings, Lincoln found himself surrounded by verse and rhythm. Moreover, from his earliest days, Lincoln exhibited the key element that characterizes all poets—a deep feeling for the sound, rhythm, and aura of words.[3] As an old friend W. M. Butler once recalled, whenever he was asked a question, the young Lincoln "gave an answer, it was characteristic, brief, pointed, *a propos,* out of the common way and manner, and yet exactly suited to the time place and thing."[4] The copybook doggerel he wrote (probably around age 10) in his arithmetic book in Spencer County, Indiana, reflects this emerging talent.

> Abraham Lincoln
> His hand and pen
> He will be good but
> God knows when.[5]

As a teenager, in 1825 or 1826, Lincoln wrote a lengthy satirical rhyme on his friend Josiah Crawford's prominent nose that had his neighbors (excluding Crawford) in stitches. Two decades later, after a visit to Southern Indiana, he wrote a somewhat heavy-handed, if reflective, "My Childhood's Home I See Again," as well as other poems. In late September 1858, when he was staying in Winchester, Illinois, he jotted down verses in the autograph albums of two young girls: The poem "To Linnie Haggard" reads:

To Linnie—
A sweet plaintive song did I hear,
And I fancied that she was the singer—
May emotions as puir, as that song set a-stir
Be the worst that the future shall bring her.[6]

Lincoln retained this admiration for poetry all his life. When he lived in Springfield, he joined a "Poetical Society," to which he read his composi-tions. He immediately recognized the genius of Walt Whitman's *Leaves of Grass* and lauded Oliver Wendell Holmes's "The Last Leaf" as a stellar piece of work. While in Springfield, he scribbled "poem—I like this" on a stray verse by Scottish writer Charles Mackay, who would later cover the Civil War for the *London Times*.[7] But after his 1858 verses to the Winchester girls, Lincoln seems to have channeled his power of words into political rather than poetic discourse.

This chapter explores the Scottish cultural impact on Lincoln's world via the following: succinct sketches of five Scots who helped shape his life, analysis of the role of the famed New York Seventy-ninth High-land Regiment, which fought all through the conflict, a somewhat more speculative exploration of how the Scottish idea of a "covenanted nation" lay at the base of Lincoln's various proclamations of Fast Days and days of Thanksgiving, and an examination of the popular Scottish reaction to Lincoln and the Civil War.

Poet William Knox

Although Lincoln repeatedly praised Burns as the greatest poet of his day, it was another Scotsman, William Knox, who penned the verse that Lin-coln claimed to value most highly. Sometime in 1831, Dr. Jason Duncan of New Salem clipped out for Lincoln an anonymous poem in the Louisville *Evening Post* entitled "Immortality," sometimes known as "Mortality," or by its first line "Oh, Why should the spirit of mortal be proud?" Lincoln quickly committed "Mortality" to memory.

Unknown to Lincoln, this lengthy poem was written by minor Scottish poet William Knox. In heavy-handed lines of four beats to the measure with an AA/BB rhyme scheme, Knox essentially restated the themes of chapter 3 of the book of Job and chapter 1 of the book of Ecclesiastes. The essence of his message revolved around personal humility and the transience of life.[8] A comparison with a passage from Ecclesiastes shows Knox's borrowing in detail.

> The thing that hath been,
> it is that which shall be;
> and that which is done is
> that which shall be done: and
> there is no new thing under
> the sun.

In Knox's paraphrase, the same thought is restated thusly in verse 9:

> For we are the same thing
> That our fathers have been,
> We see the same sights
> That our fathers have seen,
> We drink the same stream,
> And we feel the same sun,
> And we run the same course
> That our fathers have run.[9]

Lincoln's admiration for this rather undistinguished poem knew no bounds. In 1846, he wrote his friend Andrew Johnson that he would give "all I am worth and go into debt" to be able to write such a work.[10] At various times in his life, Lincoln jotted down the poem from memory and gave it to others, including sixteen-year-old Lois Newhall of the Newhall family singers, artist F. B. Carpenter, and the wife of Secretary of War Edwin McMasters Stanton. He wrote this last version on War Department letterhead stationery.

Who was William Knox? A descendant of the renowned John Knox, William was born in 1789 on the family estate near Lilliesleaf, Roxburghshire. In a strange way, his life paralleled that of Robert Burns: Knox worked as a farmer, was moderately well educated, loved to converse, battled depression, drank heavily, and wrote Scottish dialect poetry. Two years after the publication of his first volume, *The Lonely Hearth and Other Poems* (1818), Knox left his farm for the literary world of Edinburgh. There he made modest contributions to the popular *Literary Gazette* and engaged in literary hackwork. A Professor Wilson introduced him to Sir Walter Scott, who praised Knox's modesty and conversational skills. Aware of the lost genius of Burns, Scott privately tried to assist Knox, although he personally considered his verses "grave and melancholy." But, as Scott ruefully noted, Knox became "too soon his own master and plunged into dissipation and ruin."[11] He died of a paralytic stroke in 1828 at age 36. In 1895 a grand nephew placed a tablet to his memory in the Lilliesleaf parish kirk. The tablet quoted several lines from "Mortality" and claimed that the poem was printed in golden letters and hung in a place of honor on the walls of the Imperial Palace of Saint Petersburg.[12]

Although virtually forgotten today, Knox achieved a fair degree of public recognition during his lifetime. Both Burns and Knox grew to maturity surrounded by a culture of stern Presbyterian morality. Although Burns largely cast this aside for a world of sensual pleasure, Knox possessed a sterner conscience that periodically drew him remorsefully back to biblical themes. The publication of *The Songs of Israel* (1824) and *The Harp of Zion* (1825), a series founded on the Hebrew Bible, gave him a modest reputation in Scotland as a master of sacred song. A generation later, famed Presbyterian minister George Gilfillan praised Knox as the best sacred poet in all of Scotland.[13]

Aside from the rephrasing of biblical passages, most of Knox's verse tilted toward the melancholy. Titles like "The Funeral," "The Family Tombstone," and "A Mother's Grave" are typical. His verse "The Suicide" contains the lines:

> Oft we'll weep at the tree
> Where the strangers have laid her
> But cursed be he
> The false man that betrayed her.

His most recognized poem, "Mortality," included the following:

> Oh, why should the spirit
> Of Mortal be proud
> Like a swift-fleeting meteor,
> A fast-flying cloud,
> A flash of the lightning,
> A break of the wave,
> Man passes from life to the
> Rest in his grave
>
> 'Tis the wink of an eye, 'tis
> The draught of a breath
> From the blossom of health
> To the paleness of death,

From the gilded saloon to the bier
And the shroud
Oh, why should the spirit of
Mortal be proud?

So closely was Lincoln linked to this dolorous poem that shortly after his death at least three pieces of sheet music appeared that paired the verse with various tunes. Two versions acknowledged that this was Lincoln's favorite poem, and one, published by Oliver Ditson and Company in Boston, actually claimed Lincoln as the author.[14]

During the late nineteenth century, many Scots became aware of Lincoln's admiration for Knox's poem. This fact is mentioned on Knox's 1895 tombstone, and ten years later, G. S. Aitken misinformed readers of the newspaper *Scotsman* that Lincoln had recited verses from "Mortality" on the day of his assassination.[15] By 1905, Knox's opening line "Oh, Why should the spirit of Mortal be Proud?" had graduated to the rank of "familiar quotations."[16]

At least twice, Lincoln asked friends to be certain to tell him if they ever uncovered the identity of the author. In 1864, James Grant Wilson traced the verse back to Knox and told the president. Later, Wilson sent Lincoln a copy of the 1847 edition of Knox's poems that contained "Mortality." Lincoln must have been delighted to finally discover Knox's identity, but, it should be noted, he praised none of the other Knox poems, including those that deal with similar themes.

Although contemporaries did not seem especially bothered by Lincoln's poetic preferences, historians have been somewhat puzzled by his deep admiration for the mediocre "Mortality." Historical aesthetic styles are hard to define, and poetry, like artichokes and rutabaga, remains an item of personal taste. Thomas Jefferson, for example, admired the works of the Celtic bard Ossian, which were usually considered fraudulent.

In retrospect, however, it seems clear that Lincoln's intense admiration for "Mortality" reflected two aspects of his world view. First, Knox's stanzas marched "with a stately funeral-like pomp, full of terrible admonition of man's mortality," and this resonated both with Lincoln's periodic depressions and with his more sustained tragic view of life.[17] Historian Maurice Boyd argues that Knox spoke both to Lincoln's propensity to melancholy and to his sense that Divine Providence directed both individual and national destinies. In Boyd's view, Knox's "Mortality" provided Lincoln "with spiritual substance in moments of anxiety."[18] Lawrence Weldon, who traveled the Illinois Circuit with Lincoln, agreed. He felt that Knox provided "a reflex in poetic form of the deep melancholy of his soul."[19] Second, Knox's heavy-handed verse form also provided a ready model for Lincoln's own poetic aspirations, both in meter and content. A few critics have gone so far as to suggest that young Lincoln's poetry revealed a "potentially major literary talent." Historian Wayne C. Temple has also defended Lincoln's poems as bordering on excellent.[20] But these are decidedly minority opinions. With Knox providing the main model, Lincoln's verses never ranked higher than B-minus.

In February 1846, Lincoln returned to his southern Indiana boyhood home, and he wrote three or four cantos by way of a poetic response. The relentless four-beats-to-the-measure verses (in the first and third lines) echo Knox's influence. The opening verse of "My Childhood-Home I See Again" reads:

> My childhood-home I see again,
> And gladden with the view;
> And still, as mem'ries crowd my brain,
> There's sadness in it too.[21]

Lincoln's brooding, twenty-four-verse recollection of southern Indiana reflects the central theme of "Mortality" as well, as verse 9 shows.

> I hear the lone survivors tell
> How nought from death could save,
> Till every sound appears a knell,
> And every spot a grave.

Some historians argue (probably correctly) that these 1846 verses reveal Lincoln's belief that the fundamental characteristic of humankind lies in the realm of reason alone, the topic of verse 8.

> I've heard it oft, as if I dreamed,
> Far distant, sweet, and lone—
> The funeral dirge, it ever seemed
> Of reason dead and gone.

Lincoln's sanguine verses on "The Bear Hunt" (September 26, 1846?) also are influenced by "Mortality." In this twenty-two-verse poem depicting a wild bear chase, Lincoln again recalls his boyhood Indiana in verse 2.

> When first my father settled here,
> 'Twas then the frontier line
> The panther's scream, filled night with fear
> And bears preyed on the swine.[22]

Twelve years later, one of Lincoln's last recorded poems—the 1858 verses he scribbled into the autograph album of his young Winchester admirer Rosa Haggard—falls in the same camp.

> To Rosa—
> You are young, and I am older;
> You are hopeful, I am not—
> Enjoy life, ere it grow colder—
> Pluck the roses ere they rot.
> Teach your beau to heed the lay—
> That sunshine seen is lost in share—
> That *now's* as good as any day—
> To take thee, Rosa, ere she fade.[23]

As long as Lincoln relied on Knox as his poetic model, his literary aspirations were unlikely to rise higher than their source. But from the mid-1850s forward, as he grappled with more-monumental themes, Lincoln began to turn to other literary models—the King James Version of Scripture, Shakespeare, and Robert Burns—and to the medium of prose rather than poetry. With this, his literary star began its upward journey.

Presbyterian Pastor James A. Smith

A second Scot who helped shape Lincoln's world was James A. Smith, author of *The Christian's Defense* (1843), as well as other works, and pastor of the First Presbyterian Church in Springfield from 1849 to 1856. Unlike Knox, Smith lived a rather dramatic life. Born in Glasgow in 1801, he was orphaned at an early age and raised by an aunt and uncle to enter the family business. After some university education, Smith rejected the business world, married Elizabeth Black, and emigrated to Cincinnati, where he engaged in free-lance writing and occasional teaching. Well read in the Comte de Volney and Thomas Paine, Smith had become a confirmed deist at the time of his emigration, convinced that all religion was a fraud perpetuated by the ruling classes. In early 1825, however, Smith attended an Indiana camp meeting and was converted by Cumberland Presbyterian minister James Blackwell. Afterwards, he began seriously to study theology and scripture and in October 1825 was licensed to preach by the Logan, Kentucky, Presbytery of the Cumberland Presbyterian Church. Of all the major branches of American Presbyterianism, the Cumberland Church had the most flexible requirements regarding formal theological training. The Old School and New School Presbyterians both demanded far more formal education for their pastors. Of the fifteen Old and New

School Presbyterian clergy who served in Illinois from 1816 to 1836, for example, fourteen were college graduates.[24] Still, the various branches of the American Presbyterian Church maintained fellowship with one another, and there were numerous transfers among them.

For five years, Smith worked as a Cumberland pastor and circuit rider in Indiana and Kentucky. In 1830, he moved to Nashville, Tennessee, to pastor a church and edit the major denominational journal, the *Cumberland Presbyterian*. A prolific writer, he had already compiled a two-volume collection of the sermons of fellow frontier clergyman James McGready, and he later wrote a lengthy *History of the Christian Church*. His goal was to create a vigorous publishing empire to set forth the Cumberland Presbyterian position in earnest detail.[25] During this time, Smith spent many hours preaching at various locations across the south. During the winter of 1839–40, he preached at Columbus, Mississippi, a small town not far from the Alabama line. Columbus boasted its own resident "infidel" Charles G. Olmsted, author of *The Bible Its Own Refutation*, and Olmsted's followers eagerly challenged Smith to debate their mentor. Smith accepted, and after a year's preparation—he had to send to Europe for various theological treatises—the debate took place in April of 1841.

Antebellum America abounded with public theological exchanges of this sort. Alexander Campbell, the Scottish-born founder of the Disciples of Christ, raised these disputes to an art form. In 1829, he staged a week-long public debate with Freethinker Robert Owen, recently arrived from New Lanark, Scotland, to establish the utopian village of New Harmony, Indiana. (Because the exchange involved not one but two Scotsmen, Smith may well have attended.) In 1837, Campbell staged a similar weeklong dispute with John B. Purcell, the Roman Catholic bishop of Cincinnati. Such public debates probably convinced few to alter their theological views, but they formed an integral part of a world in which "the people" were expected to make up their own minds on all religious matters. Many of Campbell's exchanges were models, with some of the disputes later published as books.[26] Thus, the 1841 Smith-Olmsted theological debate followed precedent. A major undertaking for both sides, the clash involved nineteen evenings of hearty give-and-take in the Columbus, Mississippi, Presbyterian Church. Discussion ranged from Genesis to Revelation, from the physical existence of Jesus to the veracity of the New Testament. A sympathetic writer for the *Union Evangelist*, who attended every session, termed it "an intellectual feast." Smith later reworked his portion of the lectures into *The Christian's Defense*, which was published in 1843.[27] He also aligned himself with the Old School Presbyterians and in March 1849 accepted a call to pastor Springfield's two-hundred-member First Presbyterian Church. There he came to know the Lincolns.

During the fall of 1849, Abraham and Mary Todd Lincoln visited relatives in Lexington, Kentucky, and Lincoln picked up a copy of *The Christian's Defense* from the Todd family library. Unable to finish it, he borrowed the book upon his return to Springfield from Smith himself. Yet, it was the tragic loss of the Lincoln's youngest son, Eddie, on February 1, 1850, that really brought the two men together. Mary had been attending the Episcopal Church with her sister, but because the Episcopal priest was out of town, she asked Smith to preach Eddie's funeral sermon. Moved by both his compassion and his well-chosen words, Mary soon joined the First Presbyterian Church. The Lincoln family purchased pew 20, which they retained until their move to Washington eleven years later.

Lincoln respected Smith on a number of fronts, perhaps because Smith was likely the first educated clergyman whom Lincoln knew first hand. Reverend David Elkin, the Baptist pastor who had preached Lincoln's mother's funeral sermon, could barely read and write. Samuel Brostow and Young Lamon, two other Indiana Pigeon Creek pastors, whom Lincoln also surely heard, had no formal theological training of any sort. Although the Campbellites and the itinerant Methodists of his youth called for a dramatic, immediate experience of grace, the Old School Presbyterians constantly maintained that the Christian faith was eminently reasonable. Thus, as Smith set forth at length in *The Christian's Defense*, faith could be rationally and logically defended. We know that Lincoln read at least parts of Smith's tome. As he once remarked to his friend John H. Littlefield, "Now you take the subject of predestination; you state it one way, and you cannot make much of it; you state it another, and it seems quite reasonable."[28] Smith's book made a good case for the latter position.

The lives of Lincoln and Smith share a number of parallels. Each lost a parent at an early age, passed through an aggressive deist phase, and lost a child. Each kept a fount of stories and anecdotes to readily prove a point. They also shared similar views—in general noncondemnatory—on temperance issues; Lincoln contributed funds to help publish one of Smith's sermons on that theme, *A Discourse on the Bottle—Its Evils—and the Remedy* (1853). Each enjoyed reading Burns and Shakespeare, and Smith loaned (or gave) Lincoln a copy of a Shakespearean play. Their main disagreement was in the realm of politics. Smith remained a pro-Southern Democrat (although not a secessionist); Lincoln was a Whig and Republican. One contemporary spoke of "a mystic cord uniting the minister and the lawyer."[29]

Some observers suggest that Smith's arguments actually brought Lincoln into the Christian fold. Lincoln's brother-in-law, Ninian W. Edwards, so claimed in an 1872 interview. Edwards recalled Lincoln said he had been reading one of Smith's works on the evidences of Christianity, had heard him preach and converse on the subject, and was "now convinced of the truth of the Christian religion."[30] Smith himself also claimed that *The Christian's Defense* had brought Lincoln closer to the Reformed faith.[31]

Historians usually dismiss these claims. Lincoln never enjoyed metaphysical speculation, and he showed little interest in theology. A distinct political context shaped almost all of Lincoln's public observations on religion. Although he referred at times to "the Savior," none of his printed works mentions the name of Jesus, all of which makes the various statements of conversion problematic. Still, many Calvinist Baptists and Old School Presbyterians of Lincoln's day, without necessarily downplaying Jesus, placed an equal emphasis on biblical morality and on the all-encompassing role of Divine Providence. For example, the October 1863 resolutions from the Wisconsin Baptist State Convention—sent to Lincoln in response to the preliminary Emancipation Proclamation—never mentioned Jesus either. Rather, the "Christian men" of Wisconsin acknowledged God's chastening the nation for its sins and praised the president for recognizing the role of "righteous and merciful Providence" in his actions.[32] If, indeed, Lincoln made these comments about Christianity to Edwards and Smith, a "providential morality" may well have been what he was referring to. As Smith later recalled, at his request, Lincoln addressed the annual meeting of the Bible Society of Springfield on the importance of having a Bible in every Illinois household. Lincoln closed, Smith recollected, by saying that the Bible contained a divinely inspired, perfect moral code, applicable to all conditions of life.[33] If that was what Lincoln meant by "Christianity," then the statements by Edwards and Smith may well be more accurate than historians have supposed.

In 1856, Smith resigned from the First Presbyterian Church. After briefly working for Peoria University, plus taking a short trip to Scotland in 1859, he purchased a ten-acre farm near Brookhaven, Mississippi. The 1860 election campaign, where he almost surely spoke out for Lincoln, cost him his farm and forced him back to Chicago. At Mary's urging, Lincoln appointed Smith U.S. consul to Dundee in 1861, but Smith initially declined in favor of his son, Hugh. After Hugh resigned the post because of alcoholism, Smith took over in 1862 and was appointed full consul the next year. He served with distinction until the end of the war. After Lincoln's assassination, Mary again turned to the aged pastor for solace. But here the cause lay less with her grief than with her anger and humiliation. On November 16, 1866, William A. Herndon delivered his infamous fourth lecture on Lincoln in Springfield. Claiming that he knew Lincoln better than any other person, Herndon entitled his speech "A. Lincoln–Miss Ann Rutledge, New Salem-Pioneering, and the Poem Called 'Immortality'—or 'Oh, Why Should the Spirit of Mortal Be Proud'" and therein introduced the themes of Lincoln's religious infidelity, his lifelong passion for Ann Rutledge, and his loveless marriage to Mary into the public realm. From Scotland, Smith denounced Herndon in a blistering reply to the *Dundee Advertiser*, and this was picked up by the *Chicago Tribune* shortly afterwards. Terming Herndon a "false friend," Smith decried his "malignant attack" upon Mary and the two Lincoln sons. Declaring that the family circle (to which Herndon was never invited) rather than the law office was a better arena to judge a man's bearing toward his wife, Smith claimed that he knew a great deal more about Lincoln's domestic affairs than did Herndon. Smith said that during his seven years in Springfield, he saw the Lincolns on an average of every two weeks. As he was a frequent household guest, he could report that Lincoln treated Mary with "a heart overflowing with love and affection."[34]

Two years later, Smith invited Mary and Tad to visit him in Scotland, and in July 1869, they spent seven glorious weeks touring the home of her ancestors. (She came from Covenanter stock and had named their third son after the Scottish hero William Wallace.) Mary waxed eloquently on the sights of "dear Old Scotia," especially Burns's cottage, Highland Mary's grave, and the Royal Castle at Balmoral. Although Smith proved somewhat feeble at sixty-eight, he spent as much time with her as he could. After she departed, and surely at her urging, he began lobbying various U.S. Senators regarding her pension. He lived two more years and died in 1871 at age seventy.

Smith's seven-year relationship with the Lincolns had a number of consequences. First, he was available at a parent's most difficult time—the loss of a child. In crises such as this, people usually turn either toward or away from faith, and Lincoln, however haltingly, seems to have taken the former path. Smith's presentation of the Old School Presbyterian version of Scripture, emphasizing God's overriding Providence and a biblical, transcendental code of ethics, also resonated with Lincoln on a number of fronts. But Lincoln's friendship with the Scot had long-term political repercussions as well. His awareness of Smith's three-week theological debate with Olmsted—which he surely must have heard about—may well have been the inspiration for his 1858 challenge to Stephen A. Douglas to hold a similar set of debates regarding the expansion of slavery.[35]

Editor James Gordon Bennett

In the world of mid-nineteenth-century journalism, the name of James Gordon Bennett rivals only that of Horace Greeley, the famed editor of the New York *Tribune*. Born into a Roman Catholic family in New Mill, Banffshire, Scotland, Bennett trained for the priesthood in Aberdeen before emigrating to Nova Scotia in 1819. Drifting to New York in 1823, he became a staunch supporter of Andrew Jackson and a free-lance writer. He also worked briefly from 1822 to 1823 on the *Charleston* [South Carolina] *Courier*, and this experience gave him a staunch pro-Southern point of view, which he retained throughout his life. Moving back to New York City, he began the *New York Herald* in 1835 on borrowed money and soon turned it into one of the nation's first—some insist the best—popular tabloid. Bennett printed dramatic, even sensational, stories of crime, sexual scandal, and murder. He also attacked his own Catholic Church, often denouncing New York Archbishop John Hughes. He even suggested that America should elect its own pope.

Such blatant coverage cost Bennett his local standing with both the clergy and the respectable business community, but his "Satanic Majesty" guided the *Herald* to the largest circulation in the nation by the 1850s. The daily print run approached eighty-four thousand copies, most sold by newsboys on the street for two cents each. By 1856, he could claim two thousand European readers as well.[36] He was probably the only American editor recognizable by sight in Great Britain. His motto was, "Never be more than a day ahead of the people and never an hour behind."[37] Physically, Bennett proved impressive at six feet tall, with a long face fringed by white whiskers. He kept a strong Scottish accent all his life. In essence, he served as a prototype of Andrew Carnegie (without the libraries): a poor immigrant Scots youth who amassed a gigantic fortune through his ability to anticipate the American public's needs. His main detriment was that he was severely cross-eyed. As cub reporter William A. Croffut once recalled, "When he looked at me with one eye, he looked at the City Hall with the other."[38] Because of his fierce reputation, many people were afraid of him.

Bennett's politics shifted with the wind. He remained decidedly anti-English, which delighted his numerous Irish readers, pro-Southern, and anti-abolitionist; he steadfastly refused to adhere to any party line. He initially supported President Franklin Pierce but when a promised position as minister to France fell through, turned against him. He seemed to favor those of Scottish ancestry and usually (but not always) spoke well of James Buchanan and Ulysses S. Grant. As expected, he was a great fan of Robert Burns. Initially, Bennett had opposed Lincoln in the election of 1860 but during the lame-duck months of the Buchanan administration, repeatedly urged Lincoln to come forth with major policy statements. When the war broke out, Bennett continued to display a strong pro-Southern stance. He predicted widespread public outrage over Lincoln's call for seventy-five thousand volunteers and was stunned when an angry mob gathered in front of the *Herald*'s offices to demand that he display the U.S. flag, which he eventually did late that afternoon. The rival New York press, which had long despised him as a "foreigner," was delighted. Newspaper cartoonists eagerly depicted Bennett as shutting up shop and sailing back to Scotland in disgrace. But that did not happen. Sensing a shift in public opinion, he began to tack with the prevailing winds.

Ever conscious of the crucial role of public opinion, Lincoln realized that he needed Bennett on his side, especially because of the *Herald*'s overseas readership. He is "powerful for mischief," Lincoln once observed, and "can do us much harm if hostile."[39] Influencing the mercurial Scot proved a challenge, however, and in 1861 and 1862, Lincoln found himself virtually wooing Bennett. He sent Albany editor Thurlow Weed as an intermediary to negotiate with him, and, in turn, Bennett sent his star reporter Henry Villard as an intermediary to relay his personal response. Bennett, Villard reported, was willing to support the Union cause. He would begin by donating his yacht to the government, with the understanding that his son, James Gordon Bennett Jr., would receive a commission in the navy. This was quickly done.[40]

In turn, Bennett began to woo Mary Todd Lincoln, sending her occasional flowers, to which she responded with an invitation to a White House ball on January 1, 1862. In December 1861, the *Herald*'s Washington, D.C., reporter Henry Wikoff was somehow able to telegraph the *Herald* an early copy of Lincoln's first annual message to Congress (that is, before it was delivered), for which he was promptly thrown into jail. Wikoff said that John Watt, a White House gardener, had memorized the speech and revealed the contents to him, but it seems obvious that Wikoff obtained it from Mary.[41]

Bennett saw clearly that the Civil War would rank as the greatest story of his generation, and he determined to supply readers with the latest news available. Here again he proved prescient. His Fort Sumter issue sold 135,000 copies, and the fall of Richmond issue about the same number. Union soldiers eagerly read the *Herald*, and Southerners sought out smuggled copies. During the war, Bennett sent out as many as sixty-three field correspondents to cover the fighting and usually kept the *Herald* on the side of the Union. But he also criticized Lincoln on a variety of occasions. In May of 1862, Lincoln wrote him to correct a wildly speculative editorial regarding a forthcoming cabinet split because of General David Hunter's overruled emancipation declaration. Bennett responded with a courteous reply, declaring he would soon visit Washington, although that does not seem to have occurred. Most of Lincoln's encounters with Bennett came via intermediaries, as they seem never to have met face-to-face.

A staunch anti-abolitionist, the Scotsman only grudgingly accepted the Emancipation Proclamation, which freed the slaves in states still in rebellion, but in 1864, he urged the swift passage of the Thirteenth Amendment, which abolished slavery. Inconsistency remained his long suit. In February 1864, Bennett denounced Lincoln as a "joke" in an exceptionally bitter editorial and began to push for Ulysses S. Grant to succeed him as the Union Party candidate. On May 20, 1864, in an even more shocking editorial, he referred to Lincoln as the "head ghoul at Washington." But in 1864, Grant showed no interest in politics, and shortly afterwards Bennett changed his mind (again) and began to urge support for Lincoln.

A Chicago editor had earlier advised Lincoln on Bennett by suggesting that the Scotsman desired social prestige above all else. Lincoln took that advice to heart. He began by appealing to the New York editor's honor and his sense of his own role in history. In a July 1864 letter (intended to be shown to Bennett), Lincoln stated that because the forthcoming presidential campaign would likely be a contest between a Union and Disunion candidate, the issue was "momentous for all people and all time; and whoever aids the right, will be appreciated and remembered."[42] He also let Bennett know in February of that year that he planned to appoint him minister to France, a position for which he was well qualified as he spoke fluent French and had established the *Herald*'s European office in Paris. Flattered although he must have been, Bennett declined the appointment on the grounds of age. After Lincoln's assassination, the *Herald* became one of his staunchest supporters. It played an unwavering role in turning Lincoln into the martyr of the nation.[43] But for much of his Washington career, Lincoln had to handle the mercurial Scotsman James Gordon Bennett and the *Herald* with kid-gloves attention.[44]

White House Scots: John Watt and Alexander Williamson

Given its harsh climate and volatile weather, Scotland has long accorded the profession of gardener a high degree of prestige. Scots gardeners played crucial roles in establishing major public parks in Saint Louis, Missouri, Salt Lake City, Utah, and San Francisco, California. The same was true for Washington, D.C. The Lincolns kept on Buchanan's Scots émigré John Watt as public gardener for the White House grounds.

Watt proved a troublesome figure. He initially held Southern sympathies, as did his chief assistant. Because Mary seemed strangely partial to Scots, early on she confided in Watt regarding her ever-present financial woes. Eager to please, Watt charmed Mary with bouquets of flowers. He also padded his White House expense account and returned some of the funds to the First Lady. Years later, he petitioned Congress to reimburse him for funding one of Mary's many buying trips to Boston. Rumors also abounded that Watt held three incriminating letters written to him by Mary, with which he hoped to blackmail Lincoln—allegedly on Mary's financial "infidelity"—but these letters have never surfaced. In any case, Watt soon found himself in trouble. A committee revoked his appointment as lieutenant in the Union army on grounds of disloyalty, and he was forced to reenlist as a private in the Thirteenth New York Artillery. Only in 1866, after he had proven his loyalty, did Watt regain his former rank.[45]

Alexander Williamson is a much more attractive person. Born in Edinburgh to a middle-class family that fell on hard times with the death of the father, Williamson studied at Edinburgh University, married Barbara Donaldson, and emigrated to the States around 1855. He taught in both Virginia and Maryland before settling permanently in the District of Columbia. An early advocate of Republican Party principles, he and Barbara fed and housed as many as thirty-five soldiers from the famed Seventy-ninth New York Highlanders when they were billeted in the city after the debacle of First Bull Run.

Williamson's fellow Scot, Lieutenant Colonel Thomas L. Alexander, served as acting governor of the Soldiers' Home, located about three miles north of the Capitol building. The lieutenant commander touted Williamson's teaching skills to Mary Todd Lincoln in early March, and shortly afterwards she asked that Williamson call upon her. When he visited the White House, she asked if he would like to tutor Tad and Willie—Robert was away at prep school—as there were then no public schools in Washington. Always conscious of money, Mary paid Williamson no salary but through her husband secured a government position for Williamson as a clerk in the post office. Thus, Williamson worked at the post office in the mornings and taught Tad and Willie in the afternoons. The two young children of Judge and Mrs. H. M. Taft, Horatio Nelson Taft Jr. and Halsey Cook Taft, occasionally attended as well.[46]

When first introduced to Lincoln, *London Times* reporter William Howard Russell wryly observed, "A person who met Mr. Lincoln in the street would not take him to be what—according to the uses of European society—is called a 'gentleman.'" Similarly the Scottish-born Williamson initially described Lincoln as "very far from what we call courtly." But Russell left his initial meeting with the president impressed by Lincoln's shrewdness, humor, and natural sagacity, and Williamson felt the same way. He praised the president's long working hours and his great tenderness of heart: "He was as kind hearted as a woman."[47] Williamson was also present when the Free Church of Scotland came out officially against slavery. Because the Southern Presbyterians had aided the Free Church financially during the Great Disruption of 1843, they expected some sympathy when they appealed to their fellow Scottish Presbyterians for moral support during the Civil War. Mild though the rebuke of slavery was, it brought Lincoln to tears "so deeply was he moved to find that, in spite of her *apparent* sympathy with the South, Scotland was still sound on the question of slavery."[48]

Williamson was delighted at how enthusiastically Willie enjoyed learning. William Wallace Lincoln shared his father's memory and his love for poetry as well. When an old family friend from Springfield, Colonel Edward Dickinson Baker, died, Willie wrote a verse in his honor. To the youngster's delight, the *National Republican* published it. Williamson tutored Willie for about five months until he died unexpectedly on February 20, 1862. The Scottish tutor was much less successful with Tad. Youngest of the Lincoln boys, Thomas (Tad) remained a problem for much of his youth. Afflicted with a severe speech impediment, a common characteristic of the Todd family, Tad also suffered what might today be considered a learning disability (perhaps attention deficit disorder). Some historians even suggest that he was slightly retarded. In any case,

Tad proved unable to concentrate on anything for any length of time. He spent his days racing wildly through the White House causing mischief. He was eight before he mastered the alphabet and nine before he could fully dress himself. Williamson soon concluded that he could do little with Tad other than babysit. So, he played with him, and together they attended the theater on several occasions. Eventually tiring of this role, Williamson assumed a full-time position as secretary to Isaac Newton, head of the Department of Agriculture. With that, as historian Wayne C. Temple notes, Williamson moved from tutor to that of "trusted family friend." Other tutors replaced him, but none lasted long or accomplished much with Tad, who remained incorrigible.

Williamson stayed close to the Lincolns after he shifted to the auditor's office in 1863. In 1864, his eighty-one-year-old mother sent Lincoln a shepherd-check plaid as a gift, to which the president graciously replied. He often wore the plaid while riding. And after his assassination, Mary gave to Williamson Lincoln's carpet slippers, his dressing coat, a copy of H. R. Helper's *Impending Crisis*, and the inkwell said to be the one used to sign the Emancipation Proclamation.

On the night of April 14, 1865, Williamson and his son also attended Ford's Theater to enjoy *Our American Cousin*. Watching the assassination in horror, he raced to the White House where he met Tad on the stairs and then hurried back to the Peterson House, where the president had been carried. E. H. Miller's painting, "The Last Moments of Lincoln," depicts Williamson standing at the foot of the dying president's bed.

Mary trusted Scots and, as she did with Pastor Smith for support after tragedy, turned to Williamson after Lincoln's death for yet-another assignment. Deep in debt and beside herself with grief, Mary enlisted Williamson to lobby Congress on her behalf, both for a pension and for the remainder of her late-husband's salary. In addition, she urged Williamson to adopt Mary's chosen penname of "Charles Forsythe" (it sounded "aristocratic") to solicit wealthy Republicans for contributions on her behalf. The goal was to establish an endowment, the Mary Lincoln Fund, which would allow her to live as she aspired. Williamson's contingency fee was $35 for every $1,000 he raised.[49]

From 1865 to 1867, Mary peppered Williamson with letters. Her missives were filled with minute financial instructions, and he essentially assumed the role of her financial advisor, the man responsible for sorting out her financial chaos, which proved considerable. Although he later passed much of this assignment on to Judge David Davis, the officially designated administrator of the Lincoln estate, Williamson had to approach the respected D.C. jeweler M. W. Galt and Company about accepting a return of Mary's gold earrings, a breastpin with Grecian pattern, and two gilt clocks. Diligent and honest though Williamson was, most of his efforts came to naught. He successfully returned trinkets and fended off creditors, but he was unable to raise any money on her behalf. Although Mary insisted that she had "the interests of all the widows and orphans, in the land, at heart," her letters to him gradually ceased when he could produce no funds. Afterwards, the Scot worked at various bureaucratic jobs in Washington until 1886, when he moved to New York City to work for a shipping line. He died in 1903 at age eighty-nine.[50]

Detective Allan Pinkerton

Of all the contemporary Scots who helped shape Lincoln's world, Allan Pinkerton's name remains the most recognized. Indeed, the detective agency he founded—with its motto of "the eye that never sleeps"—is still active today.

Born in Glasgow in 1819, Pinkerton and his new wife, Joan Carfree, moved to Canada in 1842 and shortly afterward settled in the primarily Scottish town of Dundee, Illinois, about forty miles north of Chicago. Pinkerton, who had trained as a cooper, was gathering staves for his barrels and stumbled upon a band of counterfeiters, whom he helped capture. In 1850, the strongly abolitionist Scot moved to Chicago, where he began working as a detective.[51] He soon came to the attention of the Illinois Railroads, which hired him to catch a variety of crooked employees. Using both male and female agents, Pinkerton soon apprehended a number of the worst offenders. From August 1861 to November 1862, he was in charge of the Secret Service department of the army.

It was through the railway work that Pinkerton heard rumors of a Confederate plan to assassinate Lincoln as he passed through Baltimore in February 1861 on his way to Washington, D.C., to be inaugurated. According to Pinkerton, the leader was an Italian barber named Cypriano Ferrandina who had loudly claimed that the only way to save the Southern way of life was to assassinate Lincoln and that he was willing to give his life in the effort. Pinkerton's friends had also heard rumors of a Maryland man who had sworn an oath that Lincoln would never arrive in Washington.[52] The detective had always considered the border city of Baltimore as dangerous. Moreover, the rail lines were laid out so that Lincoln would have to transfer by carriage from one Baltimore station to another to catch the train to Washington, D.C. This mile-long journey, presumably in an open carriage, was scheduled to travel through a narrow underpass, where the act would allegedly occur. Pinkerton always felt that Lincoln himself was terribly naïve on security matters. "I could not believe that there was a plot to murder me," he once said.[53] This naiveté continued during his four years in office. A later bodyguard noted that Lincoln flatly refused to have military guards accompany him when he went to church or places of entertainment.[54] But in 1861, when Lincoln received information from three independent sources that a potential assassination effort existed, he changed his mind and agreed to travel to Baltimore and Washington on earlier trains than had been announced.

Lincoln first journeyed from an engagement in Philadelphia to Harrisburg, where he met with the Pennsylvania state legislature. Although it was difficult to extract him from the crowd at Coverlie's Hotel in Harrisburg, Pinkerton picked him up by carriage, presumably to take him to the governor's mansion where he was to spend the night. Instead, that February 22, Lincoln boarded a special night train—one passenger car long—to West Philadelphia. From there, he took the 11:00 P.M. train to Washington via Baltimore. None of the train officials knew he was aboard.[55] As an added precaution, the manager of the American telegraph office sent a lineman to cut and ground all telegraph wires on the Northern Central Railroad line from Harrisburg to Baltimore.

When Lincoln stepped off the train in Washington, on a chilly February 23, 1861, he was wearing a soft felt cap, not his usual stovepipe hat, as well as a heavy overcoat and muffler. Still, he was easily recognized. By no means had he donned a disguise. Nevertheless, rumors swept through Washington that in "the flight of Abraham," the president-elect had sneaked into the city in disguise, wearing "a Scotch cap and a heavy military cloak." Reporters and (especially) Democratic party cartoonists, seized on the Scotch-cap theme. It soon became the talk of the city. *Vanity Fair* and *Harper's Weekly*, among other journals, printed hard-edged cartoons depicting Lincoln in his Scotch cap, sometimes wearing a Scots kilt. London *Times* reporter William Howard Russell found himself baffled at the furor caused by this inconsequential matter. Lawyer Lawrence Weldon later dismissed the felt-hat agitation as "mere stuff."[56]

It is not now possible to determine whether a true conspiracy lay in wait for Lincoln in Baltimore. No one was arrested in the matter, and the relevant Pinkerton materials all burned in the 1871 Chicago fire. Several newspapers felt that Pinkerton had concocted the plot to enhance his own reputation. Lincoln's bodyguard, Ward Lamon, similarly dismissed the idea as fiction when he wrote his biography of the president. Lincoln himself seems to have had some doubts as well. Pinkerton remained adamant, however. In an 1868 defense of his actions, he praised his agent Timothy Webster—executed by the Confederates in 1862—as being the first to uncover the assassination plot. As the 1868 compilation of relevant letters showed, Pinkerton had a case.[57] Baltimore in early 1861 abounded with Confederate sympathizers. The Seventy-ninth New York Highlanders were jeered when they marched through the city on their way to defend the Capitol, and the appearance of a Massachusetts regiment shortly afterwards provoked a riot that caused several deaths. Pinkerton himself argued that the Baltimore assassination conspiracy was far better organized than the one that eventually succeeded four years later. Had he been on duty then, he bragged, he could have prevented John Wilkes Booth from carrying out his mad scheme. Although it cannot be absolutely proven, the evidence strongly suggests that Scottish immigrant Allan Pinkerton had the ultimate impact on Abraham Lincoln's career. In early 1861, he saved his life.

The Scots Soldiers

Much of the tangled history of Scotland has pivoted on the outcome of major conflicts, usually against England. From the Battle of Bannockburn to the Border Wars to violent clan quarrels to the Stuart uprising known as the Forty-five, Scottish society has long respected the skills of the fighting man.[58] Indeed, Scottish soldiers formed an integral part of the expansion of the British Empire from the late eighteenth century forward.[59] This historic military tradition also migrated to the United States, and memories of Scottish heroism helped recruit scores of volunteers from Chicago and New York, each of which formed distinctive (largely Scottish) military commands.

The Highland Guards were organized in Chicago in 1855. Much in demand for the celebration of Burns's birthday four years later, they staged a striking procession through downtown Chicago. The Highland Guards answered Lincoln's call for troops with kilts and pipes and became one of the most colorful units of the day. As Company E of the Nineteenth Illinois Voluntary Infantry, they fought bravely at the Battle of Stones River. A Scottish supporter named Chamberlain created a song for them.

Not without thy wondrous story
Illinois, Illinois
Can be writ the Nation's glory
Illinois, Illinois[60]

The most famous Scottish military group, however, was the famed Seventy-ninth New York Highlanders, which boasted the motto: "Stand Fast, Craigellachie." Raised largely in New York City, the unit first organized as a company—really a social club—called "the Highland Guard," which consisted chiefly of men of Scottish birth or ancestry. Initially, they sported kilts, which, as the historian of the unit noted, produced "an extra share of attention" when they marched through Philadelphia.[61] Starting with the Battle of Blackburn's Ford on July 18, 1861, the Seventy-ninth were involved in twenty-six engagements. These included First and Second Bull Run, Antietam, Fredericksburg, Knoxville, the Battle of the Wilderness, and Spotsylvania Courthouse, among others. Up to their mustering out in 1864, they suffered severely: 108 casualties, along with 82 who died of disease and about 450 wounded. Figures for their second period of service—June 1864 to July 1865—where they were central to the brutal assault on Petersburg—are not available.[62]

The loss of 25% of their men at First Bull Run—higher than any other regiment of the division—brought the Seventy-ninth close to demoralization, and the unit mutinied. According to Julia Taft Bayne, however, who witnessed the event as a young girl, the real cause of the mutiny came from the order to discard their plaids, kilts, and sporrans for regular Union army uniforms. The mutiny soon turned ugly, and in mid-August 1861, an armed line of Army regulars assembled, with orders to fire if the mutineers did not fall back into line. At the last minute, the rebels capitulated, but their regimental colors were taken away as punishment. For fear of harming enlistments, the story of the mutiny never reached the press. Taft begged her older brother, a surgeon in the Signal Corps, not to tell Lincoln, and it is possible that he never knew of the situation.[63] Still, the Highland unit was viewed with contempt for several months until their colors were finally restored. Eventually, Lincoln's first secretary of war, Scotsman Simon Cameron, who had lost his only brother, Colonel James Cameron, with the regiment at Bull Run, took the unit under his wing. Probably because of his influence, they were then sent to the Sea Islands off the coast of South Carolina. There as the soldiers of Master Lincoln, as the president was called by the islanders, they were greeted as liberators.

Their hands and feet were kissed by the escaped slaves, although almost none of the soldiers initially favored Lincoln's use of Black troops.[64]

Both North Carolina and South Carolina similarly reflected the historic Scottish military heritage. Local North Carolina Confederate units termed themselves "the Highland Boys," "the Highland Rangers," "the Scotch Greys," and the "Scotch Tigers." Charleston also boasted at least two primarily Scottish units. The most famous, the Charleston Highlanders, traced their roots to a militia company that had been formed by immigrants in 1806. The company banner sported the Arms of South Carolina on one side and the Scottish thistle on the other. During the conflict, the Scots fought as part of the First South Carolina Battalion. While on duty in South Carolina, the New York Seventy-ninth Highlanders learned that the Confederate Charleston Highlanders had been assigned to guard South Carolina's mainland. Thus, they found themselves in a state of "armed neutrality" against their fellow Scots. When the Seventy-ninth captured a Confederate Scottish lieutenant, he was greatly relieved at his kind treatment, jesting that he should have worn his kilts.

In a scene that cries out for a novelist, Scottish immigrant Alexander Campbell of the Seventy-ninth New York faced his younger brother James Campbell of the First South Carolina Battalion on June 16, 1862 in the Battle of Secessionville on James Island, South Carolina. Similarly, the color bearer of the Seventy-ninth heard rumors that his Confederate brother was also stationed nearby. Six days before this fateful encounter, Alexander Campbell wrote to his wife, "This is a war that never was the like of before Brother against Brother." As the historian of the Seventy-ninth ruefully noted, "Truly this was a fraternal strife."[65] Lincoln visited the Seventy-ninth at least twice, once after First Bull Run and again after Antietam. In April 1864, Lincoln, the cabinet, and several generals reviewed them from the balcony of Willard's Hotel, the last glimpse of the president that most of the soldiers would ever have.

The final Scottish group interaction with Abraham Lincoln came when the presidential funeral train, on its sad route back to Springfield, retraced his 1861 inaugural journey. The Caledonian Club of Philadelphia called an emergency meeting to express submission to God's will and to condemn "the atrocious act" of assassination. They also marched in the Philadelphia funeral procession. When the cortege filed through the streets of New York City, Scots were also highly visible. The Saint Andrews Society, the Caledonian Club, and many former Seventy-ninth Highlanders also marched in the funeral parade, with their two pipers "wailing out a melancholy pibroch."[66] In 1918, pro-Union Southerners erected a monument to the Seventy-ninth regiment, New York Highlanders, in Knoxville, Tennessee.

The Influence of Scottish Covenant Thought

If individual Scots, such as, Knox, Smith, Williamson, Bennett, and Pinkerton, plus the men of the Seventy-ninth, helped shape the contours of Lincoln's world, so, too, did the broader, albeit more speculative, Scottish idea of a "covenanted nation." This view—very much a part of the Scottish past—maintains that God had selected certain nations to play specific roles in world history. Covenant thought emerged during the late sixteenth century. Based in part on John Calvin's theology, it argued that the grace of God manifested itself in the form of a "compact" or contract between the Divine and the community. (Such religious ideas initially meshed easily with the traditional Scottish world of a Laird-Tenant relationship; both involved responsibility in exchange for loyalty.) Like ancient Israel, many Scots believed they had established a covenant with the Lord of Scripture, by which they were commanded to fulfill God's laws. Should the nation fail in this regard, God's wrath would fall upon the people. Thus, Scotland's fear of possible punishment from God existed side by side with a firm conviction of God's special favor.

To understand the political ramifications of this concept, it is necessary to add a bit of background. Excluding only the Radical Reformation of the Hutterites and Mennonites on the continent, the Scottish Reformation of the 1560s proved the most extreme. In their assault on all "popish images," angry Calvinists burned Roman Catholic statues and smashed stained-glass windows. Mobs tore down the remaining walls of the majestic Elgin Cathedral in Moray, while the impressive cathedral in Glasgow was spared only because a loyal counter-mob surrounded it at a crucial moment. In addition to the visible destruction, the Scottish Reformed clerics dismantled the ritual means by which the Catholic clergy had structured time for their followers. Gone were morning prayers, noon prayers, vespers, and the like. Gone, too, were the seven sacraments that guided a person through the stages of life: baptism, confirmation, the Mass, confession, marriage, holy orders, and extreme unction. In the Reformed tradition, only baptism and the Lord's Supper remained. Simultaneously, under John Knox's leadership, the Scots began to create a new sense of national destiny. Like ancient Israel, they felt "called" to play a central role in God's plans for the betterment of the human race. The thousands who signed the National Covenant in Greyfriars Church in Edinburgh in 1638 testified to this sense of special chosenness.[67]

Chosen or not, no society can survive without some form of shared social ceremony. Individuals and nations both need appropriate rituals as they confront their enemies and move inexorably through time. Gradually, the radical Protestant Scots devised a new set of ceremonies to replace the discarded Catholic ones. On an individual basis, this meant that a person who erred needed only to publicly *confess* his or her sins. Afterwards, he or she would be accepted back into the church fold. So, too, on a national level. A nation could sin (break God's covenant) as easily as an individual. A community, thus, needed similar rituals of reconciliation, and these emerged as ceremonial days of fasting and humiliation, interspersed with days of praise. Both confessing humiliation and giving praise helped restore an erring society to national wholeness.

The ceremonies of Fasting Days and Thanksgiving are usually associated with the New England Puritans, another Reformed people who shared an equal sense of Covenantal "chosenness." From 1620 to 1700, the New England colonies held numerous days of fasting and humiliation. The Pilgrims' first Thanksgiving in 1621 has, of course, become a central mythological legend of the modern United States. When the American Revolution broke out, these Reformed covenantal ideas received new life. During the era of the Revolution, the Continental Congress proclaimed seven days of Thanksgiving and seven days of fasting and prayer. Afterwards, Congress proclaimed days of Thanksgiving to celebrate the British surrender at Yorktown (October 19, 1781) and the adoption of the Constitution (November 26, 1789). President George Washington asked for a day of Thanksgiving on February 19, 1795, after suppression of the Whiskey Rebellion, and John Adams called for a fast day in 1798. James Madison called for Thanksgiving on April 3, 1815, the day of his official notification of the peace treaty with England, and John Tyler set aside May 14, 1841 as a day of fasting and prayer upon the death of William Henry Harrison. Without authorization of Congress, Zachary Taylor also issued a recommendation of a national fast on the first Friday of August 1849 because of cholera.[68]

The Covenantal idea of chosenness and the new rituals emanating therefrom proved far more pervasive than has generally been recognized. Historians Marilyn Westerkamp and Leigh Eric Schmidt have argued that the eighteenth-century colonial-American revivals trace their origins to the Communion observances of the Scots and the Scotch-Irish.[69] By the time of the Civil War, such ideas had become nationwide. Consider this comment from an 1861 sermon: "Geographically placed between Europe and Asia, we [the United States] were, in some sense, the representatives of the human race. The fortunes of the world were in our hand. We were a city set upon a hill, whose light was intended to shine upon every people and upon every land."[70] One might assume that this observation came from a New England Puritan, but the author was South Carolinian Southern Presbyterian J. H. Thornwell, a fiery secessionist. If such ideas shaped Southern Presbyterian Thornwell's views, we can be certain they were not exclusively held by New Englanders alone. But the Puritans were not the only means by which the ideas of a covenanted nation reached the New World. Thousands of Scots and Scotch-Irish emigrants of similar Reformed background brought these concepts to the farms of Pennsylvania, Virginia, and the Ohio River Valley.

As later events would show, the ideas of a national covenant formed much a part of Lincoln's world view. Where did he first come upon them? The most likely explanation is that he absorbed them from frontier Baptist or Presbyterian sources rather than from Yankee Congregationalists. Illinois had no Congregational Church until 1833, and although Yankees established a number of local colleges, their settlements were limited to Chicago, Galesburg, and a few other Northern Illinois towns. The atmosphere of Lincoln's southern Indiana and Springfield resembled a "transplanted Kentucky" far more than it did a transplanted New England.[71] During his years in Illinois, Lincoln witnessed a number of local and state reenactments of this covenant-based communal ritual. Illinois Governor Thomas Ford proclaimed a state day of Thanksgiving and worship on November 28, 1844, and his successor August C. French declared the same for November 25, two years later. In 1856, Illinois Governor Joel A. Matteson set aside November 20 "to be observed as a day of Thanksgiving and prayer." Illinois' first Republican governor, William H. Bissell, did the same for November 26, 1857. Mayors of Springfield proclaimed local Thanksgivings in late November in 1858 and 1860, in gratitude that the city had been spared much of the suffering that had afflicted other towns due to the recession.[72] The most famous pre–Civil War proclamation of this type came from lame-duck President James Buchanan, who, on December 14, 1860, set aside Friday, January 4, 1861, "to be kept as a solemn fast." Buchanan's proclamation of a day of national humiliation led to a variety of sermons by clerics of all faiths, one compilation of which broke into print. But, the editor ruefully noted, "One cannot but see first the difference which now divides the North and the South is not a mere misunderstanding; that there is real and profound difference of opinion."[73]

Today, the themes of Thanksgiving and Fast Days, with their respective emphasis on praise versus humiliation and prayer have fallen into different camps. Indeed, except for New Hampshire, the latter has completely disappeared from public view, while the former has turned into a major shopping opportunity for retailers. But the two ideas of Thanksgiving/ Humiliation were much more closely intertwined during the first part of the nineteenth century. The link, of course, revolved around the shared belief that God's providence controls the entire world and that, in Lincoln's words, the "almost chosen people" of the United States needed to acknowledge God's sovereignty with humility as well as praise. For this generation, national actions, be they sinful or virtuous, had to be acknowledged as a *collective* enterprise. The Abraham Lincoln Papers contain over thirty requests that Lincoln proclaim a national day of fasting and humiliation.[74] During the Civil War, it is clear that the covenant idea had spread far beyond its original Calvinist origins. An 1862 request from Philadelphia contained the endorsements of Presbyterians, Old and New School Episcopalians, Methodists, Baptists, German Reformed, and Jews. These groups all agreed that the nation required "repentance for our grievous sins and our need of His guiding and sustaining help."[75]

During his over four years in office, Lincoln requested a number of such days of national retrospection. For example, by special request of Congress, Lincoln appointed the last Thursday of September 1861 "as a day of humiliation, fasting and prayer for all the people of the nation." The Scottish Covenanter community in Iowa urged James Harlan, one of their senators, to push Lincoln toward what eventually became his March 30, 1863, Day of National Humiliation, Fasting, and Prayer. Similarly, again by special request of Congress, Lincoln set aside the first Thursday of August (the fourth) 1864, as a day of prayer that the Rebellion would be suppressed and the Constitutional laws of the land restored. Equally important was the plea to God "not to destroy us as a people, nor suffer us to be destroyed by the workings or connivance of other nations, or by obstinate adhesion to our own counsels which may be in conflict with His eternal purposes, and to implore Him to enlighten the mind of the nation to know and do His will."[76] Of this last proclamation, Attorney General Edward Bates noted in his diary, "Surely no people ever stood more in need of self-abasement" than the American people.[77] After Lincoln's assassination, President Andrew Johnson declared June first as a day of national humiliation and prayer as well.

During his administration, Lincoln issued eight proclamations of fasting or thanksgiving. In a brilliant passage from *Lincoln at Gettysburg*, historian Garry Wills contrasts the crusading militancy of Julia Ward Howe's poem "Battle Hymn of the Republic" with the humility of Lincoln's Fast Day proclamations.[78] The balance between official days of humiliation and official days of Thanksgiving also echo the Scottish/Puritan concept of a national ritual, as demanded by the covenants. Lincoln's famous February 5, 1864, statement on proposed loyalty oaths for ex-Confederates similarly reflected covenantal ideas: "On principle I dislike an oath which requires a man to swear he has not done wrong. It rejects the Christian principle of forgiveness on terms of repentance. I think it enough if a man does no wrong *hereafter*."[79]

If the periodic Fast Days have quietly faded from public view, Lincoln's proclamation of a national Thanksgiving remains much a part of contemporary national life. The standard version of this story credits New Hampshire editor Sarah Josepha Hale for the idea. Hale began her crusade for such a day in 1827 as editor at *Ladies' Magazine* in Boston. Later, as editor of *Godey's Lady's Book,* she wrote numerous editorials on the concept, as well as personal letters to all the state governors. Because *Godey's* had a circulation of 150,000, these views reached many homes. Hale also wrote a special letter to Lincoln on September 28, 1863, and five days later, on October 3, 1863, he issued his Proclamation for Thanksgiving. On three occasions in 1864, Lincoln issued similar proclamations to commemorate victories of the Union army. His October 20, 1864, proclamation, which set aside the last Thursday in November, suggests that he may have been thinking of the holiday in annual terms.[80] Hale was not the only person to urge Lincoln to establish a day of Thanksgiving. The Lincoln papers at the Library of Congress contain over forty letters—several from overseas—with similar suggestions.[81] The precise time of year did not seem to matter. One New Englander suggested April 19—the anniversary of the Battle of Lexington. Another correspondent recommended April 20. An autumn date—which echoed a harvest celebration—proved much more common, and Thanksgiving eventually emerged as a late-November holiday. The selection of a date in late November, however, had an unanticipated effect on Scottish American culture. Thanksgiving fell close to Saint Andrew's Day (November 30) and essentially crowded the latter off the national calendar. In its place, the Scottish American community turned to Robert Burns's birthday. From the Civil War era forward, January 25—rather than November 30—became the central date for Americans to celebrate the Scottish American experience in all its contradictions.

Thus, it seems clear that Abraham Lincoln's world was shaped not only by the verse of Robert Burns but also by the activities and ideas of hundreds of his fellow Scots as well.

Scottish Opinion on Lincoln and the War

Most historians who have dealt with the United States and Great Britain during the Civil War have focused on London, home of the British government, the American minister Charles Francis Adams, and the influential pro-Southern London *Times*. But to focus on English opinion exclusively is to neglect the sentiments of the other "nations" that composed Great Britain of that era: Wales, Ireland, and Scotland.

Even though Scotland had merged its monarchy with England in 1603 and its parliament in 1707, it remained very much a separate country. Scotland boasted its own national Presbyterian Church, its own legal system, and a much more democratic pattern of education. This ensured that Scottish public opinion on Abraham Lincoln and the war often remained very distinct from that of its larger southern neighbor.

Centuries of Scots and Scotch Irish immigration across the Atlantic Ocean meant that many Scots kept abreast of American affairs. The antebellum growth of the antislavery movement deepened this connection. Noted Black orator Frederick Douglass delivered a number of abolitionist speeches in Scotland in 1847, where he was acknowledged as a gentleman of intellect and character.[82] He filled numerous halls with his denunciation of the Free Church solicitation of money from the slave-holding U.S. Southern Presbyterian churches. "Send back that money" was his rallying cry. Douglass's impassioned speeches put the powerful Free Church in an embarrassing position. Although they condemned slavery as an institution, the Free Church did not consider all slaveholders as necessarily sinful. When Douglass accused them of violating principle solely for financial gain, their public discomfort was thoroughly relished by the more antislavery denominations, the Church of Scotland, the Congregationalists, the Quakers, and others. So popular was Douglass that the Edinburgh publishing house of Adam Black and Charles Black brought out its own edition of Douglass's first autobiography *My Bondage and My Freedom*.[83]

Author Harriet Beecher Stowe was even more successful. Following the triumph of *Uncle Tom's Cabin*—the first American novel to sell over a million copies—Stowe visited Scotland in 1853 where she met a hero's welcome. The Workingmen of Glasgow composed and sang a composition for her entitled "Scottish Workers to Harriet Beecher Stowe," and British publishers reprinted her famous book with several additional engravings. "Less than a year ago," marveled the *Scotsman*, "the name of Harriet Beecher Stowe was unknown in Britain; it is now a household word in every home in the country."[84] When the train carrying her party arrived in Lockerbee, the crowd at the station cried out for her to come to the window. "Ye're welcome to Scotland," admirers shouted. In Glasgow, representatives from several surrounding communities introduced themselves and showered her with flowers and fruit. She shook hands with citizens from Paisley, Greenock, Dundee, Aberdeen, and Edinburgh. The Duchess of Sutherland, in whose London home she had stayed, presented her with a gold bracelet. After a two-hour train ride from Glasgow to Edinburgh, Stowe and her party were met by the Lord Provost at the door of the car, and he presented her with the magistracy of the city. He gave her a carriage tour of the city; the crowd shouted and cheered when she went by. In Old Town, gangs of young boys raced alongside the carriage and shouted, "That's her, see the *courls*." As it was deemed improper for women to address a mixed audience, the city arranged a tea party in her honor instead, where she met hundreds of antislavery admirers.[85] She returned in 1856 for a stay at Inverary Castle and shortly afterwards wrote her account of the visit, *Sunny Memories of Foreign Lands*. All in all, Harriet Beecher Stowe's journey through Caledonia proved a triumphant procession. Only later did her naïve support of the Sutherland clearances bring forth harsh criticism from certain circles.

Stowe's *Uncle Tom's Cabin* touched Scottish sentiment on a number of fronts. First and foremost, her book struck a familiar chord of public moralism. "I could not control the story," Stowe later said. "It wrote itself." On another occasion, she said that the Lord was really the author and that she had served as but a humble instrument in His hand.[86] The elevated, moral tone of *Uncle Tom's Cabin* cut across Scottish social-class boundaries. The embarrassment of Free Church acceptance of Southern Presbyterian moneys could be momentarily forgotten. The crowds who cheered her were reassured that their nation "is thoroughly sound at heart, and ready to respond with any truly great and generous impulse."[87] Several years later, a traveling African American speaker filled Edinburgh halls with the claim that he had served as the chief model for her character of Uncle Tom.[88]

The abolitionist speeches of Frederick Douglass and Harriet Beecher Stowe paved the way for Scottish understanding of the deepening American crisis. But it took four more years before Scots became aware of Lincoln. On Friday, September 7, 1860, the *Scotsman* first mentioned the name of Abraham Lincoln. Terming him a self-made man who had begun life as a "blacksmith," the paper characterized the Republican presidential nominee as "obscure as Mr. Preston Brooks before he bludgeoned Mr. [Charles] Sumner." Arguing that "the curse of slavery" had long haunted the American republic, the *Scotsman* supported Lincoln's candidacy, hoping that his election on a no-expansion-of-slavery platform would eventually result in the complete eradication of the institution.[89] With this modest introduction, Edinburgh's premier newspaper began what would emerge as the most extensive Scottish coverage of Lincoln's activities. The newspaper defended Lincoln's arrival in Washington in a "Scotch cap and plaid cloak." After the First Inaugural, the *Scotsman* observed that his policy decisions called forth as much interest in Scotland as in the American South. The editors interpreted his 1863 call for three hundred thousand volunteers as a sad collapse of Northern support for the cause.[90] The *Scotsman* sent its own correspondent to cover the conflict but as his letters sometimes took as long as six months to reach Edinburgh, the paper was forced to rely heavily on the pro-Southern coverage by London *Times* reporters.[91] In 1863, the *Scotsman* printed the Emancipation Proclamation in full and covered all the major Civil War battles and troop movements in detail. The election of 1864 was depicted as a contest between peace and war.[92]

Although the *Scotsman* remained a moderate Lincoln supporter throughout the conflict, the same could not be said for many of the other Scottish publications. Several Scottish newspapers, including the *Glasgow Herald* plus the two most prominent literary quarterlies, the *Edinburgh Review* and *Blackwood's Magazine*, remained staunchly pro-Southern. Even the radical newspapers, such as, the Glasgow *Sentinel*, the voice of the Glasgow trades council, supported the Confederacy. When Andrew Carnegie returned to his hometown of Dunfermline, he was astounded to discover that his former radical associates, as well as the respected Dunfermline *Journal*, all favored Jefferson Davis over Lincoln. Carnegie found virtually no support for the Union cause among his old comrades. Historian R. J. M. Blackett recently concluded that British support for the Confederacy extended far more widely than previously suspected.[93] There is considerable evidence for this position. Scottish poet Charles Mackay, chief reporter for the London *Times* in the States, also proved decidedly pro-Southern in his dispatches. The Church of Scotland made no official statement one way or the other. *Blackwood's* ridiculed the Union cause with regularity. For example, they described the secession of Virginia as pivoting on Lincoln's response to a last-minute peace visit by three Virginia delegates. When one delegate asked Lincoln to loan him "his finger and thumb"—a reference to some form of statement of reassurance—Lincoln allegedly replied, "My finger and thumb, what would you do with them? Blow your nose?" With that, the delegation left, and Virginia seceded.[94] As late as 1874, a writer in *Blackwood's* described American slaves as the most "moral, orderly and respectable peasantry" in the world.[95]

Outside of Edinburgh, the two strongest pro-Lincoln sections of the country were located in the west of Scotland and the far Northeast. In the west of Scotland, the pro-Union advocates were concentrated in two areas. The first was Glasgow, home of the largest abolition organization, the Union and Emancipation Society. This group sent a letter of congratulations to American minister to Britain Adams on the Congressional passage of the Thirteenth Amendment. A subsidiary antislavery society existed in the weaving hamlet of Newmilns, Ayrshire, about twenty miles from Burns's home, and historically an area with a strong radical Covenanter tradition. The Newmilns group, led by political radical John Donald, actually seems to have been more active than the larger Glasgow society. Scottish radicals saw the American republic as the model toward which they wished to push their own country. And from a Covenanter perspective, there was no question that slavery was a sin. The Newmilns society met regularly to praise Lincoln as a man sent from the working class with a God-given destiny to end chattel slavery. Their sentiments were also duly forwarded to Adams in London. Local legend maintains that Lincoln sent an American flag to Donald and Newmilns in appreciation of their support, but that has never been substantiated. Still, in December 1864, John Brooks, an African American, did present the community with a U.S. flag. When Newmilns flew the flag at a subsequent celebration, the *Glasgow Herald* sneered that the community had just sworn allegiance to the "Federal President and the Federal Constitution."[96] The other pro-Union segment in the West of Scotland lay with the tiny Quaker movement. Glasgow Quakers infiltrated the Clydeside shipyards and, almost surely, were the ones who gave the list of Confederate ships under construction to John Bright, British Member of Parliament, that he read aloud in session in hopes of embarrassing the Henry J. T. Palmerston administration. Quaker radicals also alerted the press in 1864 about the Clyde-built ram Pampero and halted its impending sale to the South.[97]

In the agrarian Northeast, pro-Union sentiment was led by the *Dundee Advertiser* and the influential Aberdeen paper, the *Aberdeen Free Press and Buchan News*. Self-exiled Aberdonians wrote letters from the States to the *Free Press* praising Lincoln and the Union cause. Émigré William Grieg wrote regularly from New York in 1861 and 1862, and the "Colorado Scot" later echoed his views. From January 1864 through the end of the war, the Milwaukee-based "Wisconsin Scot" wrote regularly to denounce Mackay's descriptions in the *Times* and to give voice to Lincoln's wartime goals.[98] Among the Scottish nobility, the Duke of Argyle and the Duchess of Sutherland also gave Lincoln their support. The London-based pro-South *Index* circulated in Scotland, but it is impossible to estimate its influence. When pro-Confederate speakers reached Scotland, however, they usually attracted considerable audiences. The cottonworkers and shipworkers of Glasgow were much affected by the economic dislocation of the war. At the request of two hundred Glaswegians, John Spence of Liverpool filled Glasgow's City Hall with a speech advocating Southern independence. Arguing that secession was a God-given right, Spence denounced Lincoln as a despot who could have freed the slaves in the loyal Border States but chose not to. He proclaimed the Emancipation Proclamation a "farce" and predicted that the first consequence of Union victory would be an American war on Great Britain. His audience gave him a vigorous ovation.[99]

His compatriot, Joseph N. McDowell, who had spoken at Queen Street Hall in Edinburgh ten days earlier, had a much more difficult time. Currently serving as inspector of Confederate hospitals, McDowell marched to the podium to a chorus of mixed cheers and hisses. In his speech, he termed Lincoln a fraud, which was countered with loud cheers and hisses and a voice, "Fraud! What do ye mean?" Lincoln deserved this appellation, the speaker said, because had he honestly stated in 1860 that he planned to eradicate the South's domestic institutions, he never would have been elected. McDowell argued that the South had the right to secede, based on both the Constitution and the Declaration of Independence. Why did Lincoln persist in allowing loyal slaveholders in the Border States to keep their property? Because he was duplicitous. The Edinburgh audience showed that it was conversant with American affairs, so much so that someone challenged McDowell on almost every point he made. The more he tried to explain, the louder the mixed boos, cheers, and vocal outbursts. Eventually, the tumult caused the speaker to conclude early, closing with the prediction that the South would yet be free. In spite of the considerable opposition, the audience gave McDowell three cheers for his performance.[100]

On the other side, Lincoln supporter Henry Ward Beecher filled the Free Church Assembly Hall on October 14, 1863. The gathering was described as one of the most crowded ever held in Edinburgh. Beecher also met with a mixed chorus of cheers and hisses as he presented the Union case.[101] In 1863, Scottish public opinion on Abraham Lincoln was clearly not of a single mind. This situation disappeared overnight, however, when word arrived in late April of 1865 of Lincoln's assassination. The *Aberdeen Free Press*, the *Herald*, and the *Scotsman* all printed scores of articles on Lincoln in the wake of the tragedy. Many of the comments came in the form of poems, including a reprinting of the famed "Abraham Lincoln" apology from *Punch*. The May 6 (Saturday) edition of the *Glasgow Weekly Herald* included a separate portrait of the late president, a relative rarity for the times. "In short," reported the *Herald,* "no similar event has created such a profound impression since the day on which William the Silent was slaughtered in his palace" [in 1584].[102] Scots were so agitated over the assassination that detectives arrested an incoming passenger who resembled John Wilkes Booth. The unfortunate man arrived via the ship *Edinburgh* and was immediately apprehended at Queens Ferry.[103]

Public praise for Lincoln's steadfast pursuit of his goals became commonplace. His homely phrase "pegging away" evolved into a Scottish idiom. In 1865, the *Herald* concluded that as he was neither genius nor hero, Lincoln was ideally suited to the ultimate leadership of a republic.[104] In a lengthy biographical sketch of the martyred president, the *Scotsman* said, "In person he was tall, much beyond the common run of men, and ungainly in face and frame; but he looked, nevertheless, a man of thought and power."[105] Some Scottish papers wondered if Northern officers could restrain their Black troops from taking revenge on Southern Whites after the assassination. They similarly noted that Confederate officers and soldiers in Libby Prison in Richmond passed resolutions that "they were soldiers and applauded no assassins."[106] The newspapers also printed the comment of an *Index* supporter that the Confederate government had not been involved in the murder.

In late April and early May 1865, with the issue of American slavery resolved, the question of Southern secession quashed and the poignancy of the assassination still fresh, the mixed British feelings regarding America began to solidify. Within a fortnight, they merged into a feeling of universal sympathy. In England, the House of Lords and the House of Commons both passed appropriate resolutions. Queen Victoria sent a personal letter to Mary Lincoln, a heartfelt message from one widow to another. But perhaps the best indication of the shift in Scottish popular opinion can be seen in the spontaneous public meetings that sprang up in almost every town of any size, including Leith, Hawick, Dundee, Montrose, and Aberdeen. The crowds for these gatherings included all classes of Scots.[107] As the *Herald* had received several letters asking for such a meeting, the mayor of Glasgow filled Saint Georges's hall on Thursday, April 27, 1865. American citizens in Glasgow also sent a special message to Charles Francis Adams. Another public meeting of largely workingmen filled the Trades Hall for the same purpose. Noting the long trade and immigration links between Glasgow and America, the resolutions sent "our most cordial sympathy with the people of America" and promised "to do our utmost to encourage them to meet their present trial with fortitude, and with wisdom, with Christian forbearance."[108] One Scot complained that, as a workingman, he could not attend any afternoon public meetings, but, as a member of the people, he wished to make his voice of sympathy known as well and, therefore, urged the holding of evening meetings so as to include the working classes.[109] The public meeting at the Music Hall in Edinburgh on May 3 brought an equally poignant response. A large audience heard the Lord Provost praise Lincoln's magnanimity. Although Scots had differed on the Civil War, he said, on this day there existed a common feeling of repudiation of the act of assassination and sympathy for the American people. Regardless of previous political positions, noted another speaker, Scots could come together now on the grounds of common sorrow.[110]

The *Scotsman*'s special correspondent extensively described the Lincoln funeral obsequies in New York, where between 50,000 and 70,000 people marched in solemn procession. He reported that an estimated 120,000 viewed the open coffin in City Hall, with the silent crowd composed of old and young, men, women, and children, rich and poor. A humble Irish woman laid a small cross at the foot of the coffin with the whispered comment, "God preserve your soul."[111] Only after the close of the hostilities, aided by the overwhelming mood of sorrow, did the legend of Abraham Lincoln begin to deepen its affinity with Scottish history.

5

Burns and Lincoln in Historical Memory

Writing comparative history, a cynic once observed, demands twice as much effort for half the results. But some historians rush in where angels fear to tread, and in this chapter I plan to do precisely that. During the nineteenth century, Robert Burns and Abraham Lincoln each evolved into mythological figures. They did so in ways that not only paralleled one another but overlapped as well. In each case, "the people" led the crusade. Eventually, their governments placed their respective images on currency, stamps, and scores of heroic statues. Both scholars and amateurs added thousands of books, essays, and speeches to the mix. The result was to merge man with nation, as each became the representative symbol of his native land. As the *Scotsman* noted in 1884, émigré Scots found their "national sentiment condensed and idealized in Burns."[1] Moreover, Scots could recognize the American appreciation of Lincoln because he similarly approximated "a national type."[2] Simultaneously, the emerging parallel mythologies also became intertwined with each other. For years, numerous speakers on both sides of the Atlantic continued to emphasize the overlap of Scottish and American social goals. Perhaps the best examples of this sentiment may be seen in the heroic Lincoln statue in the Old Calton Hill Burial Ground in Edinburgh and the twelve Burns statues that grace various American cities. It is rare for a country to erect a statue to a foreign national who has never set foot on its soil.

This overlapping, of course, went through a number of stages. Immediately after his death, Lincoln's contemporaries often interpreted him through a Burnsian lens, a movement that lasted until shortly after World War I. From the 1920s forward, however, Burns's message seemed to be much less central to the American experience. By the time of the Great Depression, Burns's reputation had become largely restricted to the Scottish American community. The average American lost familiarity with his classic verses. The 1959 bicentennial of Burns's birth was hardly noticed in the United States; neither was the bicentenary of his death. Instead, in 1959 Americans eagerly celebrated the sesquicentennial of the birth of Lincoln. In the States, Lincoln had simply surpassed Burns as the voice of democratic aspirations. After World War II, few outside of the academy could recall their previous interconnections.

The First Comparisons

Because the life and legend of Robert Burns functioned almost as a category of thought for many Victorian Americans, it is no surprise that Lincoln's contemporaries initially tried to fit him into this framework. As one 1861 visitor to the White House suggested, there was something in Burns's rough life that had great appeal to the president.[3] Several of Lincoln's early biographers held to this view as well. Ohio Republican Joseph H. Barrett opened and closed his 842-page study with this theme. He began by comparing the prospects that William Burness faced in Scotland with those of Thomas Lincoln in Kentucky. Over eight hundred pages later, he concluded, "What Robert Burns has proverbially been to the people of his native land and to a certain extent all lands as a bard, Abraham Lincoln seems to have become to us."[4] In his now-classic memoir, *Six Months in the White House* (1869), F. B. Carpenter made a similar link. He felt that Lincoln's nobility of character perfectly illustrated his favorite poet's words:

> The rank is but the guinea's stamp
> The man's the gold for a' that.

Carpenter's version—"gold" for "gowd"—probably reflected common parlance.[5] But Burns's career as category of thought proved generational and did not long survive the century. One of the final overt comparisons came in 1909 in Francis Grierson's memoir: "The people [at one of the Lincoln-Douglas debates] stand bewildered and breathless under the natural magic of the strangest and most original personality known to the English-speaking world since Robert Burns."[6]

Perhaps the last proponent of this view was William E. Barton, Congregational minister turned historian. Born in Illinois in 1861, Barton grew to maturity among people who had known Lincoln personally; he later served as a teacher and circuit-riding preacher in the hill country of Kentucky. There he dealt with farmers who lived very close to the ways that the Lincoln family had lived. Thus, he knew full well the social ambience that surrounded American pioneer culture. In his two-volume *The Life of Abraham Lincoln* (1925), Barton began by comparing the "auld clay biggin" in Ayr with the recently monumentalized Lincoln log cabin in LaRue County, Kentucky. A year later, the American consul in Edinburgh observed that both Lincoln and Burns had been cut from the same cloth: they were born to the peasantry and grew up as provincials. The consul added that both were raised to their respective heroic positions by the love of their fellow men.[7]

Barton had few successors along this line. The next generations of professionally trained biographers—James G. Randall, Benjamin P. Thomas, David Herbert Donald, Stephen B. Oates, Douglas L. Wilson, Allen C. Guelzo, Gabor S. Boritt, William E. Gienapp, and others—all pointed to Lincoln's admiration for Burns's poetry but stopped at that. The indexes of all the recent studies of the sixteenth president devote far more attention to Ambrose Burnside than they do to Burns. Even books treating Lincoln's mastery of the language tend to give Burns short shrift. There are two main reasons for this shift. First, by the 1920s, the ethnic composition of the nation had shifted so extensively that the Scots and Scotch Irish influence seemed much less crucial in shaping the national identity. In addition, by the late 1920s, Burns's literary star had fallen drastically in mainstream American culture. He was no longer viewed as the "poet of American democracy," as he had been a generation earlier.[8] By the early twentieth century, America had (finally) produced a bevy of poets all her own: Walt Whitman, James Russell Lowell, Henry Wadsworth Longfellow, Oliver Wendell Holmes, Emily Dickinson, Robert Frost, Edna St. Vincent Millay, Langston Hughes, and so on.

Although Scottish American enthusiasm for Burns remained as strong as ever, the new generation of literary scholars had begun to "demote" Robert Burns from his initial lofty position as one of the world's finest writers. By the late 1920s, few critics outside of Scotland ranked him among the world's greatest: Goethe, Shakespeare, or Cervantes. Rather, by about 1925, Burns had assumed the status of fine "regional" poet but no longer a world-class master. In 1972, literary critic Raymond Bentman complained bitterly that Burns's poetry had been virtually ignored by English literary scholars for a quarter of a century.[9]

The 1909 Birthday Celebrations

Burns and Lincoln were born almost exactly fifty years apart. This meant that the 1909 centenary of Lincoln's birthday also marked the sesquicentenary of Burns's. Thus, from approximately 1896 (the centenary of Burns's death) to 1909, writers and speakers in Britain and the United

States devoted a good deal of attention to both men's lives. For example, the American ambassador to Britain, Joseph H. Choate, delivered a series of lectures on famous Americans, speaking to the Edinburgh Philosophical Institution in 1900 on Lincoln. When he published the essays in 1910, he prominently featured Lincoln's name in the title.[10] That same year, a Scottish writer argued that Burns and Lincoln shared similar goals: one to sing a song that would remain in the memory of his countrymen; the other to "distinguish himself by some great service to mankind."[11]

The year 1909 produced a wave of Lincoln celebrations all across the United States. February 12 was observed as a general holiday, and Judge James S. Ewing estimated that admirers delivered over fifty thousand speeches that day on some aspect of Lincoln's life.[12] In the New York City area alone, over 560 public schools staged some form of celebration. The mayor of New York presided over one meeting at Cooper Union Hall, while a former Civil War officer presided over another at Carnegie Hall. Perhaps the greatest public interest focused on President Roosevelt as he laid the cornerstone of the Lincoln Memorial Building near Hodgenville, Kentucky, scheduled to house the log cabin in which Lincoln had been born.[13] Naturally, Lincoln's hometown of Springfield, Illinois, boasted the largest celebration. Joining a host of dignitaries, James, Lord Bryce, British ambassador to the States, spoke to the crowd, emphasizing Lincoln's British heritage and his masterful use of the English language. Although American by birth, Bryce noted, Lincoln had become a figure who now belonged to all of humankind.[14] Because the local Black community had been ignored in the official proceedings, the comments by Reverend L. H. Magee at the Springfield African American Episcopal Church proved especially poignant. Lincoln, said Magee, was clearly used as an instrument of God in setting four million people free; like Jesus of Nazareth, his life was sacrificed that they should so remain. In the eyes of the church members, Lincoln remained synonymous with the concept of freedom.[15]

In the years flanking 1909, American writers also devoted a fair amount of attention to the 150th birthday of Robert Burns. From 1905 to 1909, national magazines carried over twenty articles on various aspects of Burns's life. Even the sparsely populated territory of New Mexico ordered that the American flag be flown at all schools on January 25.[16] Scotland, of course, commemorated Burns's 1909 birthday in a spectacular manner. The celebrations were encouraged by the Burns Federation in Ayrshire, which, by 1885, had begun to formalize the January 25 celebrations. Aided by its annual *Burns Chronicle* (founded 1892), the federation assumed the mantle of overseeing (and recording) all official ceremonial functions. The society loomed prominently in Scotland's formal celebrations of the centenary of his death and the sesquicentennial of his birth. The 1909 celebration of his birthday—by now every Scot's "January obligation"—called forth endless restatements of the poet's greatness.

These celebrations of 1896 and 1909—only thirteen years apart—marked the high point of the American commemoration of Burns's life. In 1896, the governor of Massachusetts oversaw the Boston Burns gala, while a spokesman for the New York gathering noted with pride that "the Americans present seemed to appreciate the entertainment nearly as much as the Scotch folks." As the *Scottish-American* reported of the Buffalo, New York, Burns gathering in 1909, everyone felt "Scottified to the teeth."[17]

Spokesmen of the Lincoln-Burns Link

Given this heady turn-of-the-century Burnsian atmosphere, it was inevitable that someone from the Scottish American community would try to refurbish the historic Burns-Lincoln connection. The three most prominent figures to make this effort were industrialist Andrew Carnegie, diplomat Wallace Bruce, and lawyer Alexander McKnight. By the early 1890s, the diminutive Carnegie had achieved international fame as "the richest man in the world." A young railway supervisor during the Civil War, he had a passing brush with Lincoln, whom he admired greatly. Idealist as well as practical businessman, Carnegie had long placed Burns on a similar pedestal. Much in demand for various Scottish celebratory occasions, in 1912 Carnegie delivered the dedication address at the unveiling of a heroic Burns statue in Melrose, Scotland. In this oration, he put a high gloss on the Burns-Lincoln link: "As a lad at school he [Lincoln] fortunately had a Scotch schoolmaster who adored Burns. The boy was carried away by the Bard, and it is recorded that when still a youth wagers were made that no one could call upon him for a recitation from Burns which he could not give from memory. In his mature years he lectured on his favorite poet, and, as usual, drew the masses of the people."[18] Exactly where Carnegie acquired this information is unclear—no researcher has been able to identify any Scottish schoolmaster or Lincoln lecture on Burns—but because of Carnegie's reputation, the speech received a good bit of publicity. In 1911, the aged Carnegie, not surprisingly, listed both Lincoln and Burns among his list "21 World Movers"—those who have helped humankind.

Carnegie's contemporary and friend Wallace Bruce continued along similar lines. A wealthy businessman of Scottish origins, Bruce served as

U.S. consul to Edinburgh in the early 1890s, where he became the driving force behind the erection of the city's famed Lincoln statue. Early in his term as consul, the widow of a Scottish émigré who had fought for the Union and later returned to work in the local mills in Scotland approached Bruce regarding the possibility of a pension. Bruce decided to go a step further beyond just getting the widow her pension. Drawing on his extensive social connections, he secured 602 subscriptions of $100 each to "erect a statue to the greatest man of the age—Lincoln—in the most beautiful city in Europe—Edinburgh."[19] Edinburgh city officials quickly warmed to the idea. They viewed the statue as both a memorial to Scottish émigrés who had lost their lives fighting for the Union as well as a celebration of the idea of the self-made man. Editorial comments noted that Carnegie, who contributed his share, reflected this ideal, as did the Edinburgh chair of the Lincoln Memorial Committee, Sir William Arrol, who had begun life as a blacksmith and rose to become the builder of the Firth of Forth Bridge. Arrol was "a true Scot, and a self-made man, such a man as Lincoln would like to have known," said the *Scots Magazine*.[20]

The statue, which depicted Lincoln standing over a grateful ex-slave, was the first Lincoln statue to be erected outside the United States. Formally unveiled in the Old Calton Hill Burial Ground in 1893 during a fierce shower, most of the ceremony proper had to be postponed until the banquet that evening. But in the speech of dedication, Bruce noted that the depiction of Lincoln freeing the slaves represented the culmination of Saxon freedom and reflected the democratic idealism shared by both countries.[21] For years, Scotland took great pride in housing the only statue to Lincoln in all of Europe. As late as 1912, it remained one of the most popular tourist destinations in Edinburgh for American visitors.[22]

Throughout his lengthy career, Bruce tried his best to strengthen these Scottish American links. He oversaw the presentation of a facsimile of the Declaration of Independence to the Canongate Lodge in Edinburgh, and he contributed heavily to a frieze honoring Burns in Ayrshire. At the completion of the Ayr Burns statue, he reminded the audience that not just Scottish Americans but Americans in general considered Burns the poet laureate of all people. Bruce also served as the driving force behind the efforts to erect a replica of the Burns cottage at the 1904 Saint Louis World's Fair, to ensure the presence of a "Scottish nook" that acknowledged the Scots' roles in the rise of America.[23] In addition, Bruce also gained fame as a collector of Burnsiana, and his elegant Brooklyn home on Stuyvesant Avenue housed one of the largest collections of first editions, as well as a holograph manuscript of "the blue-eyed lassie." His prize possession was a piece of the bed on which Burns had allegedly breathed his last.

Wallace Bruce's official efforts to connect Lincoln and Britain echoed on a governmental level for the next three decades. In 1917, when the *New York Times* requested a tribute from Prime Minister David Lloyd George on Lincoln Day, he replied that the Allied cause—a war against slavery and for the cause of freedom—was identical to Lincoln's cause of fifty years previous.[24] In 1920, at an unveiling of a Saint Gaudens Lincoln statue in Britain (the second overseas), Lloyd George seized on the same theme: Lincoln was "an American no longer"—now he belonged to "the entire world."[25]

To honor the American contribution to the fighting in the Great War, the British Navy drew from Burns's most famous song. As the American fleet sailed out of the Firth of Forth for home, the British fleet lined up in double columns for about thirty miles. All hands stood on deck to bid the Americans farewell by singing "Should Auld Acquaintance Be Forgot." This gesture, boasted John Gribbel of Philadelphia—the man who donated Burns's Genriddle manuscripts to Scotland—did more to cement relations with the two countries than all the treaties ever made.[26]

The most steadfast advocate of a revived Burns-Lincoln connection came from long-term Duluth, Minnesota, resident Alexander G. McKnight. Born in Ayrshire, Scotland, in 1878, young Alexander emigrated to the states when he was fifteen. After attending several universities, he joined the Minnesota Bar in 1904. For years, he remained active in Duluth civic affairs and in the national Democratic Party.[27] In April 1934, President Franklin D. Roosevelt appointed him as chief of the litigation division of the National Recovery Administration (NRA) in Washington, D.C. He served in that capacity for twelve months, resigning only when the U.S. Supreme Court declared the NRA unconstitutional. Afterwards, he accused the court of stepping "beyond the boundaries of constitutionality."[28]

In addition to his civic and political careers, McKnight devoted a good deal of time to Scottish American affairs. He subscribed to his hometown Ayrshire newspaper for forty-eight years and in 1936 was elected honorary president of the Robert Burns Club, World Federation. He also served as president of Clan Stewart, Duluth, and as the National Royal Chief of the Order of Scottish Clans. A popular presenter, he was much in demand as a public speaker.[29] On his departure for Washington, the Duluth *Herald* termed him "one of the leading Scotsmen of the United States."[30] McKnight pursued his avocation with intensity. He compiled the largest collection of Burnsiana in Minnesota, wrote essays for various publications on the Scottish bard, and penned his own poetic verses celebrating Ayrshire.[31] Local editors invariably described him as an "authority" on Burns as well as Lincoln.[32] In the course of his research, McKnight contacted all the major Lincoln experts of his day to compile evidence of the Burns-Lincoln connection. He wrote Helen Nicolay, daughter of Lincoln's former secretary, to tell her that he had discovered two letters in which Lincoln had quoted Burns (1837 and 1861), although Lincoln scholars remain dubious.[33] McKnight also promoted the doubtful claim that Lincoln had scribbled a Burns stanza from memory into one of the books in his library. The quotation written in the book closes with "man's inhumanity to man / makes countless thousands mourn!" to which Lincoln allegedly added "and enslaves his fellow men." This source has never been verified either. McKnight pestered James G. Randall so much that Randall referred to McKnight as "somewhat of a fanatic" on the subject.[34] Over the years, McKnight published four modest pamphlets on Burns or the Burns-Lincoln relationship. These all appeared in minor venues with limited circulation, although several were later reprinted as pamphlets. McKnight's interpretation was hardly new. He defended Burns on all counts and noted that the poet's most famous phrase on equality "would have given eternal fame had he never written another line."[35]

But McKnight proved the last of a breed. By the onset of the Great Depression of the 1930s, American boys and girls were not learning Burnsian phrases from each other, as in Ralph Waldo Emerson's day. Nor were they studying Burns in school. In 1939, famed American Burnsian scholar DeLancey Ferguson complained that his scholarship on Burns seemed to be met with "an almost passionate apathy." By the late 1920s, the popular appeal of Scotland's most famous bard had become largely restricted to the Scottish American community. As anthropologist Celeste Ray has shown in *Highland Heritage* (2001), even the Burns's Nights suppers—especially in the South—celebrated "Scottish culture" in general far more than the specific words of the poet.[36] The arrival of the 1959 Lincoln/Burns anniversaries reflected this shift in emphasis. From 1957 to 1959, American magazines published only four articles on Robert Burns. During the centennial year, American publishers brought forth no new books on Burns—neither biographies nor new editions of his poems. (A Scottish bookseller of that year could only list seventeen editions of his works and only twenty-two books about him.)[37]

On the other hand, in 1959, Americans could not get enough of Abraham Lincoln. The list of Lincoln books, essays, and speeches for that year is overwhelming. In 1957, Congress created a bipartisan Sesquicentennial Committee, and on December 29, 1958, President Dwight D. Eisenhower officially designated 1959 as Lincoln Year. The Library of Congress hosted an appropriate exhibition of Lincoln materials, and in February 1959 alone over nineteen foreign nations and fifteen states staged some form of ceremony. By the close of the year, about ninety nations had held various ceremonies. The American press of 1959, however, hardly mentioned that the year also commemorated the 250th birthday of Robert Burns. A fourteen-hundred-person gathering of Scottish Americans in Chicago seemed to be the main U.S. event in this regard. During the era of the Cold War, Burns's appeal as poet of equality had bypassed the United States. The Scottish commemoration, of course, reversed the tables of celebration. The National Library of Scotland staged a major exhibit of Burnsian artifacts, and a reviewer termed his poetry "the best of its kind." No book of poems, he said, had ever been reproduced so often as the Kilmarnock Burns. In spite of Burns's reputation on religious matters, Saint Michael's Church, Dumfries, which Burns had attended, held a special service for him, and a statue was unveiled at Arbroath. A Scot in Belfast criticized the British government for not issuing a special stamp in Burns's honor: "Woe betide our London Government if they ever try to slip a Willie Shakespeare stamp over on us." In Edinburgh, two hundred people attended a wreath-laying ceremony at the Burns memorial on Calton Hill. A gigantic procession marched along High Street in Old Town from the City Chambers to Saint Giles Cathedral. In the memorial service at the cathedral, the Reverend H. C. Whitley made only a brief reference to the recent decision by the cathedral board to reject a Burns memorial plaque because "there was no room."[38]

Just as Lincoln's birthday was commemorated across the world, so too was Burns's. Rome, Paris, London, Germany, New Zealand, and Australia all held ceremonies, with the citizens of the Soviet Union greeting the Burns's bicentenary with special vigor; over 613,000 copies of his verses had been sold since the 1917 revolution, and a secretary of the Soviet Embassy in London laid a wreath at Ayr on a plinth of a Burns statue.[39] Although the Soviets could not easily celebrate Lincoln, they could, indeed, commemorate the works of the Scottish poet.

Historical Memory

Both Burns and Lincoln had emerged from the ranks of "the people," and it was the people who turned them into national icons within a generation after their deaths. Interestingly, however, the process was initiated by two different segments of "the people." Burns's Kilmarnock edition sold well in Ayrshire, but 612 copies does not a reputation make. It took the Edinburgh reprint of 2,800 and the enthusiastic celebration by the Edinburgh literary elite to launch him on his road to national fame. Only then did the Scottish plowboys and maidservants begin to devour his writings. Thus, the Scottish *aristocracy* essentially began the process that catapulted the ultimate democrat into the public realm as the key representative of the Scottish national ethos.

With Lincoln, the opposite proved true. The first group to invest him with iconic status were the ex-slaves, who immediately hailed him as their savior. Only after his assassination did Illinois farmers and other Union supporters begin to forge the cosmic legend that exists today. The White South held back for at least three generations. Gradually, however, each man came to represent far more than simply a literary or political figure. Instead, each man evolved into the very embodiment of his nation's hopes and fears for the future, calling forth, as one commentator phrased it, "a praise akin to worship."[40]

As has been recently noted, the forging of social memory relies on a widespread, shared knowledge of the past. Although many streams feed into this sentiment, the most powerful means of shaping historical memory rests with the commemorative ceremony. This is even more effective if it occurs on an annual basis and involves active physical participation by supporters.[41] The memories of Burns and Lincoln thus became commemorated in virtually identical ways: celebration of their birthplaces and final resting places; creation of birthday holidays; the placing of their images on currency and stamps; and the erection of hundreds of heroic monuments.

Burns lived in a variety of Scottish locales, and Alloway, Edinburgh, and Dumfries could all equally claim his mantle. He died in Dumfries in 1796, but his widow, Jean, chose to live in their comfortable house until her own death in 1834. During this time, she opened her home to the constant stream of visitors who sought her out for the next thirty-eight years. In 1851, their son Colonel William Nichol Burns purchased the house and later donated it to the Dumfries Education Society. In the mid-1930s, the town council renovated it to reflect Burns's era. Today, visitors may tour his house without charge, as well as the Burns Grecian mausoleum in the nearby Saint Michael's Churchyard. Still, it was not until the opening of the elaborate Burns Center in 1986 that Dumfries began to seriously cultivate Burnsian tourism. For years, critics had accused Dumfries of ignoring the bard. Naturally, Ayrshire established the strongest claims to his memory, as it housed the birth cottage in Alloway, the various family farms, and the largest Burns monument. These venues have drawn tourists for over two centuries to view a variety of artifacts, including the two-volume Bible that Burns gave to Highland Mary, as well as a lock of Mary's hair. "I think you love him in America a'most as well as we do oursels," an Ayrshire landlady remarked in 1893. "It's very seldom the English come to see anythin' about him."[42]

The Edinburgh celebration of the city's Burnsian locales proved somewhat tardy. In 1936, the *Scotsman* observed that although no official marker existed, "every little Lawnmarket urchin could tell visitors precisely where Burns had stayed while he lived in Edinburgh in 1786."[43] The founding of the Writers' Museum in Lady Stair's house in the early 1950s accelerated the Edinburgh ceremonial process. Today, guidebooks allow a person to retrace (literally) every step that Burns took throughout Edinburgh (and all of Scotland).[44]

American efforts to commemorate the various Lincoln sites moved at a similar irregular pace. Following the assassination, Mary Todd Lincoln found it too painful to return to their two-story home in Springfield, and after her death, Robert Todd Lincoln donated it to the American people, with the stipulation that no one should ever be charged admission. The National Park Service manages it today. From 1865 onward, the Lincoln family tomb north of Springfield has drawn countless visitors, ranging from foreign dignitaries to the merely curious. On November 28, 1924, for example, sixteen hundred schoolchildren arrived via special trains to pay homage in what was then termed "the most spectacular pilgrimage of the kind ever staged in America."[45] Beginning in 1934, the Lincoln Life Insurance Company of Fort Wayne, Indiana, began to seriously encourage the nation's Boy Scout troops to make annual pilgrimages to the closest Lincoln statue, usually on his birthday—a practice that continues to this day. The most concerted efforts to memorialize Lincoln's name occurred in the early twentieth century. During the second decade of the twentieth century, entrepreneur Carl G. Fisher conceived of a coast-to-coast road (U.S. 30) that later was designated the "Lincoln Highway." In 1932, English immigrant Robert Watchorn created an extensive memorial shrine in Redlands, California (now a museum and reference library), and five years later, the Lincoln Tunnel connecting New York with New Jersey received its first traffic. Twenty-five counties, twenty-four cities, and about six-hundred schools also carry his name.

The most impressive local monuments, however, involved the re-creation of his birthplace log cabin near Hodgenville, Kentucky, the rebuilding of New Salem, Illinois, the reestablishment of the Lincoln family farm in Lincoln City, Indiana, and the erection of the Lincoln Memorial in Washington, D.C. At the time of the assassination, Thomas Lincoln's log cabin home at Sinking Spring, Kentucky, had long fallen into disuse, and none of the various "logs" later reassembled could ever be thoroughly authenticated. Still, in 1894, a New York businessman purchased the old Lincoln homestead and had what passed for the cabin moved there. But shortly afterward, the logs were dismantled and stored in a warehouse; later they were reassembled for a traveling exhibition that toured a number of American cities. In 1906, a citizens group raised $350,000 by popular appeal to build an impressive marble and granite memorial over the re-created log cabin. This rather strange juxtaposition—a log cabin enshrined in a pseudo–Greek temple—was formally dedicated in 1911. A destination point for thousands of visitors each year, the site near Hodgenville, Kentucky, became a national park in 1916 and was officially designated the Abraham Lincoln Historic Site in 1959.[46]

The re-creation of New Salem, Illinois, followed shortly after. Like the original log cabin, the small town where Lincoln had lived from 1831 to 1837 had quietly melted back into the earth. By the 1870s, however, tourists and souvenir hunters had begun to ransack the region for artifacts. In 1906, publisher William Randolph Hearst purchased sixty acres of the original town site and gave it to a local organization. In 1919, the locale was reconstituted as a state park. During the Great Depression of the 1930s, the Civilian Conservation Corps did a masterful job of reconstructing various buildings, including sawmills and grist mills, and of planting hundreds of trees to reestablish the wooded setting. Meanwhile the New Salem Lincoln League began to gather period piece artifacts. The first theatrical festival—"Out of the Wilderness," designed to celebrate his New Salem Days—was staged in 1940. Today, New Salem functions as a Midwestern Williamsburg, and with a new visitors center (1992) and superb history reenactors, the site attracts thousands of visitors annually.[47]

The memorialization of the Lincoln farm in Indiana, where the family lived from 1816 to 1830, began in 1879 with the official marking of the grave of Nancy Hanks Lincoln. In 1925, the Indiana Department of Conservation began to develop the site by acquiring part of the Lincoln homestead and making various improvements to the trails and landscape. In the wake of the sesquicentennial of Lincoln's birth in 1959, the area was reconstituted in 1963 as Indiana's first national park. Although touted as the "premier Lincoln site in Indiana," archaeologists and historians have verified no historic Lincoln artifacts, other than the ownership of the land itself. Essentially, the farm functions as a "period piece" to reflect early pioneer life. Even so, it attracts about 170,000 visitors a year. Today, the states of Kentucky, Indiana, and Illinois have their Lincoln memorials firmly in place. One can also follow the path that the Lincoln family took from Kentucky westward.[48] A new study by historian Ralph Gary goes even further. *Following in Lincoln's Footsteps* (2001) allows the reader to explore *all* the locations visited by Lincoln during his fifty-seven years.[49]

The most striking of the Lincoln commemorative sites, of course, is the gigantic Lincoln Memorial in Washington, D.C. Although the idea for a national shrine was voiced as early as 1867, nothing happened until 1911, when Congress appointed a special commission to that effect. After endless discussion of how to memorialize the president, the commission finally decided on a gigantic statue by sculptor Daniel Chester French, whose standing Lincoln (1912), located at the west side of the capitol in Lincoln, Nebraska, had already become a tourist attraction. Over several years, French sculpted a massive, seated Lincoln within a modified Grecian temple. Former president William Howard Taft presided over the dedication in 1922.[50]

Over time, the Lincoln Memorial has evolved into one of the four most recognized symbols of the United States, ranking with the Capitol dome, the Washington Monument, and the White House. It far outranks the (Episcopal) National Cathedral, the Supreme Court building, or the Jefferson Memorial in terms of international recognition. Indeed, as historian Christopher A. Thomas notes, the Lincoln Memorial has become for most foreigners a symbol of American values, as well as a metaphor for the nation itself.[51]

Heroic Statues

Erecting scores of heroic statues became yet another way by which Scotland and America mythologized their heroes. From the eighteenth century up to, perhaps, the 1930s, when a community wanted to celebrate an historic figure, the most common means involved creating a monument or heroic statue of the person. Because the twenty-first century is awash with visual imagery, it is hard to appreciate the role that these centrally placed statues played for a pre–mass-culture society. But the various statues and monuments long formed the keystone of public art, an art that imposes itself on all passersby. One simply could not avoid seeing these monuments. Community after community erected such statues to merge nation and man into a single unit.

Designers and builders believed that these statues would have a beneficial impact on those who saw them. Glasgow-born Wyoming philanthropist Mary Gilcrist phrased this idea well. Erecting a statue to Robert Burns in downtown Cheyenne, she said in 1929, "would exert a tendency to direct thought in the community to wholesome consideration of his sweet gentle philosophy."[52] American admirer Edward Goodwillie, who painstakingly documented the placement of hundreds of Burns statues worldwide, went further. Creating a monument to Burns's memory, he stated, would serve "as a speaking symbol of those Christian, humane, manly, patriotic and nature-loving instincts, which . . . he translated into inimitable, imperishable verse."[53] Goodwillie carefully detailed the stories of all the world's Burns monuments, statues that range from the modest to the towering: the cenotaph in Alloway (whose foundation was built in 1820); the Burns monument on Calton Hill, Edinburgh (1830), the statue of which was later moved to the National Portrait Gallery in Edinburgh; the Thames Embankment statue (1884); and the statue in Aberdeen (1892), to name just a few. The formal dedication of a Burns monument in Scotland always called forth gigantic crowds. Six thousand witnessed the unveiling of the Aberdeen statue in 1892; the dedication of the Leith statue drew thirty thousand. It was, the *Scotsman* reported, "a popular demonstration in which all classes of the community joined."[54] The faces of the Burns statues were invariably based on the classic portrait by James Nasmyth.

But Scotland was not the only country to erect heroic statues to Robert Burns. Dunedin, New Zealand; Belfast, Ireland; Toronto, Canada; and Adelaide, Australia, among others, also joined in. Scottish vaudeville entertainer Harry Lauder, who traveled around the world, once remarked that there were more monuments to Burns than to any other person in history.[55]

America certainly contributed its share. New York City erected the first monument to Burns outside of Scotland with its Central Park statue (1880). Albany, New York; Barre, Vermont; Denver, Colorado; Chicago, Illinois; San Francisco, California; Milwaukee, Wisconsin; Boston, Massachusetts; and Cheyenne, Wyoming, soon followed. Saint Louis, Missouri, created a replica of the Burns birthplace cottage for the World's Fair of 1904 (the cottage was later moved to Portland, Oregon); Atlanta built a like cottage in 1910. Supporters attempted to erect another replica birth cottage on

Long Island during the mid-1920s, but that effort fell through. By 1925, however, America housed at least twelve heroic statues of Scotland's premier poet. The speakers at these unveilings in the United States almost always tied Scottish and American ideals into a single package. At the unveiling of the first American Burns statue in Central Park, orator George William Curtis observed that Lincoln and Burns were both products of "the people" and that "America is trying to make the ploughman's words true." The orator at the 1901 unveiling in Barre, Vermont, declared that immigrants would be better Americans for being better Scots because the United States was "dedicated to the very principle for which Burns sang his earnest song."[56] The statue in Denver (1904) was unveiled on Independence Day, and the dedication in Cheyenne (1929) occurred on Memorial Day. From 1928 to 1934, New York Scottish organizations staged elaborate, formal parades to the New York Burns statue, where speakers discussed such issues as disarmament, international understanding, and world peace. All were touted as Burnsian themes.[57] William R. Smith's Washington, D.C., collection of Burnsiana was praised as "as much a Capitol institution as the Smithsonian or the Congressional Library."[58] It is now housed in a local Masonic temple.

American cities, of course, memorialized Lincoln with even greater enthusiasm. San Francisco erected the first Lincoln heroic statue in 1866, and by 1899, fourteen more had made their appearance across America. Historians counted eighty-two U.S. Lincoln statues by 1952. Naturally, Illinois boasts the largest number at fifteen, but New York houses eight and Wisconsin, seven. It is, perhaps, significant that the 1874 monument in Springfield was largely subscribed by African Americans; the Black community also contributed the cost of the Washington, D.C., monument (1876). Until 2003, Border States Maryland and Missouri (one each) and Kentucky (three) were as far South as the movement went. Scotland claimed the first foreign Lincoln statue, but England later added its own in London and Manchester. Oslo, Norway, and Florence, Italy, joined in as well. Mexico put up a statue in 1966.

If the handsome Naysmith-derived face graces most Burns statues, American sculptors faced the "unique problem" of depicting Lincoln's rugged features and awkward frame in an appropriately dignified manner.[59] Although it took effort, most succeeded. The young Lincoln holding book and axe at the entrance to the New Salem State Park, the lofty statue in the square in Hodgenville, Kentucky, and, of course, the Lincoln Memorial—visited by over four million tourists every year—all convey great dignity. The main exception lies with the statues designed by George Grey Barnard, in Louisville, Kentucky, and Manchester, England, where a scowling, rather-unkempt Lincoln presides.[60]

Heroic statues of Lincoln were never well received by the White South. Thus, it came as a bit of a surprise when the National Park Service announced in late 2002 that it planned to unveil a depiction of Lincoln and his son Tad at the service's Civil War Visitor's Center in Richmond, Virginia. The local Sons of Confederate Veterans protested the decision, terming it a "slap in the face" to loyal Confederates who were defending their homes against the "invasion of Virginia." Other opponents called Lincoln a Marxist and a war criminal. They urged instead that a statue to assassin John Wilkes Booth be placed in front of the Lincoln Memorial. On April 5, 2003, when the statue was formally dedicated, mounted police remained on patrol for the entire ceremony. A pro-Confederate group chanted in derision all through the proceedings, and a small plane flew by trailing the banner "Sic Semper Tyrannis," the phrase that Booth had shouted to the audience as he fled from Ford's Theater in 1865.[61]

Judging fame by counting statues is risky business, but if one includes heroic busts in this compilation, Burns wins hands down. The reason is that Andrew Carnegie insisted that every library he helped erect—2,507 in total, with 1,681 in the States—contain a prominently displayed bust of Robert Burns.[62]

Stamps and Coins

Part of the commemoration process involved national currency and coinage, but here the two stories diverge sharply. Ever since its creation in 1783, the American republic had scrupulously avoided placing any head of state on its coins, preferring, instead, various representations of Liberty or, from 1864 onward, Plains Indians. Lincoln's image appeared on several 1862–63 Native American peace medals, on privately produced medals and tokens, and on a rare government silver-certificate bill, but these were few and far between. Then came the centenary of his birth in 1909.

That year, President Roosevelt commissioned sculptor Victor D. Brenner to design a coin for the occasion, and the famed Lincoln penny was officially released on August 2, 1909, the first to carry a presidential image. Although the Philadelphia Mint had stockpiled about twenty-five million coins for nationwide distribution, the demand proved overwhelming. Hastily scrawled "No more Lincoln pennies" signs appeared in front of several subtreasury locations. "The common, homely face of Honest Abe looks good on the penny," observed writer Carl Sandburg, "the coin of the common folk from whom he came and to whom he belongs."[63] In 1959, the sesquicentennial of Lincoln's birth, the reverse side of the penny was redesigned, with the Lincoln memorial replacing the original Illinois wheat shafts. Released on February 12, 1959, the huge lines of people waiting to buy the new penny reminded older mint officials of the 1909 issue, but this time there was no shortage. The Philadelphia Mint produced 600 million, and the Denver Mint 1.2 billion, or about seven cents per citizen.

For reasons that remain unclear, republican ideology seemed far less concerned over the danger of placing presidential images on paper currency or stamps. Lincoln appeared on the ten-dollar bill in 1862 and 1863 and on a fifty-cent note; later, his portrait was used on the one-hundred-dollar bill and the five-hundred-dollar bill. The various U.S. five-dollar-bill series have carried the Mathew B. Brady image of Lincoln since the 1920s.[64] From 1866 forward, Lincoln was also, sporadically, on over fifty national stamps, including a five-cent (1902) version and an even more popular 1909 two-cent stamp, the latter coordinated with the release of the Lincoln penny. The 1959 sesquicentennial of his birth, setting the stage for the centennial of the Civil War itself (1861–65), produced a barrage of Lincoln-related stamps: the Lincoln-Douglas debates, Emancipation Proclamation, various famous photographs, as well as a variety of first-day covers (envelopes with a special stamp) for collectors. Many young people began their stamp-collecting careers with these Lincoln stamps. A number of African nations, including Liberia, Cameroon, and the Central African Republic, have also issued Lincoln commemorative stamps.

Burns has not fared so well in these departments. Although he appears on privately minted medals, the faces of the Hanoverian monarchs grace all British coins. Today, Burns's image appears only on the five-pound note, put out by the Scottish Clydesdale Bank. The famous mouse he disturbed with his plow graces the reverse.

Burns's image did not appear on a postage stamp until 1959, the bicentenary of his birth. Ironically, it was the Soviet Union, rather than the United Kingdom, that issued the first Burns commemorative stamp; British postal policy did not then allow for the celebration of individuals on postage. The Soviets issued a handsome set of Burns commemoratives and acknowledged his birth with an exuberance usually reserved for Karl Marx and Vladimir Lenin. Seven years later, Britain reversed its policy and minted two Burns commemoratives. With the bicentennial of his death in 1996, Britain issued four more commemorative Burns stamps. In this category of bills, coins, and stamps, however, Lincoln wins hands down.

Birthdays

The annual celebration of each man's birthday formed, perhaps, the lynchpin of the memorialization process, and here Burns has fared somewhat better than Lincoln. In 1867, the *Scottish-American Journal* noted that Saint Andrew's Day (November 30) was celebrated more enthusiastically in the States than in Scotland proper.[65] But Lincoln's 1863 proclamation of an annual Thanksgiving gradually edged Saint Andrew's Day off the national map. In its stead, Burns birthday dinners on January 25 emerged as the chief Scottish American holiday. Elaborate guides were published to ensure that the Burns ceremony was conducted in a "proper" fashion. Still, one commentator wondered in 1900 whether Burns clubs or golf clubs had proven the better means of spreading Scottish culture abroad.

Celebrating Lincoln's birthday proved a bit more irregular. On Monday, February 12, 1866, the House of Representatives set aside an official day to commemorate Lincoln, and historian George Bancroft delivered a lengthy address on his life.[66] Southern states were hesitant to join the chorus. Some southern writers argued that because Lincoln was an atheist, his values were antithetical to the south as the home of Christian civilization.[67] The southern Black churches, however, celebrated February 12, 1866, with singing, prayer, and orations. Said one speaker at Zion Church in Charleston, South Carolina, "It is a notorious fact, that the colored population, with a few exceptions, are the only truly loyal people here."[68] In 1866, Illinois observed a fast day on the anniversary of his assassination, an occasion also commemorated by the Freedmen of the South. President Andrew Johnson closed all departments for the day, and the Senate adjourned until the next Monday.[69]

But commemorating a date of death lacks the power of commemorating a day of birth, and the regular observance of April 15 soon faded. Still, official state celebrations of February 12 proved irregular. In 1867, New Jersey formerly acknowledged Lincoln's birthday but even northern celebrations remained erratic until 1891, when Hannibal Hamlin of Maine, who had been Lincoln's first vice-president, urged that February 12 be turned into a national holiday. This idea grew steadily as the centenary of his birth approached, and subsequently, really for the first time, southern states joined in the celebration.[70] But the commemoration of his birthday continued to remain sporadic. In 1909, President Roosevelt declared February 12 a legal holiday in the District of Columbia and the U.S. territories. By 1938, twenty-seven states had also made February 12 a legal holiday. Still, even at the 1959 sesquicentennial of his birth, Lincoln's birthday was officially celebrated in only about thirty states. His birthday did not become an official national holiday until 1971, when Congress decided to combine it with Washington's birthday (February 22) and to set aside the third Monday of the month as President's Day. Currently, the celebration of Burns's birthday is more precisely defined than that of Lincoln's.[71]

Collectors and Forgers

Because both men had evolved into semi-sacred national icons shortly after their deaths, it should not be surprising that souvenir hunters began to cart away anything that they could find. By the late nineteenth century, a distinct collectors' market had emerged, and "Burnsiana" and "Lincolniana" became two of the most highly desired subcategories.[72]

Original letters became the most sought-after items. In each case, hundreds were available. Burns generously recopied his poems for admirers so three or four copies of the same poem exist in his handwriting. Lincoln also copied several of his classic documents for friends. Each man wrote hundreds of letters as well. Given this demand, prices began to rise. The Octavo Kilmarnock edition of *Poems, Chiefly in the Scottish Dialect*—which initially sold for three shillings—became one of the most sought-after items on the book-collectors' market. In 1892, George Collins, a bookbinder, stole a copy from a London bookseller, for which he received a twenty-month jail sentence, the first for thievery of this kind. As one commentator noted in 1902, a "single letter or versicle by Burns is now almost worth its weight in diamonds."[73]

Thus, it did not take long for various forgers to enter the picture, the most famous of whom were Alexander Howland "Antique" Smith, who forged Burns items, and Wilma Frances Minor and Joseph Cosey, who reproduced Lincoln. During the late 1880s, the collecting craze approached "manic proportions." Around this time, a young solicitor's clerk named Alexander Howland Smith was asked by his elderly employer to clear away documents in preparation for a move. Smith stumbled on an authentic manuscript of a poem in Burns's distinctive handwriting, which he sold to a respected Edinburgh antique bookdealer, James Stillie. In the course of the negotiations, Stillie may well have mentioned that he would gladly purchase any similar artifacts. A talented but unscrupulous painter and calligrapher, Smith immediately went to work. He purchased authentic late-eighteenth-century theological treatises for a song, unbound the books, treated contemporary ink with acid or an iron solution to age it, and began a lively career of forging Burns documents. He also created items allegedly written by Mary, Queen of Scots, the Duke of Argyll, Bonnie Prince Charlie, Flora MacDonald, and a host of other important Scottish figures. Always in need of money, Smith sold these documents to various Edinburgh dealers, including Andrew Brown and Stillie. The extent of Stillie's knowledge of this enterprise is still under dispute, but he eagerly resold the documents—many to wealthy American collector John S. Kennedy of New York. Kennedy graciously donated about $20,000 worth of Burnsiana to various American libraries and museums. But when all but one of Kennedy's 202 purchases from Stillie were eventually declared forgeries, Kennedy sued. He only withdrew his suit because of the bookseller's advanced age.[74] A reporter from the *Edinburgh Evening Dispatch* raised local suspicion, and it was not long before the Edinburgh police knocked on Smith's door and put him under arrest. When the trial hit the newspapers, the British public was outraged. The *Daily Telegraph* stated, "Punishment sufficiently severe for the Scotsman who would forge letters and poems by Scott and Burns in order to beguile the inexperienced collector could hardly be either imagined or invented. Hurling him from the top of Castle Rock at Edinburgh would be far too mild for the offense."[75]

Smith pleaded innocent. His lawyers argued that there was no crime in *reproducing* antique documents and that any infraction of the law belonged to the sellers, not Smith. After a six-month trial, followed closely by Edinburgh newspapers, the jury reached a decision. In 1893, the High Court of Scotland found Smith guilty on all counts, but the judge, following the jury's pleas for mercy, sentenced him to only a year in prison. Everyone involved agreed that the Antique Smith trial produced "one of the most remarkable cases of manuscript forgeries on record."[76] After serving his sentence, Smith set himself up on George Street in Edinburgh as a dealer of antique books and manuscripts and enjoyed a modest career. Whether he returned to his earlier forgeries has never been determined. As late as 1986, however, a (probable) product of his art—a letter from Burns to an engraver—was sold at auction in Glasgow for a considerable sum. The shadow cast by Antique Smith has proven a long one.

The same demand for documents affected collectors of Lincolniana, and here even more material was available. During his lifetime, Lincoln wrote over a million words. There are, for example, five copies of the Gettysburg Address in his handwriting. In her diligent research in the 1890s, biographer Ida Tarbell uncovered dozens of forgotten Lincoln documents. By the early twentieth century, Lincoln forgers began to appear on the scene as well. The most notorious involved Californian Wilma Francis Minor and an Iowa printer named Joseph Cosey.

In the spring of 1928, California writer Wilma Francis Minor announced that she had discovered a set of love letters written between Lincoln and Ann Rutledge. She said that she found them in the materials of Matilda Cameron, a cousin and confidante of Ann, along with Matilda's own diary. When Minor informed the *Atlantic Monthly* of her discoveries, editor Ellery Sedgwick became enthralled. Biographers Bruce Barton, who saw only Photostats, and Ida Tarbell, who actually examined the originals, initially declared the materials genuine, although Barton expressed some private reservations. Minor's collection—ten letters written by Lincoln and four by Ann Rutledge (the first of their kind)—seemed to prove the oft-told story of their love. It took little persuasion for Minor to agree to a three-part publication in the *Atlantic*, with a hefty book contract to follow. The *Atlantic* published the first installment in December 1928 under the title "Lincoln the Lover."[77] The carefully chosen phrase echoed a popular 1914 photoplay with identical title and theme. In the film version, Lincoln accidentally stumbles across Ann in the arms of her lover and "for a month never smiled again."[78]

By now, however, a number of Lincoln scholars, including Barton and Paul M. Angle of the Lincoln Centennial Association in Springfield, had become convinced the letters were forgeries. True, the paper seemed authentic, but Angle found numerous small errors of fact in the documents themselves. Although a surveyor, Lincoln referred to "section 40," but the American system contained only 36 sections. He spoke of a family leaving for Kansas when the region was as not yet known as "Kansas," nor was it open to White settlement. Confronted with this evidence, Minor signed a modest confession, which revealed that she had drawn on her mother's mystical communications with the departed Matilda Cameron, which she later copied onto authentic paper from the era. This episode remains one of the *Atlantic Monthly*'s most embarrassing moments.[79]

Thanks to Angle, Minor was exposed immediately, but the work of Joseph Cosey remains at large to this day. From the 1930s to the mid-1940s, he flourished as the foremost Lincoln forger of all times. Joseph Cosey—and that may not be his real name, because he used at least six aliases—began his career as a journeyman printer who worked at various towns in Iowa and in Peoria, Illinois. While in Iowa, he discovered a ledger of paper watermarked "Moinier's 1851." Realizing that Lincoln had written on this same paper, he began using it extensively for extremely sophisticated forgeries. Like Antique Smith, Cosey doctored contemporary ink with iron to age it and found various ways to age the paper as well. As befits a professional forger, the tale of Cosey's entry into the field comes in two versions. In one telling, he filched an authentic Lincoln letter from the Library of Congress. In another, he stole a Benjamin Franklin pay warrant from the New York Public Library. In either case, however, when he tried to sell the pilfered item to a New York manuscript dealer, the dealer dismissed the document as a fraud. Incensed, Cosey began to forge various Lincoln documents—the most sought-after of all American signatures—which the same dealer later eagerly purchased.[80]

Unlike many other forgers, Cosey did not limit himself to mere signatures. Like Smith and Minor, he created full letters, multipage documents, and even a Lincoln record book, dated 1858. His masterpiece included several letters to Alexander H. Stephens, later the vice-president of the Confederacy. One New York expert claimed that Cosey was the cleverest forger he had ever seen. Cosey was so prolific that he flooded the collectors' market with bogus material, and collectors' magazines began to caution their readers about him. So brazen was he that he allowed a *Saturday Evening Post* reporter to interview him. He even challenged the law to apprehend him: "I never said the stuff was genuine. I approach dealers with: 'I found this in a trunk. Is it worth anything?'" "I never impose on innocence," he bragged, "only greed."[81] During his heyday, Cosey saturated the market with bogus Lincoln, Franklin, Edgar Allan Poe, and even Mary Baker Eddy documents (he is the only known Mary Baker Eddy forger). In 1934, the *New York Times* warned Lincoln collectors that they should have an outside expert's opinion before they purchased any item.[82]

Sometime around 1945, Cosey disappeared from the record, but his legacy remains. Recently the Lincoln National Life Foundation in Fort Wayne, Indiana, knowingly purchased one of his best forgeries for its extensive collection. At his prime, Joseph Cosey was compared, for skill and arrogance, with the master, "Antique" Smith.[83]

National Icons

The memorialization process gradually melded Burns and Lincoln into the symbols of their respective nations. It seems no accident that Scotland's national newspaper, the *Scotsman*, published its first edition on Burns's night in 1817. As early as 1866, historian George Bancroft had suggested that

Lincoln *was* America.[84] On July 19, 1872, the *Scotsman* similarly termed Lincoln as the central figure of his time. Two generations later, William Howard Taft described the Lincoln Memorial as a "universal shrine," where all could come to worship. A turn-of-the-century reminiscence termed Lincoln "indeed the First American." In 1939, Carl Sandburg declared that Lincoln had become "the symbol of America."[85]

The combination of the 1959 sesquicentennial of Lincoln's birth and the ensuing Cold War with the Soviet Union furthered the identification for a generation. The United States Information Agency (USIA) produced a comic-book version of his life, *Abraham Lincoln*, that was distributed gratis in numerous languages, including Indonesian, Nepalese, Thai, Vietnamese, and classical Arabic. The simplified text reiterated the basic theme that Lincoln had become the symbol of humanity and democracy. To know Lincoln, the booklet informed countless foreign readers, was to reach out and touch the soul of the American nation.

The same proved true for Robert Burns. As one admirer declared, "Robert Burns is Scotland condensed into a personality."[86] In 1892, the respected *Scotsman* observed that the nation's patron saint was no longer Saint Andrew but Robbie Burns. A generation later, another *Scotsman* writer struck the same chord. Said Lord Sands at the Perth Burns Club, "Burns, more perhaps than any other memory, was the cement which bound the Scottish race together."[87] On January 21, 2007, the newspaper *Scotland on Sunday* acknowledged that Burns was "universally recognized as a symbol of all that is good about an egalitarian Scotland." Thus, the countless birthday speeches, statues, coins, and stamps celebrated not simply the individual but also a hoped-for set of national social goals as well.

Because of this merger, it is no surprise that each country turned to its respective icon in times of crisis. This proved especially true during the first and second world wars. American cartoonists drew heavily on Lincolnian themes during the 1914–17 conflict, and Vachel Lindsey's poem "Abraham Lincoln Walks at Midnight" received several public readings. A year after the armistice, *Nation* writer Carl Van Doren observed that the American people had looked to Lincoln during the conflict "more by far than most people realized, for words which would quiet our bitter tears and doubts, and for instructions on how to act in a time so nearly parallel to his."[88]

The dedication of the Lincoln monument in 1922 accelerated this process. During the 1940s, the classic antifascist play was Robert Sherwood's *Abraham Lincoln in Illinois* (1939). Denied use of a DAR venue because of her race, Black contralto Marian Anderson's famed 1939 Easter Sunday concert was held in front of the Lincoln Memorial, as was Civil Rights leader Martin Luther King Jr.'s equally classic "I Have a Dream" speech twenty-four years later. President Dwight D. Eisenhower was once observed praying there. In a powerful image surrounding the 1963 John F. Kennedy assassination, cartoonist Bill Mauldin depicts the Lincoln Memorial statue holding his head in his hands. In 1964, President Lyndon B. Johnson observed the 155th anniversary of Lincoln's birthday by speaking from the memorial to remind the nation that as long as any American citizen was denied full human dignity, "Lincoln's work—our work—will be unfinished."[89] The list could be extended.

So, too, in Scotland. In 1917, Reverend Donald MacMillan published a pamphlet setting forth Burns's "message to Scotland" in times of war.[90] Another commentator observed, "Had Burns been alive in 1914 he would have been one of the first to go, and his verse would have added speed to the laggard and heart to the brave."[91] During World War II, Peter Esslemont's collection of Burnsian sayings, subtitled "A Minute a Day with Burns," sold thirty-seven thousand copies.[92] When Glaswegian children were evacuated to the countryside during the bombing raids of 1940, some of the bairns were given copies of Burns poems to tuck into their few possessions. Public speakers linked the Lincoln/Burns themes on many occasions during the interwar years. In 1927, Americans of Scottish ancestry and sympathy donated to a memorial in Edinburgh for those lost during the Great War. Soon, it became customary to hold an annual service there. At the eighth such ceremony, a speaker spoke of "the mystic chords of memory" that united Americans with Scotland. Americans understood that the greatest poem of democracy was "A man's a man for a' that."[93]

The Opposition and the Shift in Reputations

Charting public fame is a delicate business, but it is clear that the reputations of both Burns and Lincoln have shifted considerably over time. Some Scottish clerics continued to denounce Burns well into the twentieth century. Perhaps the climax of this antagonism occurred in 1959, when the managing board of Saint Giles Cathedral in Edinburgh refused to allow a plaster plaque honoring Burns to be placed there. This widely unpopular move evoked many angry responses. Surprisingly, the opponents of Burns's legacy had earlier received some rather unexpected aid from a most unlikely source, Scottish Marxist poet Hugh MacDiarmid (G. M. Grieve). In scathing prose, MacDiarmid attacked the Burns Clubs for concentrating on the eccentric minutia of the poet's life rather than the rich tradition of authentic Scottish verse.[94] Said MacDiarmid: "The Burns cult must be killed stone-dead and would be instantly if a single fighting flash of the spirit of Burns were alive in Scotland—home or colonial."[95]

In the second decade of the twentieth century, angry suffragettes attempted to set alight the Burns cottage. In the 1980s, Scottish feminists arose to denounce Burns's treatment of women, Jean in particular. At the moment, there are only two statues to Jean—in Mauchline (2002) and Dumfries (2004). Kirk people have often remained skeptical of his reputation. In general, however, this represents the minority view. From the 1930s to the present, the downward spiral of Burns's American reputation can be traced less to direct opposition than to benign neglect. The 1959 U.S. celebration of the overlapping bicentenary and sesquicentenary of the Burns and Lincoln births, respectively, focused, of course, on Lincoln. Burns virtually disappeared from public view. Robert Hillyer gave a formal 1959 lecture on Burns at the Library of Congress, but that formed the extent of the U.S. official celebration. The contrast with America's extensive 1859 commemoration of his birthday is striking. Things did not improve over the rest of the century. A 1971 exhibition and catalogue at Northern Illinois University in DeKalb and a 1996 North American Burns Conference held at the University of South Carolina, Columbia, formed the only major celebrations. The G. Ross Roy Collection of Scottish materials at the University of South Carolina ranks among the nation's finest, but only specialists are aware of it. By the opening of the twenty-first century, Burns had completely lost his status as "America's poet." Academics solemnly complained of the "scandalous neglect" of the Bard.[96]

Not so in Scotland. Here the revival of Scottish nationalism served to enhance his already-elevated reputation. In 1995, a new Burns National Heritage Park was dedicated in Alloway, and on July 21, 1996—the two hundredth anniversary of his death—the Burns cottage was festooned with a thousand flowers. That same year, the Edinburgh Burns monument on Regent Road, long closed to visitors, was reopened to the public. In the wake of the bicentennial of his death (1996), the Mitchell Library in Glasgow produced a comprehensive catalogue of their Burns holdings and dedicated a Burns Room for special concerts and programs. Since 1990, the University of Strathclyde has inaugurated its annual Burns Conference programs, which have an international following. In the late 1990s, the Saint Giles Cathedral finally erected a stained-glass window in his honor and installed a plaque on the floor that describes Burns as "the poet of humanity." When vocalist Sheena Wellington opened the first gathering of the Edinburgh Scottish Parliament in 1999 with a sing-along rendition of "A Man's a Man," it proved a moment of high drama that brought tears to the eyes of many. Although Burns Day celebrations tend to gather larger crowds in the Lowlands than on Shetland, Orkney, or the Western Isles, the bard still embodies Scottish hopes and aspirations far more than any other historical figure.

In the latest edition of the poet's works—*The Canongate Burns* (2001)—editors Andrew Noble and Patrick Scott Hogg suggest that Burns was trying to re-create in the Britain of the 1790s a multiple democratic nationalism composed of Welsh, English, Scottish, and Irish dimensions. Literary critic Robert Crawford terms Burns a "cultural broker" and celebrates his intermingling of English and Scots words as the beginning of a truly British literature. (If, from a sympathetic outsider's point of view, this sounds more like the 1990s than the 1790s, it still reflects the never-ending appeal of Scotland's greatest poet.)[97] The ever-flexible image of Robert Burns seems today to have almost bridged the yawning Scottish gaps of region, religion, and social class.

Ironically, the Lincoln image may be headed in the other direction. The reason rests less with region, religion, or social class than with the nation's premier social dilemma: race.[98] The South was conspicuously tardy in acknowledging Lincoln's greatness; a South Carolina extremist in the 1940s actually compared him to Adolf Hitler. In the 1960s, as America waded steadily into the murky waters of religious and ethnic pluralism, Lincoln's ideas of a sacred national unity based on Covenantal imagery drawn from the King James Version of the Bible seems to have diminished appeal. White Southerners might be edging slowly into the mythological Lincoln camp, but some sectors of African American opinion appear to be leaning in the other direction. Black views of the sixteenth president, of course, have shifted greatly over the years. When the Emancipation Proclamation was read in the twenty Philadelphia Black churches on January 1, 1863, the reaction struck abolitionist Benjamin Rush Plumly as a combination of the solemn joy of Passover, the sentiments of Thanksgiving, and the zeal of the Year of Jubilee. When rumors circulated that forced Black colonization might follow, one woman cried out, "God won't let him." Another responded: "God's in his heart." It is a great thing, Plumly wrote the president, to be enshrined in the religious sense of a people.[99] Over two years later, when Lincoln first entered Richmond in early April of 1865, he arrived without fanfare, but, still, the Black servants and dockworkers learned who the tall, angular man wearing the lofty top hat really was. Soon, a largely Black crowd began to follow him with jubilation. "Thank you, dear Jesus, that I behold President Linkum," cried one woman. Another jumped up and down shouting, "Glory! Glory! Glory!" Another shouted out, "Bless the Lord!"[100] The crowds surged forward with such intensity that at times, Lincoln could make no headway. Eventually, the embarrassed president spoke a few words to the throng, urging the ex-slaves to use their newfound freedom wisely. Shortly thereafter, on April 11, thousands of ex-slaves gathered at a public rally in Arlington House, Virginia, Lee's former home, to sing "The Year of Jubilee."[101] In early April 1865, the jubilation of the ex-slaves knew no bounds; within days, their sorrow knew no depths. When news of the assassination spread, a numbed crowd gathered in front of the house where the president was dying. Gideon Wells noted that Black "people especially—and there were at this time more of them, perhaps, than of whites—were overwhelmed by grief."[102]

As African American historian Benjamin Quarles observes, "Lincoln became Lincoln" largely because of Black people. The ex-slaves were the first Americans to invest Lincoln with salvific qualities. As Jesus had saved them from sin, so Lincoln had saved them from slavery.[103] Many Capitol City Black families skipped a meal to buy household mourning crepe or mourning clothing. When the cortege was drawn through New York City, a Black contingent marched in the three-hour parade bearing a banner, "We mourn our Emancipator." In 1895, African American educator R. R. Wright suggested that Lincoln shared many traits usually associated with his race: a gentle disposition, patience in the presence of great wrong, a spirit of forgiveness, and an incredible struggle for bread and learning. He concluded, "May it not be stated that the two typical Americans are Abraham Lincoln and Frederick Douglass?" In 1928, when Black historian Carter Woodson began Negro History Week in February (now Black History Month), he did so to tie African American history to the birthdays of both Lincoln (February 12) and Frederick Douglass (February 14). But a deep-rooted Black countercurrent regarding Lincoln has also been firmly in place for years. As Frederick Douglass noted at the 1876 dedication of the African American–sponsored Freedmen's Memorial Monument in Washington, Lincoln considered Blacks his "stepchildren." Many statues, such as those in Washington, D.C., and Edinburgh with their supplicating slaves at Lincoln's feet, are politically embarrassing today. The advent of the Civil Rights Movement in the 1950s has elevated Martin Luther King Jr. into the national pantheon, and his birthday has become an official holiday. In a strange way, the emergence of the King image has somewhat diminished Lincoln's reputation among the Black community. (King faces the same dilemma with White audiences but in reverse.) Historian Guelzo points to "the slow, almost unnoticed withdrawal" of African Americans from the group of Lincoln admirers.[104]

A recent hostile view of Lincoln has emerged from the pen of African American editor Lerone Bennett Jr. In a famous *Ebony* article (February 1968), he asked, "Was Abe Lincoln a White Supremacist?" After years of research, he published *Forced into Glory: Abraham Lincoln's White Dream* (2000), in which he argues that Lincoln was both a racist and a supporter, via colonization, of the "ethnic cleansing" of Blacks. Bennett has given numerous speeches on this theme as well.[105] Recent emphasis on what has been termed "the politics of regret"—national recognition of the nation's maltreatment of minorities—has given this position considerable play. Collective memory, of course, shifts over time but as sociologist Barry Schwartz notes, negative sentiments rarely become embodied in permanent historical or commemorative forms.[106] As Boritt, Harold Holzer, and others observe, Lincoln voiced concern that the expansion of slavery into the territories would also restrict the opportunities of free White laborers to improve their station. Simultaneously, however, he repeatedly reminded audiences in 1856 and 1858 that Black people held natural rights, the crucial one being the right to control the fruits of their own labors.[107] Given the bitter politics of Illinois, had he taken a more radical position, he never could have been elected to anything.

It should come as no surprise that Lincoln did not share twenty-first-century views on racial matters. He was, after all, born in 1809. Thus, critics who claim that Abraham Lincoln did not share a contemporary attitude on race and equality are correct. But, it should also be noted that neither did anyone else in the 1860s, even the radicals. People of past times invariably share far more in common with one another than they do with their historical descendants. If we could miraculously bring back an 1864 New England abolitionist and a Virginia planter for coffee, we would discover that our knowledge of genetics, psychology, the welfare state, aircraft, subatomic physics, two world wars, DNA, computers, and atomic weapons had created an unbridgeable gap of understanding. Obvious disagreement aside, they would feel much more comfortable with each other than with any one of us.

But Lincoln does not lack for supporters regarding his handling of racial issues. His defenders maintain that one must view the Civil War racial situation in its historic context. They acknowledge that Lincoln shared the crude racial attitudes and language of his era but argue that he also transcended them. He might have used the mildly derogatory term *cuffie*—for which he was gently reprimanded by a young abolitionist—but he also equalized pay for Black army workers when he thought the time was ripe. And he never generalized about Blacks, even after being attacked by a group of slaves on his first trip to New Orleans. True, he argued for voluntary Black colonization and slave-owner compensation plans, but he also greeted Frederick Douglass as a friend and a true critic of the republic. He had an audience with Black abolitionist Sojourner Truth as well. Civil War historian Boritt argues that Lincoln spoke of colonization largely *before* emancipation rather than after and that Black service in the military—the Victorian era's ultimate test of national loyalty and citizenship—seemed to have settled the issue as far as he was concerned.[108]

Nailing down the proper terms to describe Lincoln's evolving views on race has never been easy. Historian Philip Shaw Paludan calls him a "process-based egalitarian" who insisted on working out his social goals through existing governmental institutions. James Oakes terms him a master practitioner of the possible, carrying out only what the law and public opinion allowed him to do.[109] Guelzo terms him the nation's last Enlightenment president, driven by both a faith in reason as well as a sense of the eighteenth-century virtue of prudence, or moderation—a far cry from the insistence on immediate moral absolutes of later years. Guelzo even suggests that Lincoln had distinct plans for emancipation from the moment he took office.[110] Yet, on April 4, 1864, Lincoln wrote, "I claim not to have controlled events, but confess plainly that events have controlled me."[111] This discussion is not likely to end soon.

All analyses of Lincoln's views on race and equality must be firmly anchored in the gritty world of mid-nineteenth-century politics. Whatever else he might have been, Lincoln was first and foremost a politician. His old antagonist Roger B. Taney—the author of the 1857 *Dred Scott* decision that Lincoln viewed as a perversion of the Constitution—remained as chief justice of the Supreme Court until his death in October 1864. If any early federal proclamation or emancipation legislation had reached the Court, Taney would surely have ruled against it.[112] Aside from their crucial April 1862 decision to free the slaves in the District of Columbia, with compensation to owners, plus the passage of two Confiscation Acts regarding slaves owned by Rebels, the members of Congress stalled as well. Similarly, the contentious legislatures of the four Border Slave states—Missouri, Kentucky, Maryland, and Delaware—consistently refused to accept any federal compensation/emancipation bills, in spite of the president's urgent recommendations. Thus, simultaneously drawing upon a deepening understanding of God as a mysterious providence, whose ways remained hidden from humankind, and his elected capacity as commander in chief of the army and navy, Lincoln issued his two famous Emancipation Proclamations.[113] In so doing, he realized full well the impact on the nation. As he later told artist F. B. Carpenter, who was commemorating the event in a formal White House portrait, "As affairs have turned, *it is the central act of my administration, and the great event of the nineteenth century*" (italics in original).[114] Although generally viewed in this light for over two generations, the proclamation is seldom so acknowledged today. No federal holiday graces the first of January. In African American circles, June 19—"Juneteenth"—when Galveston slaves, supposedly the last to hear the news, learned of their freedom—has assumed a holiday atmosphere, but it is celebrated only regionally.

Every year on February 12, one can be assured that all the complex issues surrounding Lincoln's presidency will be aired once again for a new generation. Famed historian Ved Mehta once argued that history is essentially "argument without end," and it is likely that future Americans will continue to debate Lincoln's evolving views as long as the republic survives.[115] His positions on social equality, race, and religion are abundantly documented in the various collections of his writings. Yet, sometimes personal anecdotes can reveal as much as a formal speech, for they serve as shifting metaphors of understanding rather than hard, textual "proof." Of all the incidents that illuminate Lincoln's view of race, probably none is more revealing than the following stories, both of which might also be interpreted as echoing his early reading of the verses of Robert Burns. Carpenter reported that in 1863 a Colonel Mckaye of New York, Robert Dale Owen of Indiana, and others, had been assigned to investigate the condition of the freedmen off the coast of South Carolina and the Sea Islands. When the investigators returned from Hilton Head, they visited the White House, where Mckaye told the following tale. According to Mckaye, the slaves had a distinct sense of the power of the "master" and of the higher power of God. When Union forces arrived on the island, they drove off the residents' old masters by drawing upon yet-another power the slaves termed "Massa Linkum." During a meeting in the islanders' humble "praise house," several ex-slaves asked their leader, "the praise man," to tell them precisely what "Massa Linkum" was. "Brederin," he said, "you don't know nonsen' what you'se talkn' 'bout. Now you just listen to me. Massa Linkum he eberywhar. He know eberyting." Then solemnly looking up, he added, "He walk de earth like de Lord!" Lincoln was much affected by Mckaye's story. After he heard it, he did not smile but rose and strode across the room. After resuming his seat, he said, "It is a momentous thing to be the instrument, under Providence, of the liberation of a race."[116]

Several months later, on Tuesday April 4, 1865, Lincoln journeyed to Richmond, Virginia, with Tad by his side. Escorted by army and navy officers and easily visible because of his height and his tall black silk hat, he walked about two miles up the Main Street to the former executive mansion of the Confederacy. Most of the doors on the Richmond streets remained closed to him in a gesture of defiance, but one opened furtively, and a woman's hand extended with a bouquet of flowers, which he accepted. The contrast with the sentiment of the Richmond Black community could not have been more striking. Crowds of African Americans milled around him, singing and shouting his praises. One old Black man, eyes filled with tears, raised his hat when he stood before Lincoln, bowed, and asked God to bless the president. In turn, Lincoln removed his own hat and bowed to the man in silent reply. This simple gesture constituted "a bow which upset the forms, laws, customs, and ceremonies of centuries."[117] "A man's a man for all that," indeed.

Epilogue: The Dilemmas of Democratic Fame

The lives of Robert Burns and Abraham Lincoln have been intertwined for almost two centuries. When Lincoln first discovered the poet's verses while living in southern Indiana during the 1820s, he met a writer whose images, ideas, and cadences remained with him for the rest of his days.

After the poet's death in 1796, it took the people of Scotland and the Scottish diaspora about a generation to turn Burns into the national representative of Scotland. It took even less time for the people of the United States to do the same with Lincoln after his assassination in 1865. But no national mythology can ever be all encompassing. Numerous Presbyterian clerics in Scotland and Confederate sympathizers and—later—African American intellectuals in the United States refused to accept the prevailing sentiment. Although this opposition is unlikely to disappear, it has remained peripheral. For most people, Burns and Lincoln are sacrosanct, reflecting a variety of positions: natural genius, "Nature's nobleman," the representative "Western man," the consummate democrat, and the ultimate symbol of their nation's highest aspirations.

The legends of Burns and Lincoln have each faced potential "rivals": Sir Walter Scott, on the one hand, and George Washington on the other. The towering gothic monument to Scott on Princes Street in Edinburgh (erected 1846) and the stark Washington monument in the District of Columbia (begun 1836 and completed 1885) are easily recognized as representing their respective cities. Scott's residence of Abbotsford on the River Tweed and Washington's Mount Vernon plantation on the Potomac River continue to rank among the most visited tourist sites of their respective lands. Yet there is a difference between Burns and Lincoln and their rivals.

It is as far metaphorically from Burns's rude Ayrshire cottage to Abbotsford as it is from Lincoln's Hodgenville log cabin to Mount Vernon. While Scott and Washington are much admired, Burns and Lincoln are *loved*. Each of the latter two sports a nickname—"Rabbie" and "Abe"–whereas nicknames for the other two are unimaginable. If James Grant Wilson is to be believed, Lincoln once jested that if Washington "was loafing around here now, I should be glad to have a tussle with him, and I rather believe that one of the plain people of Illinois would be able to manage the aristocrat of old Virginia."[1] When Harriet Beecher Stowe spoke on *Uncle Tom's Cabin* in Scotland in 1853, she observed that the crowds remained silent whenever she mentioned Scott but erupted in loud cheers whenever she spoke of Burns. Scottish poet Charles MacKay commented in 1874 that no name proved more central to the memory of Scots in exile than that of the Bard.[2] The ever-evolving mythoi of Burns and Lincoln embody an inclusiveness that eludes the other pair. Each man suffered tremendously, and perhaps only those who have suffered ever become genuinely loved by the people. Over time, each life has extended far beyond simple biography; each has become a "semi-cosmic" story through which ordinary citizens might interpret their own sufferings, hopes, and victories.[3]

As literary critic Leo Braudy notes, Burns and Lincoln represent a type of "democratic fame" that has largely bypassed the other national figures. Ever since the French and American revolutions, Braudy argues, the nature of fame has drastically shifted. The emergence of "democratic fame" demands a spokesperson whom people can see as reaching out to the latent potential in *everyone*. The persistent Boy Scout pilgrimages to the various Lincoln statues and the annual Burns Day celebratory dinners achieve their purpose through this means. Each allows ordinary people to partake of the Lincoln/Burns aura, not unlike the wearing of a famous athlete's jersey. The more contradictions a person contains within himself, Braudy asserts, the more famous he or she can become. Each generation interprets the contradictions through the lens of the moment.[4] "That's a funny thing about Lincoln," said one observer about 1945. "Everybody wants to prove Lincoln was the same thing he is."[5]

In 1891, Carl Schurz observed that it was the mutual understanding and empathy between Lincoln and the nation's "plain people" that gave him his particular power as a public man: "To Abraham Lincoln the people became bound by a genuine sentimental attachment. . . . It was an affair of the heart, independent of mere reasoning." This sentiment has not altered significantly since then. It has even broadened. As Robert L. Kincaid, president of Lincoln Memorial University in Harrogate, Tennessee, said in 1948, the common people of the world never tire of learning about Lincoln. He has evolved into the symbol of all their hopes and ambitions.[6] Perhaps that is why in 1959 the United States Information Agency distributed millions of free comic-book biographies of Lincoln to underdeveloped countries. To understand the United States, all one had to do was to comprehend Lincoln.

Both Burns's and Lincoln's lives were rife with contradictions. The "heaven-sent ploughman" oscillated between sexual libertine and a man of honor with women, religious skeptic and humble reader of Scripture, believer in witches and man of reason, hard drinker and energetic collector of ancient folk songs. Indeed, contemporary Irish poet Seamus Heaney traces Burns's most powerful lyrics to "the submerged quarrel between the reasonable man in Burns and the city of demons he contained." Burns identified fully with Scotland's embattled past, raged against an aristocratic social order, considered the mouse a "fellow mortal," and expressed hope for "everyman," even the devil himself.[7] The "prairie lawyer from Illinois" contained an equal number of contradictions. Although Lincoln had no problems with alcohol, like Burns he was decidedly a man of honor and struggled to meet the demands of upper-class women. And, he, too, was simultaneously skeptic and believer, respecter of social position and democrat, superstitious and man of reason. Fellow lawyer Henry Clay Whitney, who traveled the Eighth Illinois Circuit with him, once noted that Lincoln always had a reply to queries, that they were always on the mark, and that they frequently sent his listeners into hysterics. Newspaper reporter Horace White, who knew him from 1858 forward, put it thusly:

> Mr. Lincoln was a many sided man and one who presented striking contrasts. He was the most humorous being I ever met, and also one of the most serious. . . . As a master of drollery he surpassed all of his contemporaries in Illinois, and yet his solemnity as a public speaker and a political and moral instructor was like that of an Old Testament prophet. . . . "He combined within himself," says Mr. Henry C. Whitney, "the strongly diverse roles of head of the State in the agony of the Civil War, and also that of court jester."[8]

These anomalies, however, fit well with the demands of democratic fame, especially before the rise of mass media and our contemporary obsession with celebrity. Because of these contradictions of character, the Burns and Lincoln legends have reached out to the latent potential of every citizen. In this sense, as Rhode Island Chief Justice Frank J. Williams notes, both men continue to serve as our ever-present contemporaries.[9]

Next, one comes to their use of language. Burns wrote in two languages—Scots and English—and laced his letters with a variety of French phrases. As befit his day, he often bolstered his argument by drawing upon classical allusions. Although Lincoln never studied a foreign tongue, Helen Nicolay states, he also spoke two languages: the American folk vernacular and a lofty, majestic prose akin to poetry.[10] Unlike Burns, however, Lincoln drew upon no classical allusions. Instead, he made his points through rural, frontier metaphors. Three examples: Once, the British minister to Washington, Lord Lyons, urged the president to join him at table. "No, Lyons, I have had my dinner," Lincoln responded with a smile. "If anything comes which is inviting, I'll browse around." At the Astor House in New York, he introduced a Democratic politician as a man so mild mannered that the two of them could "eat out of the same rack, without a pole between us."[11] Or, more bitingly: when he referred to a top official plotting against his 1864 reelection, Lincoln said that the plotter, "like the blue-bottle fly, lays eggs in every rotten spot he can find."[12] Each man possessed the incredible ability to compress a moral truth or a piercing insight into human nature in a handful of words. It is hard to improve on their choice of words.

Although each of them was responding to the specific crises of his day, readers continue to find within their statements a universal message: the fight against entrenched social convention; a scorn for hypocrisy; a biblical, but not a denominational, religious outlook; a sense of overriding Providence; a faith in the integrity and purpose of the nation; and a confidence in the basic worth of ordinary people. By about 1850, Burns's most famous quotation was surely, "A man's a man for a' that." Similarly, after the 1856 Republican campaign, Lincoln spoke of the "central idea" behind American public opinion as reflecting the equality of man. Thus, it is obvious that each viewed the quest for social equality as the ultimate national goal. Each emphasized the *quest* rather than the actual *condition* of equality. Both Burns and Lincoln were well aware of the powerful historical circumstances that had forged the boundaries of their lives. Neither lived in peaceful times. Burns cast his lyrical statements of equality in general rather than specific terms in order to keep his government job as an excise man, lest his family starve. Lincoln similarly realized that all governing involves compromise. Laws—even unjust ones—should be obeyed until changed via the democratic process; any other system would devolve into chaos and anarchy.[13] Thus, Lincoln tempered his actions on slavery until he felt certain that public opinion—in his view the ultimate judge in a democratic republic—would sustain his decisions. As he famously phrased it, "A universal feeling, whether well or ill founded, cannot be safely disregarded."[14]

Neither Burns nor Lincoln ever fell victim to the widespread heresy that noble ideals are sufficient to justify any action. Each shared a quasi-Calvinist understanding that a mysterious Divine Providence remained in control of events, slowly (perhaps) pushing their countries toward a more democratic future. To paraphrase African American poet Langston Hughes's 1936 observation: for Burns and Lincoln, both the true Scotland and the true America eventually "will be."[15]

Coda

The ever-ongoing link between the people and their respective national icons can work on many levels. The tipsy toasts to the Immortal Memory on January 25, and the semi-coerced Boy Scout marches to various Lincoln statues on February 12 reflect only one aspect of this relationship. But periods of high emotion or extreme deprivation can call forth a far-deeper level of understanding.

The southern slaves began the process with Lincoln. In 1863, Union officers occupying the Sea Islands off the coast of South Carolina met Gullahs who spoke constantly of Jesus—who was "everywhere"—and a number of them merged Him with the American commander in chief.[16] Ex-slave Charlotte Scott contributed her first day's wages as a free woman toward erecting what became the famed Freedman's Monument in Washington D.C.'s Lincoln Park.[17] Clearly, the African Americans laid the groundwork for the emergence of Lincoln as a transcendental, national saint.

Although the Scottish people's sanctification of Burns cannot be pinpointed with the same precision, it was clearly in place by the late nineteenth century. The 1897 visitors' book at the Burns Cottage carries the following lines from a Scottish Member of Parliament:

> Creation primal stands God's greatest feat;
> The next when He His Son sent to this earth;
> The next when He, man's genius to complete,
> Ordained that Burns should in this cot have birth.[18]

As the following two stories illustrate, the people–Burns/Lincoln relationship could, in genuinely desperate times, tap into unexplained sources of authentic social power. In 1983, Tom Sutherland, a Scottish-born agricultural geneticist who had taught at Colorado State University for many years, assumed the post as dean of agriculture at the American University of Beirut. On June 9, 1985, members of an Islamic jihad organization kidnapped him and held him captive for six-and-a half years, occasionally in solitary confinement and almost always chained either to the bed or to the wall of his cell. After his release on November 18, 1991, Sutherland credited Robert Burns as crucial to his survival. Every January 25, he retold Burns's story and recited his poems to whoever was nearby. One year, he translated the verses into French for his then-cellmate, journalist Jean-Paul Kauffmann. Although they were both chained to a wall in the south of Lebanon, Sutherland later recalled, they were roaming the fields of Ayrshire in their minds' eye and eavesdropping on drawing-room conversations in late-eighteenth-century Edinburgh.[19]

During his years of isolation, Sutherland devoted countless hours to arranging the couplets of "Tam O' Shanter" in proper order and reciting every Burns poem he could recollect. He and his wife, Jean, who continued to teach at American University throughout this ordeal, shared an affection for Burns's classic love song, "O, my love is like a red, red rose," and as Sutherland later said, "Two hundred and nine years were as nothing—he [Burns] was there in the cell that night with the poem that Jean and I loved so much."[20] At his first public statement in Wiesbaden, Germany, after his release, and at Jean's urging, he began with Burns's classic comment that "the best laid schemes o' mice and men gang aft a-gley." As noted Burns scholar David Daiches later remarked to him as to the power of Burns's lyrics, "You proved it on the pulses."[21]

The saga of Prague citizen Henri Dubin reflects a similar deep, emotional link with the figure of Lincoln. During the World War II era, Dubin spent about five years in both Nazi and Soviet concentration camps. Although he had never been to the States, one evening a vision of Abraham Lincoln appeared to him in his cell, assuring Dubin that "all men are created equal," that his captors (the Soviets?) were no better than he, and that he would survive the experience. Over forty years later, at age eighty-three and showing initial signs of Parkinson's disease, Dubin flew to the States and booked a room in the Springfield Hilton Hotel. At 7:15 A.M. in mid-April 2005, Frank Walker, guest services manager, was called in to assist Dubin in finding his room. Once settled, Dubin showed Walker a 1985 letter from the then-mayor inviting him to visit Springfield and asked, in broken English, if Walker could help him. Walker promised to make the appropriate phone calls as soon as the mayor's office opened at 8:00 and turned to go. "Wait," Dubin said, "I want to read you my poem I write for Lincoln." Standing at attention and often in tears, the elderly man recited the poem, written in English. He asked Walker, "You like?" When Walker nodded, Dubin told him his story, lifting his sleeve to reveal the numbers tattooed on his arm and always crossing his hands—as if handcuffed—when he mentioned his imprisonments. He had come only for the day, he said, as he wanted to recite his poem at the Lincoln tomb and present the martyred president with a memorial wreath made of red and white carnations. A stunned Walker promised to provide all the help he could.

By chance, that week coincided with the preparations for the grand opening of Springfield's new Lincoln Museum, to be dedicated by President George W. Bush, and the mayor's office was swamped. But Walker persisted and eventually enlisted Alicia Erickson, a foreign visitors' specialist with the Springfield Convention and Visitors Bureau, to drive Dubin to Lincoln's tomb. Dubin entered very slowly, she recalled, paying very close attention to every detail. Then, standing ramrod straight, he recited his poem and laid down the wreath that he had brought from the Czech Republic. After this, he threw himself on the floor and wept. When the two departed, Erickson asked if he would like to see any other of the Lincoln sites in Springfield, his law office, his home, or the old Capitol building, but he declined. She offered to buy him lunch, but he asked only to return to the hotel, where he slept for most of the day. Later, the mayor's office sent over an official key to the city.

The next morning, Walker drove Dubin to the airport and, fearing that he might be unable to negotiate his Chicago transfer, arranged that he be declared a wheelchair passenger so that he could be escorted every step of the way. In a final gesture, the tiny Dubin grabbed Walker and said, "You are like a brother, you and Abraham Lincoln and the Lord God" and again broke into tears. "May God be with you always." His mission accomplished after only twenty-four hours in Springfield, the frail Dubin flew back home to the Czech Republic. Both Frank Walker and Alicia Erickson are still astounded by what they witnessed.[22]

These stories are not easily explained. As historian J. Frank Dobie observes in another context, popes can create saints; monarchs can create knights and dames; and presidents can distribute various honors and awards. But only the collective will of the people can give this type of power to historical figures like Robert Burns and Abraham Lincoln.[23] And when the parallel celebrations of their birthdays begin in early winter 2009, the people will have been so doing for almost two hundred years.

Appendixes

Notes

Bibliography

Index

Appendix A: Selected Burns Verses

Three Burns poems that Abraham Lincoln especially admired are "Is There for Honest Poverty" or "For A' That," "Holy Willie's Prayer," and "Tam O' Shanter: A Tale."[1] Translations of some Scottish words are at the right of the respective line in the poems.

Is There for Honest Poverty

(Tune: For A' That)

Is there for honest Poverty
That hings his head, an' a that'
The coward slave—we pass him by,
We dare be poor for a' that!
For a' that, an' a' that,
Our toils obscure an' a' that,
The rank is but the guinea's stamp,
The Man's the gowd for a' that.

What though on hamely fare we dine,
Wear hodden grey, an' a' that;
Gie fools their silks, and knaves their wine'
A Man's a Man for a' that.
For a' that, an' a' that,
Their tinsel show, an' a' that;
The honest man, tho' e'er sae poor,
Is king o' men for a' that.

Ye see yon birkie, ca'd a lord,
Wha struts, an' stares, an' a' that;
Tho' hundreds worship at his word,
He's but a coof for a' that;
For a' that, an' a' that,
His ribband, star, an' a' that:
The man o' independent mind
He looks an' laughs at a' that.

A prince can mak a belted knight,
A marquis, duke, an' a' that;

But an honest man's abon his might,
Gude faith, he mauna fa' that!
For a' that, an' a' that,
Their dignities an a' that;
The pith o' sense, an' pride o' worth,
Are higher rank than a' that.

Then let us pray that come it may,
(As come it will for a' that,)
That Sense and Worth, o'er a' the earth,
Shall bear the gree, an' a' that.
For a' that, an' a' that,
It's comin yet for a' that,
That Man to Man, the world o'er,
Shall brothers be for a' that.

Holy Willie's Prayer

Argument.

Holy Willie was a rather oldish bachelor elder,
in the parish of Mauchline, and much and justly
famed for that polemical chattering, which ends
in tippling orthodoxy, and for that spiritualized
bawdry which refines to liquorish devotion. In a
sessional process with a gentleman in Mauchline—
a Mr.Gavin Hamilton—Holy Willie and his priest,
Father Auld, after full hearing in the presbytery
of Ayr, came off but second best; owing partly
to the oratorical powers of Mr. Robert Aiken,
Mr. Hamilton's counsel; but chiefly to Mr.
Hamilton's being one of the most irreproachable
and truly respectable characters in the county.
On losing the process, the muse overheard him
[Holy Willie] at his devotions, as follows:—

O Thou, who in the heavens does dwell,
Who, as it pleases best Thysel',
Sends ane to heaven an' ten to hell,
A' for Thy glory,
And no for ony gude or ill
They've done afore Thee!

I bless and praise Thy matchless might,
When thousands Thou has left in night,
That I am here afore Thysight.
For gifts an' grace
A burning and a shining light
To a' this place.

What was I, or my generation,
That I should get sic exaltation,
I wha deserve most just damnation
For broken laws,
Five thousand years ere my creation,
Thro' Adam's cause?

When frae my mither's womb I fell,
Thou might hae plunged me deep in hell,
To gnash my gums, to weep, and wail,
In burnin lakes,
Where damned devils roar and yell,
Chain'd to their stakes.

Yet I am here a chosen sample,
To show thy grace is great and ample;
I'm here a pillar o' Thy temple,
Strong as a rock,
A guide, a buckler, and example,
To a' Thy flock.

O Lord, Thou kens what zeal I bear,
When drinkers drink, an' swearers swear,
An' singin there, an' dancin here,
Wi' great and sma';
For I am keepit by Thy fear
Free frae them a'.

But yet, O Lord! confess I must,
At times I'm <u>fash'd</u> wi' fleshly lust;   *troubled*
And sometimes, too, in wardly trust
Vile self gets in:
But Thou remembers we are dust,
Defil'd wi' sin.

O Lord! <u>yestreen</u>, Thou <u>kens</u>, wi' Meg—   *last night; knowest*
Thy pardon I sincerely beg,

O! may't ne'er be a living plague,
To my dishonour,
And I'll ne'er lift a lawless leg
Again upon her.

Besides, I farther maun allow,
Wi' Leezie's lass, three times I trow—
But Lord, that Friday I was <u>fou</u>,   *drunk*
When I <u>cam</u> near her;   *came*
<u>Or</u> else, Thou kens, Thy servant true   *before*
<u>Wad</u> never <u>steer</u> her.   *would; meddle with*

Maybe Thou lets this fleshly thorn
Buffet Thy servant e'en and morn,
Lest he <u>ower</u> proud and high shou'd turn,   *over*
That he's sae gifted;
If sae, Thy <u>han'</u> <u>maun</u> <u>e'en</u> be borne   *hand; must; even*
Until Thou lift it.

Lord bless Thy Chosen in this place,
For here Thou has a chosen race:
But God confound their stubborn face,
An' blast their name,
Wha bring Thy elders to disgrace
An' public shame.

Lord mind Gaw'Hamilton's deserts;
He drinks, an' swears, an' plays at <u>cartes</u>,   *cards*
Yet has <u>sae</u> mony taking arts   *so*
Wi' great and sma,'
<u>Frae</u> God's <u>ain</u> priest the people's hearts   *From; own*
He steals awa.

An' when we chasten'd him therefor,
Thou kens how he bred sic a <u>splore</u>,   *disturbance*
An' set the warld in a roar
O' laughin at us;—
Curse Thou his basket and his store,
Kail an' potatoes.

Lord, hear my earnest cry an' pray'r,
Against that Presbytery of Ayr;
Thy strong right hand, Lord, make it bare
Upo' their heads;

Lord vist them, an' <u>dinna</u> spare,   *do not*
For their misdeeds.

O Lord, my God! that glib-tongu'd Aiken,
My vera heart and flesh are quakin,
To think how we stood, sweatin, shakin,
And piss'd wi' dread,
While he, wi' <u>hingin</u> lip an' snakin,   *hanging*
Held up his head.

Lord, in thy day o' vengeance try him,
Lord, visit them wha did employ him,
And pass not in Thy mercy by 'em,
Nor hear their pray'r,
But for Thy people's sake, destroy 'em,
An' dinna spare.

But, Lord, remember me an' mine
Wi' mercies temp'ral an' divine,
That I for grace an' <u>gear</u> may shine,   *wealth*
Excell'd by nane,
And a' the glory shall be thine!
Amen! Amen!

Tam o' Shanter: A Tale

[It is a well-known fact that witches, or any evil
spirits, have no power to follow a poor wight any
further than the middle of the next running stream.
It may be proper likewise to mention to the be-
nighted traveler, that when he falls in with bogles,
whatever danger may be in his going forward, there
is much more hazard in turning back.—R. B.]

"Of Brownyis and of Bogillis full is this Buke."
        —Gawin Douglas

When <u>chapman</u> billies leave the street,   *packman*
And <u>drouthy</u> neibors, neibors, meet,   *thirsty*
As market days are wearing late,
And fold begin to tak the <u>gate</u>,   *road*
While we sit bousing at the <u>nappy</u>,   *ale*
An' getting <u>fou</u> and <u>unco</u> happy,   *drunk; very*

We think <u>na</u> on the lang Scots miles, *not*
The mosses, waters, slaps, and <u>stiles</u>, *gaps in walls*
That lie between us and our hame,
Whare sits our sulky, sullen dame,
Gathering her brows like gathering storm,
Nursing her wrath to keep it warm.

This truth <u>fand</u> honest Tam O' Shanter, *found*
As he frae Ayr ae night did canter,
(Auld Ayr, <u>wham</u> ne'er a town surpasses, *whom*
For honest men and bonny lasses).

O Tam! had'st thou but been sae wise,
As <u>taen</u> thy <u>ain</u> wife Kate's advice! *taken: own*
She tauld thee <u>weel</u> thou was a <u>skellum</u>, *well; rogue*
A blethering, <u>blustering</u> drunken <u>blellum</u>; *chattering; babbler*
That frae November till October,
Ae market-day thou was na sober;
That <u>ilka melder</u>, wi' the Miller, *at every meal–*
every grinding of corn
Thou sat as lang as thou had siller;
That ev'ry <u>naig</u> was <u>ca'd a shoe on</u>, *nag; a shoe driven on*
The Smith and thee <u>gat</u> roaring fou on; *got*
That at the Lord's house, evn on Sunday,
Thou drank wi' Kirkton Jean till Monday.
She prophesied that late or soon,
Thou would be found, deep drown'd in Doon;
Or catch'd wi' warlocks in the mirk,
By Alloway's auld, haunted kirk.

Ah, gentle dames! It <u>gars</u> me <u>greet</u>, *makes; weep*
To think how mony counsels sweet,
How mony lengthen'd sage advices,
The husband frae the wife despises!
But to our tale: Ae market night,
Tam had got planted unco right;
Fast by an ingle, bleezing finely,
Wi <u>reaming swats</u>, that drank divinely; *frothing ale*
And at his elbow, <u>Souter</u> Johnie, *Cobbler*
His ancient, trusty, drouthy crony;
Tam lo'ed him like a very brither;
They had been fou for weeks thegither.
The night drave on wi' sangs an' clatter;

And aye the ale was growing better:
The Landlady and Tam grew gracious,
Wi' favours, secret, sweet, and precious:
The Souter tauld his queerest stories;
The Landlord's laugh was ready chorus:
The storm without might <u>rair</u> and rustle,   *roar*
Tam did na mind the storm a whistle.

Care, mad to see a man sae happy.
E'en drown'd himself amang the nappy.
As bees flee hame wi' <u>lades</u> o' treasure,   *loads*
The minutes wing'd their way wi' pleasure:
Kings may be blest, but Tam was glorious,
O'er a' the ills o' life victorious!
But pleasures are like poppies spread,
You seize the flow'r, its bloom is shed;
Or like the snow falls in the river,
A moment white—then melts for ever;
Or like the Borealis race,
That flit ere you can point their place;
Or like the Rainbow's lovely form
Evanishing amid the storm.–
Nae man can tether Time or Tide,
The hour approaches Tam maun ride;
That hour, o' night's black arch the key-stane,
That dreary hour he mounts his beast in;
And sic a night he taks the road in,
As ne'er poor sinner was abroad in.

The wind blew as 'twad blawn its last;   *would have*
The rattling showers rose on the blast;
The speedy gleams the darkness swallow'd;
Loud, deep, and lang, the thunder bellow'd:
That night, a child might understand,
The deil had business on his hand.

Weel mounted on his grey mare, Meg,
A better never lifted leg,
Tam <u>skelpit</u> on thro' <u>dub</u> and mire,   *dashed; puddle*
Despising wind, and rain, and fire;
Whiles holding fast his <u>gude</u> blue bonnet,   *good*
Whiles <u>crooning</u> o'er some auld Scots <u>sonnet</u>,   *humming; song*
Whiles <u>glowerin</u> round wi' prudent cares,   *staring*

Les bogles catch him unawares;
Kirk-Alloway was drawing nigh,
Where ghaists and <u>houlets</u> nightly cry.   *owls*

By this time he was cross the ford,
Where, in the snaw, the chapman <u>smoor'd</u>:   *smothered*
And past the <u>birks</u> and <u>meikle</u> stane,   *birches; big*
Where drunken Charlie brak's neck-bane;
And thro' the <u>whins</u>, and by the cairn,   *furze*
Where hunters fand the murder'd bairn;
And near the thorn, aboon the well,
Where Mungo's mither hang'd hersel',
Before him Doon pours all his floods,
The doubling storm roars thro' the woods,
The lightnings flash from pole to pole,
Near and more near the thunders roll,
When, glimmering thro' the groaning trees,
Kirk-Alloway seem'd in a bleeze,
Thro' <u>ilka bore</u> the beams were glancing,   *every cranny*
And loud resounded mirth and dancing.

Inspiring bold John Barleycorn!
What dangers thou canst make us scorn!
Wi' <u>tippenny</u>, we fear nae evil;   *ale*
Wi' <u>usquabae</u>, we'll face the devil!   *whiskey*
The swats sae ream'd in Tammie's noddle,
Fair play, he car'd <u>na</u> deils a <u>boddle</u>,   *not; farthing*
But Maggie stood, right sair astonish'd,
Till, by the heel and hand admonish'd,
She ventur'd forward on the light;
And, wow! Tam saw an <u>unco</u> sight!   *wondrous*

Warlocks and witches in a dance;
Nae cotillion, <u>brent</u> new frae France,   *brand*
But hornpipes, jigs, strathspeys, and reels,
Put life and mettle in their heels.
A <u>winnock-bunker</u> in the east,   *window-seat*
There sat auld Nick, in shape o' beast;
A <u>towzie tyke</u>, black, grim, and large,   *shaggy dog*
To gie them music was his charge:
He screw'd the pipes and <u>gart</u> them skirl,   *made*
Till roof and rafters a'did <u>dirl</u>.   *rattle*
Coffins stood round, like open presses,

That shaw'd the dead in their last dresses;
And (by some devilish cantraip sleight)   *magic; trick*
Each in its cauld hand held a light.
By which heroic Tam was able
To note upon the haly table,
A murderer's banes, in gibbet-airns;   *irons*
Twa span-lang, wee, unchristened bairns;
A thief, new-cutted frae a rape,   *rope*
Wi' his last gasp his gabudid gape;   *mouth*
Five tomahawks, wi' blude red-rusted;
Five scimitars, wi' murder crusted;
A garter which a babe had strangled;
A knife, a father's throat had mangled,
Whom his ain son of life bereft,
The grey-hairs yet stack to the heft;   *stuck; haft*
Wi' mair o' horrible and awfu',
Which even to name wad be unlawfu'.

As Tammie glowr'd amaz'd, and curious,   *stared*
The mirth and fun grew fast and furious;
The Piper loud and louder blew,
The dancers quick and quicker flew,
They reel'd, they set, they cross'd, they cleekit,   *joined hands*
Till ilka carlin swat and reekit,   *witch*
And coost her duddies to the wark,   *looped/threw off; rags*
And linket at it in her sark!   *tripped; shirt*

Now, Tam, O Tam! Had thae been queans,   *these*
A' plump and strapping in their teens!
Their sarks, instead o' creeshie flainen,   *greasy*
Been snaw-white seventeen hunder linen!—
Thir breeks o' mine, my only pair,   *these; breeches*
That ance were plush, o' guid blue hair,
I wad hae gien them off my hurdies,   *buttocks*
For ae blink o' the bonie burdies!   *lasses*
But wither'd beldams, auld and droll,
Rigwoodie hags wad spean a foal,   *lean; wean*
Louping an' flinging on a crummock.   *leaping; staff*
I wonder did na turn thy stomach.

But Tam kent what was what fu' brawlie: *well*
There was ae winsome wench and waulie   *jolly*
That night enlisted in the core,   *company*

Lang after ken'd on Carrick shore;
(For mony a beast to dead she shot,
And perish'd mony a bonie boat,
And shook baith <u>meikle</u> corn and <u>bear</u>,   *much; barley*
And kept the country-side in fear);
Her <u>cutty</u> sark, o' Paisley <u>harn</u>,   *short; coarse cloth*
That while a lassie she had worn,
In longitude tho' sorely scanty,
It was her best, and she was <u>vauntie</u>.   *proud*
Ah! little ken'd thy reverend grannie,
That sark she <u>coft</u> for her wee Nannie,   *bought*
Wi' twa pund Scots ('twas a' her riches),
Wad ever grac'd a dance of witches!

But here my Muse her wing maun <u>cour</u>,   *stoop*
Sic flights are far beyond her power;
To sing how Nannie <u>lap and flang</u>,   *leaped and kicked*
(A souple jade she was and strang),
And how Tam stood, like ane bewitch'd,
And thought his very een enrich'd;
Even Satan glowr'd, and <u>fidg'd</u> fu' fain,   *wriggled with delight*
And <u>hotch'd</u> and blew wi' might and main: *jerked*
Till first ae caper, <u>syne</u> anither,   *then*
Tam <u>tint</u> his reason a thegither,   *lost*
And roars out, "Weel done, Cutty-sark!'
And in an instant all was dark:
And scarcely had he Maggie rallied.
When out the hellish legion sallied.

As bees bizz out wi' angry <u>fyke</u>,   *fret*
When plundering <u>herds</u> assail their <u>byke</u>;   *sheperds; hive*
As open <u>pussie's</u> mortal foes,   *hare's*
When, pop! she starts before their nose;
As eager runs the market-crowd,
When "Catch the thief!' resounds aloud;
So Maggie runs, the witches follow,
Wi' mony an <u>eldritch</u> <u>screech</u> and hollow.   *unearthly; yell*

Ah, Tam! Ah, Tam! Thou'll get thy <u>fairin</u>!   *deserts*
In hell they'll roast thee like a herrin!
In vain thy Kate awaits thy comin!
Kate soon will be a woefu' woman!
Now, do thy speedy-utmost, Meg,

And win the key-stone of the brig;
There, at them thou thy tail may toss,
A running stream they dare na cross.
But ere the keystane she could make,
The fient a tail she had to shake!   *devil*
For Nannie, far before the rest,
Hard upon noble Maggie prest,
And flew at Tam wi' furious ettle;   *intent*
But little wist she Maggie's mettle!
Ae spring brought off her master hale,   *whole*
But left behind her ain grey tail:
The carlin claught her by the rump,   *clutched/seized*
And left poor Maggie scarce a stump.

Now, what this tale o' truth shall read,
Ilk man and mother's son, take heed:
Whene'er to Drink you are inclin'd,
Or Cutty-sarks rin in your mind,
Think, ye may buy the joys o'er dear;
Remember Tam o' Shanter's mare.

Appendix B: Selected Lincoln Documents

The three writings by Abraham Lincoln that received the most attention in Scotland were the final Emancipation Proclamation (January 1, 1863); the Gettysburg Address, the address of November 19, 1863, at the dedication of the Gettysburg National Cemetery; and the Second Inaugural Address, March 4, 1865.[1]

Emancipation Proclamation (January 1, 1863, final)
By the President of the United States of America

A Proclamation.

Whereas, on the twenty-second day of September, in the year of our Lord one thousand eight hundred and sixty-two, a proclamation was issued by the President of the United States, containing, among other things, the following, to wit:

That on the first day of January, in the year of our Lord one thousand eight hundred and sixty-three, all persons held as slaves within any State or designated part of a State, the people whereof shall then be in rebellion against the United States, shall be then, thenceforward, and forever free; and the Executive Government of the United States, including the military and naval authority thereof, will recognize and maintain the freedom of such persons, and will do no act or acts to repress such persons, or any of them, in any efforts they may make for their actual freedom.

That the Executive will, on the first day of January aforesaid, by proclamation, designate the States and parts of States, if any, in which the people thereof, respectively, shall then be in rebellion against the United States; and the fact that any State, or the people thereof, shall on that day be, in good faith, represented in the Congress of the United States by members chosen thereto at elections wherein a majority of the qualified voters of such State shall have participated, shall in the absence of strong countervailing testimony, be deemed conclusive evidence that such State, and the people thereof, are not then in rebellion against the United States.

Now, therefore, I, Abraham Lincoln, President of the United States, by virtue of the power in me vested as Commander-in-Chief, of the Army and Navy of the United States in time of actual armed rebellion against the authority and government of the United States, and as a fit and necessary war measure for suppressing said rebellion, do, on this first day of January, in the year of our Lord one thousand eight hundred and sixty-three, and in accordance with my purpose so to do publicly proclaimed for the full period of one hundred days, from the day first above mentioned, order and designate as the States and parts of States wherein the people thereof respectively, are this day in rebellion against the United States, the following, to wit:

Arkansas, Texas, Louisiana (except the Parishes of St. Bernard, Plaquemines, Jefferson, St. John, St. Charles, St. James Ascension, Assumption, Terrebonne, Lafourche, St. Mary, St. Martin, and Orleans, including the City of New Orleans), Mississippi, Alabama, Florida, Georgia, South Carolina, North Carolina, and Virginia (except the forty-eight counties designated as West Virginia, and also the counties of Berkley, Accomac, Northampton, Elizabeth City, York, Princess Ann, and Norfolk, including the cities of Norfolk and Portsmouth[)], and which excepted parts, are for the present, left precisely as if this proclamation were not issued.

And by virtue of the power, and for the purpose aforesaid, I do order and declare that all persons held as slaves within said designated States, and parts of States, are, and henceforward shall be free; and that the Executive Government of the United States, including the military and naval authorities thereof, will recognize and maintain the freedom of said persons.

And I hereby enjoin upon the people so declared to be free to abstain from all violence, unless in necessary self-defence; and I recommend to them that, in all cases when allowed, they labor faithfully for reasonable wages.

And I further declare and make known, that such persons of suitable condition, will be received into the armed service of the United States to garrison forts, positions, stations, and other places, and to man vessels of all sorts in said service.

And upon this act, sincerely believed to be an act of justice, warranted by the Constitution, upon military necessity, I invoke the considerate judgment of mankind, and the gracious favor of Almighty God.

The Gettysburg Address (November 19, 1863)

At the Dedication of the Gettysburg National Cemetery

Fourscore and seven years ago our fathers brought forth on this continent a new nation, conceived in liberty, and dedicated to the proposition that all men are created equal.

Now we are engaged in a great civil war, testing whether that nation, or any nation so conceived and so dedicated, can long endure. We are met on a great battlefield of that war. We have come to dedicate a portion of that field as a final resting-place for those who here gave their lives that this nation might live. It is altogether fitting and proper that we should do this.

But, in a larger sense, we cannot dedicate . . . we cannot consecrate . . . we cannot hallow . . . this ground. The brave men, living and dead, who struggled here, have consecrated it far above our poor power to add or detract. The world will little note nor long remember what we say here, but it can never forget what they did here. It is for us, the living, rather, to be dedicated here to the unfinished work which they who fought here have thus far so nobly advanced. It is rather for us to be here dedicated to the great task remaining before us . . . that from these honored dead we take increased devotion to that cause for which they gave the last full measure of devotion; that we here highly resolve that these dead shall not have died in vain; that this nation, under God, shall have a new birth of freedom; and that government of the people, by the people, for the people, shall not perish from the earth.

Second Inaugural Address (March 4, 1865)

Fellow Countrymen

At this second appearing to take the oath of the presidential office, there is less occasion for an extended address than there was at the first. Then a statement, somewhat in detail, of a course to be pursued, seemed fitting and proper. Now, at the expiration of four years, during which public declarations have been constantly called forth on every point and phase of the great contest which still absorbs the attention, and engrosses the energies of the nation, little that is new could be presented. The progress of our arms, upon which all else chiefly depends, is as well known to the public as to myself; and it is, I trust, reasonably satisfactory and encouraging to all. With high hope for the future, no prediction in regard to it is ventured.

On the occasion corresponding to this four years ago, all thoughts were anxiously directed to an impending civil-war. All dreaded it—all sought to avert it. While the inaugural address was being delivered from this place, devoted altogether to saving the Union without war, insurgent agents were in the city seeking to destroy it without war—seeking to dissolve the Union, and divide effects, by negotiation. Both parties deprecated war;

but one of them would make war rather than let the nation survive; and the other would accept war rather than let it perish. And the war came.

One eighth of the whole population were colored slaves, not distributed generally over the Union, but localized in the Southern part of it. These slaves constituted a peculiar and powerful interest. All knew that this interest was, somehow, the cause of the war. To strengthen, perpetuate, and extend this interest was the object for which the insurgents would rend the Union, even by war; while the government claimed no right to do more than to restrict the territorial enlargement of it. Neither party expected for the war, the magnitude, or the duration, which it has already attained. Neither anticipated that the cause of the conflict might cease with, or even before, the conflict itself should cease. Each looked for an easier triumph, and a result less fundamental and astounding. Both read the same Bible, and pray to the same God; and each invokes His aid against the other. It may seem strange that any men should dare to ask a just God's assistance in wringing their bread from the sweat of other men's faces; but let us judge not that we be not judged. The prayers of both could not be answered; that of neither has been answered fully. The Almighty has his own purposes. "Woe unto the world because of offences! for it must needs be that offences come; but woe to that man by whom the offence cometh." If we shall suppose that American Slavery is one of those offences which, in the providence of God, must needs come, but which, having continued through His appointed time, He now wills to remove, and that He gives to both North and South, this terrible war, as the woe due to those by whom the offence came, shall we discern therein any departure from those divine attributes which the believers in a Living God always ascribe to Him? Fondly do we hope—fervently do we pray—that this mighty scourge of war may speedily pass away. Yet, if God wills that it continue, until all the wealth piled by the bond-man's two hundred and fifty years of unrequited toil shall be sunk, and until every drop of blood drawn with the lash, shall be paid by another drawn with the sword, as was said three thousand years ago, so still it must be said "the judgments of the Lord, are true and righteous altogether."

With malice toward none; with charity for all; with firmness in the right, as God gives us to see the right, let us strive on to finish the work we are in; to bind up the nation's wounds, to care for him who shall have borne the battle, and for his widow, and his orphan—to do all which may achieve and cherish a just, and a lasting peace, among ourselves, and with all nations.

Notes

Introduction

1. *Scotsman*, December 9, 2005, http://www.burnsheritagepark.com/museum-archive.php/story=33.

2. *Scottish-American Journal*, December 7, 1867.

3. Douglas Sloan, *The Scottish Enlightenment and the American College* (New York: Teachers' College Press, 1971).

4. Memorandum from John A. Morton, prisoner of war records, in the author's possession.

5. J. W. Egerer, *A Bibliography of Robert Burns* (Carbondale: Southern Illinois UP, 1964), vii–ix.

6. Thomas McMunn, "My Thirty-Three Years at the Burns Cottage," *Burns Chronicle*, 3rd series, 7–8 (1958–59): 15–17; Thomas S. McCrorie, "My Experiences at the Burns House," *Burns Chronicle*, 3rd series, 7–8 (1958–59): 12–14.

7. Tom Sutherland and Jean Sutherland, *At Your Own Risk: An American Chronicle of Crisis and Captivity in the Middle East* (Golden, CO: Fulcrum, 1996), 184–85. See also Tom Sutherland, "Burns in Beirut," *Studies in Scottish Literature* 30 (1998): 1–8.

8. John Cairney, *On the Trail of Robert Burns* (Edinburgh: Luath Press, 2000); A. M. Boyle, *The Ayrshire Book of Burns Lore* (Darvel, Scotland: Alloway, 1996); John G. Gray and Charles J. Smith, *A Walk on the Southside in the Steps of Robert Burns* (Edinburgh: Southside Museum, 1998).

9. Joyce Lindsay and Maurice Lindsay, eds., *The Burns Quotation Book* (London: Hale, 1994); Arnold O'Hara, comp., *As Burns Said* (Darvel, Scotland: Alloway, 1987; 1995).

10. Robert Crawford, ed., *Robert Burns and Cultural Authority* (Edinburgh: Edinburgh UP, 1997); Kenneth Simpson, ed., *Burns Now* (Edinburgh: Canongate Academic, 1994) and *Love and Liberty, Robert Burns: A Bicentenary Celebration* (East Lothian: Tuckwell Press, 1997); and Carol McGuirk, *Robert Burns and the Sentimental Era* (Athens: U of Georgia P, 1985). See also G. Ross Roy, "Robert Burns: Editions and Critical Works 1968–1982," *Studies in Scottish Literature* 19 (1984): 216–51; Thomas Keith, "A Discography of Robert Burns 1948 to 2002," *Studies in Scottish Literature* 33–34 (2004): 387–412; and James A. MacKay, "New Developments in Burns Biography," *Studies in Scottish Literature* 30 (1998): 291–301 (the 1998 volume is devoted entirely to Burns).

11. Andrew Noble and Patrick Scott Hogg, eds., *The Canongate Burns*, 2 vols. (Edinburgh: Canongate, 2001), 2.viii.

12. *Sunday Herald*, December 9, 2005, http://www.Sundayherald.com/39202.

13. *Scotsman*, June 27, 2005, http://www.scotsman.com/?id=705782005.

14. Egerer, *Bibliography*, xiii–xiv.

15. See the introduction by Paul M. Angle in Henry Clay Whitney, *Life on the Circuit with Lincoln* (Caldwell, ID: Caxton, 1892; 1940); and Benjamin P. Thomas, *Portrait for Posterity: Lincoln and His Biographers* (New Brunswick, NJ: Rutgers UP, 1947).

16. Ida M. Tarbell, *All in the Day's Work: An Autobiography* (New York: Macmillan, 1939), 163.

17. *Abraham Lincoln (1809): 16th President of the United States of America* (Washington, DC: GPO, 1959). See also Ferenc Morton Szasz, "The 1958/59 Comic Book Biographies of Abraham Lincoln," *Journal of Popular Culture*, forthcoming.

18. Winston Churchill, *The Crisis* (New York: Macmillan, 1901), 522.

19. The Web site address is www.lincolnbicentennial.gov.

20. The Web site address for *The Lincoln Log: A Daily Chronology of the Life of Abraham Lincoln* is http://www.thelincolnlog.org.

21. A recent survey of Scottish academics selected Burns as the "greatest-ever Scot." As Edinburgh University historian Tom Devine observed, "Burns has continuing reverence because of his belief in democracy and equality. He is a man whose beliefs allowed him to be simultaneously admired in Soviet Russia and America, the centre of the western world. He also epitomizes Scotland, particularly in his humour and egalitarian spirit" (*Scotland on Sunday*, January 8, 2006, http://scotlandonsunday.scotsman.com/print.cfm?Id=25842006).

1. Robert Burns: A Brief Biography

1. Montreal *Gazette*, January 25, 1927, scrapbook 3, Burnsiana, John M. Shaw Collection, Special Collections, Strozier Library, Florida State University, Tallahassee, Florida. The literature on Burns, of course, is enormous. An excellent brief biography is Gavin Sprott, *Robert Burns: Pride and Passion: The Life, Times and Legacy* (Edinburgh: National Library of Scotland, 1996). An older study by David Daiches, *Robert Burns the Poet* (1950; Edinburgh: Saltire Society, 1994) still retains its deserved reputation. There are equally numerous editions of his prose and poetry. Among others, I have drawn on the following: Robert Burns, *The Complete Works of Robert Burns . . . with a Memoir by William Gunnyon* (Edinburgh: Nimmo, Hay, and Mitchell, 1892), and Burns, *The Complete Poems and Songs of Robert Burns* (New Lanark, MD: Geddes and Grossett, 2001). James A. MacKay has edited *The Complete Letters of Robert Burns* (1987; Ayrshire, Scotland: Alloway, 1990).

2. Robert Burns to John Moore, MacKay, *Complete Letters*, 248–56.

3. Daiches, *Robert Burns the Poet*, 14.

4. On the impact of the King James Version, see Alister McGrath, *In the Beginning: The Story of the King James Bible and How It Changed a Nation, a Language, and a Culture* (New York: Anchor Books, 2001); Adam Nicolson, *God's Secretaries: The Making of the King James Bible* (New York: HarperCollins, 2003); and Benson Bobrick, *Wide as the Waters: The Story of the English Bible and the Revolution It Inspired* (New York: Penguin Books, 2001).

5. The plaques at Burns's birthplace in Ayrshire suggest this.

6. Robert Burns, quoted in Catherine Carswell, *The Life of Robert Burns* (1930; Edinburgh: Canongate Classics, 1990), 24. See also Gavin Sprott, *Robert Burns: Farmer* (Edinburgh: National Museums of Scotland, 1990).

7. See, for example, MacKay, *Complete Letters*, 67, 363, 426–27, 459, 466, 538.

8. *Mauchline Memories of Robert Burns* (Ayrshire: Ayrshire Archaeological and Natural History Society, 1996), 235.

9. Quoted in John Gibson Lockhart, *Life of Burns* (Edinburgh: Constable, 1828), 67.

10. See especially chapter 3, "The Kirk's Alarm," Thomas Crawford, *Burns: A Study of the Poems and Songs* (Edinburgh: Canongate Academic, 1960; 1994), 48–76.

11. John D. Ross, comp., *A Little Book of Burns Lore* (Clydebank: Lang Syne, 1926; 1991), 8.

12. When Mary's grave was exhumed in the nineteenth century, the body of an infant was found beside her.

13. Burns, quoted in L. S., "Robert Burns," *Dictionary of National Biography*, 426–38.

14. Hugh Douglas, *Robert Burns: The Tinder Heart* (Gloucestershire: Sutton, 1998), after 78.

15. James C. Currie, *The Entire Works of Robert Burns; with His Life and a Criticism on His Writings* (Glasgow: George Brookman, 1800; 1823), 44.

16. Quoted in Lockhart, *Life of Burns*, 173.

17. Quoted in *Mauchline Memories*, 235.

18. Maria Riddle, quoted in *Edinburgh Courant*, August 22, 1796, (facsimile), in Alan McNie, comp., *The Illustrated Life and Works of Robert Burns* (Rowandean, Beles, Jedburgh, Scotland: Cascade, 1995), 8.

19. Donny O'Rourke, *Ae Fond Kiss: The Love Letters of Robert Burns and Clarinda* (Edinburgh: Mercat Press, 2000). See also Graham Smith, *Robert Burns, The Exciseman* (Ayr: Alloway, 1989).

20. Robert Burns to Reverend John Skinner, October 25, 1787, MacKay, *Complete Letters*, 363. See also David Daiches, "The Facets of Genius," *Scotland's Magazine* 55 (January 1959): 46.

21. Burns, quoted in Davidson Cook, *Scotsman* (ca. 1925), scrapbook 3, Burnsiana, Shaw Collection.

22. See John Loesberg, *The Scottish Songs of Robert Burns* (Cork, Ireland: Ossian, 1994), and James C. Dick, *The Songs of Robert Burns* (London: Henry Frowde, 1903), v–viii; xv.

23. G. Legman, ed., *The Merry Muses of Caledonia* (New Hyde Park, NY: University Books, 1965).

24. The fullest explanation of his verse may be found in George Scott Wilkie, *Understanding Robert Burns: Verse, Explanation and Glossary* (Glasgow: Wilson, 2002).

25. Principal Shairp, *Robert Burns* (New York: Harper, 1900), 196–97.

26. C. M. McCoy "'Auld Lang Syne,'" *Metropolitan Review* 2 (July 1927): 10. See also David Morison, "Burns and the Scots Tongue," *Scotland's Magazine* 55 (January 1959): 40.

27. Lockhart, *Life of Burns*, 428.

28. Carswell, *Life of Robert Burns*.

29. Liam McIlvanney, *Burns the Radical: Poetry and Politics in Late Eighteenth-Century Scotland* (East Linton: Tuckwell Press, 2002), 68–69.

30. McIlvanney, *Burns the Radical*, and James Buchan, *Crowded with Genius. The Scottish Enlightenment: Edinburgh's Moment of the Mind* (New York: HarperCollins, 2003), 327–29.

31. Shairp, *Robert Burns*, 31; W. W. Buchanan and W. F. Kean, "Robert Burns's Illness Revisited," *Scottish Medical Journal* 27 (1982): 75–88.

32. Currie, *Entire Works of Robert Burns*, 37.

33. Reverend William Peebles, quoted in Donald A. Low, *Robert Burns* (Edinburgh: Scottish Academic Press, 1986), 68.

34. Quoted in G. Legman, ed., *The Merry Muses of Caledonia* (New Hyde Park, NY: University Books, 1965), xliii.

35. Robert Heron, *A Memoir of the Life of the Late Robert Burns* (Edinburgh: Brown, 1797), 8.

36. G. Ross Roy, "Some Notes on Scottish Chapbooks," *Scottish Literary Journal* 1 (1974): 50–60, http://www.sc.edu/library/spcoll/brit lit/cbooks2.html. The first quotation is from DeLancey Ferguson, *Pride and Passion: Robert Burns, 1759–1796* (New York: Russell and Russell, 1964; originally published by Oxford UP in 1939), 261; I owe the latter phrase "portable Scotland" to Robert I. Edgar of Oregon. See also the classic late-nineteenth-century biography, John Stuart Blackie, *Life of Robert Burns* (London: Walter Scott, 1888), 155–76.

2. Burns's Poetry Comes to America

1. Some of these tributes may be found in Edward Goodwillie, *The World's Memorials of Robert Burns* (Detroit, MI: Waverley, 1911); Robert Crawford, *Devolving English Literature*, 2nd. ed. (Edinburgh: Edinburgh UP, 2000), 37.

2. "Selected Poetry," *New Jersey Journal*, September 23, 1807, 4, Early American Newspapers, http://infoweb.newsbank.com/iw-search/weHistArchive?P_

action=doc&s_lastnonissueg (accessed December 22, 2005); "Robert Burns," *Poulson's American Daily Advertiser,* January 2, 1815, 2; "Robert Burns," *Salem* (Massachusetts) *Gazette,* August 19, 1823, 2; *Salem* (Massachusetts) *Gazette,* July 26, 1796, 4; Charles Augustus Murray, *Travels in North America* (New York: DaCapo, 1974; originally published, 1839), 184–85. See also the excellent overview by James Montgomery, "How Robert Burns Captured America," *Studies in Scottish Literature* 30 (1998): 235–48.

3. Robert Walsh, "Foreign Literature," *American Review of History and Politics* (January 1811): 166–67.

4. *London Herald,* 21 July 1796 (copy, Writers' Museum, Edinburgh, Scotland).

5. Archibald Monroe, "Reminiscences of the Burns Festival in 1844," *Scotsman,* July 4, 1891, 9; *Burnsiana: Speeches of Professor John Wilson* (Washington, DC: Gibson, 1877), 4–8 (copy, Illinois State Historical Library, Springfield, Illinois).

6. "Robert Burns," *Berkshire* (Massachusetts) *County Whig,* September 19, 1844, Early American Newspapers, series 1 (accessed December 22, 2005).

7. John D. Ross, comp., *Burnsiana: A Collection of Literary Odds and Ends Relating to Robert Burns* (London: Gardner, 1892), 27–29.

8. John Clive and Bernard Bailyn, "England's Cultural Provinces: Scotland and America," *William and Mary Quarterly* 11 (April 1954): 200–213. In *The Puritan-Provincial Vision: Scottish and American Literature in the Nineteenth Century* (Cambridge: Cambridge UP, 1990) and in *Fragments of Union: Making Connections in Scottish and American Writing* (New York: Palgrave, 2002), Susan Manning charts the link between Scottish and American Literature that ultimately trace to this shared sense of "cultural inferiority."

9. John M. Duncan, *Travels through Part of the United States and Canada in 1818 and 1819* (Glasgow: Glasgow University Press, 1823), 335–39.

10. Undated newspaper clipping from "Cragie," Burnsiana, scrapbook 3, box 1665, Shaw Collection.

11. John M. Duncan, *Travels,* 335–39.

12. "Burn's Club," *Baltimore Patriot* February 9, 1831, from Early American Newspapers, series 1 (accessed December 22, 2005).

13. "Robert Burns," *New Hampshire Patriot and State Gazette,* February 22, 1836, Early American Newspapers, series 1 (accessed December 27, 2005).

14. "Beautiful Eulogy on Burns," *New Bedford* (Massachusetts) *Mercury* February 23, 1838, Early American Newspapers, series 1.

15. See Vernon Louis Parrington, ed., *The Connecticut Wits* (New York: Thomas Y. Crowell, 1969); Eve Konnfeld, *Creating an American Culture, 1795–1800* (Boston: Bedford/St. Martin's, 2001).

16. Sidney Smith, review, *Edinburgh Review* 33 (January 1820): 79; Vernon L. Parrington, ed., *The Connecticut Wits* (New York: Thomas Y. Crowell, 1969), passim.

17. John Knapp, "National Poetry," *North American Review* 8 (December 1818): 169–76; Russel B. Nye, *The Cultural Life of the New Nation* (New York: Harper and Rowe, 1963).

18. *North American Review* article excerpted in *Chicago Record*, February 1, 1861, 161–62. None of the standard accounts of early-American literature acknowledges the presence of Burns. See *The Norton Anthology of American Literature* (1989).

19. "The Inventory," James Kinsley, ed., *Burns: Complete Poems and Songs* (Oxford: Oxford UP, 1969), 174. *Lan' afore* is the fore horse on the left hand in the plough, and the *Lan' ahin* is the hindmost horse on the same side.

20. John G. Dow, "Burns in America" in *Robert Burns: The Critical Heritage*, ed. Donald A. Law (London: Routledge, 1974), 439–40. See also Wallace Bruce, "The Influence of Robert Burns on American literature," *Annual Burns Chronicle* 1 (1892): 45.

21. W. R. Bonney, "American Appreciation of Robert Burns," c. 1925, undated newspaper clipping, folder 2, box 1663, Burnsiana, Shaw Collection.

22. Charles Hamm, *Yesterdays: Popular Song in America* (New York: Norton, 1979): 42–60. By and large, I disagree with many of Hamm's conclusions.

23. David Herd, *Ancient and Modern Scottish Songs, Heroic Ballads, etc.* 2 vols. (Edinburgh: John Witherspoon, 1876), vii; George Eyre-Todp, ed., *Scottish Ballad Poetry* (Glasgow: William Hodge, 1893), 1.

24. George Gilfallan, quoted in "Street Songs in Scotland," *Farmers' Cabinet* November 11, 1866, 1, Early American Newspapers.

25. Principal Shairp, quoted in W. Bruce, "Influence of Robert Burns," 92.

26. T. R. Fehrenbach, *Lone Star: A History of Texas and the Texans* (New York: Macmillan, 1968), 119 (thanks to Christopher Hitchens of the *Atlantic Monthly* for this citation); Katie Lee, *Ten Thousand Goddam Cattle* (Albuquerque: U of New Mexico P, 2001): 237–38.

27. Thomas P. Reep, *Lincoln at New Salem* (n.p.: Old Salem Lincoln League, 1927), 62.

28. Michael Burlingame, *The Inner World of Abraham Lincoln* (Urbana: U of Illinois P, 1994), 312.

29. Howard K. Beale, ed., *Diary of Edward Bates, 1859–1866* (Washington, DC: GPO, 1933), 295.

30. Ray B. Browne, ed., *Lincoln-Lore: Lincoln in the Popular Mind*, 2nd. ed. (Bowling Green, OH: Bowling Green State U Popular P, 1996), 194–95.

31. Quoted in Albert Shaw, *Abraham Lincoln: The Year of His Election* (New York: Review of Reviews, 1930), 224. See also J. Edward Murr, "Lincoln in Indiana," *Indiana Magazine of History* 13 (December 1917): 313.

32. "Visit to the Land of Burns," *New Bedford* (Massachusetts) *Mercury*, November 24, 1837, 4, Early American Newspapers.

33. Schouler, "Visit to the Cottage of Robert Burns," *New Hampshire-Sentinel,* September 16, 1846, 1, Early American Newspapers.

34. *Chicago Record,* August 1, 1857, 34.

35. *Chicago Record,* August 1, 1857, 34.

36. Nathaniel Hawthorne, "Some of the Haunts of Burns: By a Tourist without Imagination or Enthusiasm," *Atlantic Monthly,* October 1860, 386; Thomas Woodson and Bill Ellis, eds., *The English Notebooks, 1856–1860* (Columbus: Ohio State UP, 1997), 267–69; 275–85.

37. Hawthorne, "Some of the Haunts," 385–95.

38. Ferenc M. Szasz, "Jefferson Davis's 1869 and 1871 Visits to Scotland: Cultural Symbols of the Old and New Souths," *Northern Scotland* 14 (1994): 51. See also Thomas C. MacMillan, "The Scots and Their Descendants in Illinois," *Transactions of the Illinois State Historical Society* 26 (Springfield, IL: Phillips, 1919): 84; and the essays in Andrew Hook, *From Goosecreek to Gandercleugh: Studies in Scottish-American Literary and Cultural History* (East Linton: Tuckwell Press, 1999).

39. Beecher's oration may be found in Joseph Cunningham, ed., *The Centennial Birthday of Robert Burns, as Celebrated by the Burns Club of the City of New York, Tuesday, January 25, 1859* (New York: Laing and Laing, 1860); Myron W. Reed, undated newspaper clipping, Myron W. Reed file, Western Room, Denver Public Library.

40. Ebenezer Elliott, "The Character of Robert Burns," *Harper's New Monthly Magazine* 1 (1850): 114–15; "An Apology for Burns," *Harper's New Monthly Magazine* 2 (1851): 334–35. For an overview, see Ferenc Morton Szasz, *Scots in the North American West, 1790–1917* (Norman: U of Oklahoma P, 2000), and Jenni Calder, *Scots in the USA* (Edinburgh: Luath, 2006).

41. Halleck's poem may be found in Cunningham, *Centennial Birthday,* 119–23. Halleck lived long enough to attend the 1859 New York celebration of Burns's birthday; William Allan, "At the Shrine of Burns," in J. D. Ross, *Burnsiana,* 6n, 27; C. Vann Woodward and Elisabeth Muhlenfeld, eds., *The Private Mary Chestnut: The Unpublished Civil War Diaries* (New York: Oxford UP, 1984), 184.

42. Franklyn Bliss Snyder, *Robert Burns: His Personality, His Reputation and His Art* (1936; repr., Port Washington, NY: Kennikat Press, 1970), 76–77; Ralph H. Orth et al., eds., *The Poetry Notebooks of Ralph Waldo Emerson* (Columbia: U of Missouri P, 1986), 540.

43. *The Complete Poetical Works of Whittier,* ed. H. E. Scudder, 196–97, in Donald A. Low, *Robert Burns: The Critical Heritage* (London: Routledge, 1974), 44–46, 432–33.

44. Edward Wagenknecht, *James Russell Lowell: Portrait of a Many-sided Man* (New York: Oxford UP, 1971), 85, 107; Charles Eliot Norton, ed., *Letters of James Russell Lowell* (1893; repr., New York: Harper, 1947), 21–26.

45. Henry Wadsworth Longfellow, in *Life of Henry Wadsworth Longfellow*, 3 vols., ed. Samuel Longfellow (New York: AMS Press, 1966), 2:375, 3:305.

46. Daniel Mark Epstein, *Lincoln and Whitman: Parallel Lives in Civil War Washington* (New York: Ballantine, 2004), 274–305, especially 294. Not surprisingly, Epstein credits Lincoln's poetic elegance to his reading of Whitman rather than Burns. I argue, however, that Lincoln was a mature adult when he first read Whitman. He was an impressionable teenager when he encountered Burns; Gary Scharnhorst, "Whitman on Robert Burns: An Early Essay Recovered," *Walt Whitman Quarterly Review* 13 (Spring 1996): 217–20.

47. Epstein, *Lincoln and Whitman*, 309–39, especially 322; Josh Billings, quoted in A. G. McKnight, *America's Appreciation of Robert Burns* (Minneapolis, 1924), 3.

48. James Gould, comp., *Poems, Letters, and Speeches in Connection with the Centenary Birthday of Robert Burns, Commemorated in Scotland, England, Ireland, America, India, Australia, etc. January 25, 1859, with Memoirs, Reminiscences, etc.*, 4 vols. of scrapbooks, Burns Room, Mitchell Library, Glasgow, 4:82.

49. Carol McGuirk, "Haunted by Authority: Nineteenth-Century American Constructions of Robert Burns and Scotland," in *Robert Burns*, ed. Robert Crawford (Edinburgh: Edinburgh UP, 1997), 136–58.

50. Margaret Fuller, quoted in Snyder, *Robert Burns*, 55; William Frye, quoted in Snyder, *Robert Burns*, 77.

51. *New York Times*, January 26, 1856, 1; January 27, 1857, 1; January 26, 1858, 4; January 26, 1861, 8.

52. *The Burns Centenary: Being an Account of the Proceedings and Speeches at the Various Banquets and Meetings throughout the Kingdom, with a Memoir and Portrait of the Poet*, 2nd. ed. (Edinburgh: Nimmo, 1859), v. See also "Leigh Hunt on Robert Burns," *Scotsman*, January 24, 1859, 4; *Scotsman*, January 26, 1859, 4.

53. Henry, Lord Brougham, *Letter by the Right Honorable Lord Brougham, on the Occasion of the Burns' Centenary Festival, 25th January 1859 to the Honorable Lord Ardmillan in the Music Hall, Edinburgh, Printed for Those Who Attended the Banquet* (Edinburgh: 1859), pamphlet, Scottish National Library.

54. *Burns Centenary: Are Such Honors Due to the Ayrshire Bard?* (Glasgow: printed for the author, 1859); "Christian Commemoration of the Birth of Burns," *Scotsman*, February 1, 1869, 6.

55. "Dundee," *Scotsman*, January 26, 1859, 4.

56. Robert Blackley Drummond, *The Religion of Robert Burns: A Lecture* (Edinburgh: Mathers, 1859).

57. "The Burns Centenary," *Farmers' Cabinet*, January 12, 1871, Early American Newspapers.

58. *Scottish American Journal*, January 25, 1867.

59. *New York Times*, January 8, 1859; February 8, 1859.

60. *New York Times*, February 1, 1859.

61. *New York Times*, February 19, 1859.

62. Cunningham, *Celebration*, 74.

63. Cunningham, *Celebration*, 74–76.

64. *New York Times*, January 26, 1859.

65. "Burns Festival," *Littell's Living Age* 60 (January 1859): 740–49; Whittier's tribute appeared later in *Littell's Living Age* 60 (February 19, 1859): 512.

66. McGuirk, "Haunted by Authority," 136–58.

67. *New York Times*, January 26, 1859.

68. Gould, *Poems, Letters and Speeches*, 4:224.

69. Gould, *Poems, Letters and Speeches*, 4:224–25. "The Burns Centennial in New York" in *St. Louis Burnsians: Their Twentieth Anniversary and Some Other Burns Nights* (St. Louis: Burns Clubs, 1926), 74, 95.

70. Cunningham, *Celebration*, 74–85.

71. Cunningham, *Celebration*, 40.

72. "St. Andrew's Day," *Scottish-American Journal*, December 8, 1866.

73. In *How the Scots Invented the Modern World* (New York: Three Rivers, 2001), Arthur Herman argues that the idea of individual self-improvement as contained within an enlightened community—a concept that most people see as fundamentally American—is "quintessentially Scottish" (388).

3. The Lincoln-Burns Connection

1. Roy P. Basler, ed., *The Collected Works of Abraham Lincoln*, 9 vols., 2 supplements (New Brunswick: Rutgers UP, 1953–90), 3:211–12; William E. Gienapp, *Abraham Lincoln and Civil War America: A Biography* (New York: Oxford UP, 2002), 66–67.

2. David Herbert Donald, *Lincoln* (New York: Simon and Schuster, 1995), 47.

3. Although he slights Burns's contribution, on this theme see Ronald C. White Jr., *The Eloquent President: A Portrait of Lincoln through His Words* (New York: Random, 2005).

4. Noah Brooks, *Abraham Lincoln and the Downfall of American Slavery* (New York: Putnam, 1894), v–vi, 29. A good chapter on the Burns-Lincoln connection is in David J. Harkness and R. Gerald McMurtry, *Lincoln's Favorite Poets* (Knoxville: U of Tennessee P, 1959), 1–19.

5. Isaac N. Arnold, "Abraham Lincoln," in Osborn H. Oldroyd, ed., *The Lincoln Memorial: Album—Immortelles* (New York: Carleton, 1883), 33–34. See also M. L. Houser, *Lincoln's Education* (New York: Bookman, 1957), 119–20.

6. William H. Herndon and Jesse W. Werk, *Herndon's Life of Lincoln: The History and Personal Recollections of Abraham Lincoln* (New York: Boni, 1936),

44–45. For his complete poetical works, see *The Poems of Abraham Lincoln* (Bedford, MA: Applewood, 1991).

7. Robert Altor, *The Art of Biblical Narrative* (New York: Basic Books, 1981), especially chapter 1.

8. "Satire," in *The New Princeton Encyclopedia of Poetry and Poetics*, ed. Alex Preminger and T. V. F. Brogan (Princeton: Princeton UP, 1993), 1114–16.

9. Cassius M. Clay, quoted in *Reminiscences of Abraham Lincoln by Distinguished Men of His Time*, ed. Allen Thorndike Rice (New York: North American Review, 1888), 297.

10. Walter J. Ong, *Orality and Literacy: The Technologizing of the Word* (London: Routledge, 1982), 41–44; 68–69; Walter J. Ong, *The Presence of the Word: Some Prolegomena for Cultural and Religious History* (New Haven, CT: Yale UP, 1963), 21–25. See also the perceptive analysis by Ruth Finnegan, *Oral Poetry: Its Nature, Significance and Social Context* (Bloomington: Indiana UP, 1992; originally published 1977), especially 28, 133, 224.

11. Mario M. Cuomo, *Why Lincoln Matters: Today More Than Ever* (Orlando, FL: Harcourt, 2004), 20; Douglas L. Wilson, "What Jefferson and Lincoln Read," *Atlantic Monthly*, January 1991, 51–62; "Lincoln's Background of Borrowed Books," *Lincoln Lore*, October 31, 1949; "Books Lincoln Read," *Lincoln Lore*, June 20, 1932; "Borrowed Books in the White House," *Lincoln Lore*, September 28, 1931. A profound analysis of Lincoln's youth may be found in Kenneth J. Winkle, *The Young Eagle: The Rise of Abraham Lincoln* (Dallas: Taylor Trade, 2001).

12. Everett Fox, *The Five Books of Moses* (New York: Schocken, 1997), ix. Another classic text of Lincoln's youth was Aesop's Fables.

13. This was especially true of Lincoln scholars of the 1940s and 1950s, especially Paul M. Angle, James G. Randall, and Louis A. Warren.

14. William E. Barton, *The Life of Abraham Lincoln*, 2 vols. (Indianapolis, IN: Bobbs-Merrill, 1925), 1:193; Donald, *Lincoln*, 41; Carl Sandburg, *Abraham Lincoln*, 6 vols. (New York: Scribners, 1940), 1:69–71; Kenneth A. Bernard, "Lincoln and Music," in *Lincoln for the Ages*, ed. Ralph G. Newman (Garden City, NY: Doubleday, 1960), 338–43; and Kunigunde Duncan and D. F. Nickols, *Mentor Graham: The Man Who Taught Lincoln* (Chicago: U of Chicago P, 1944), 133.

15. Burns's songs often reflected the same theme.

> O Whistle, and I'll come to you, my lad!
> O Whistle, and I'll come to you, my lad!
> Tho' father and mither and a' should gae mad,
> O Whistle, and I'll come to you my lad.

See also B. Roland Lewis, *Creative Poetry: A Study of Its Organic Principles* (Stanford, CA: Stanford UP, 1931), 49, 197.

16. Cecil J. Sharp, *English Folk Songs from the Southern Appalachians*, 2 vols. (London: Oxford UP, 1932), 1:xxiii, xxv.

17. James S. Ewing, quoted in *Abraham Lincoln by Some Men Who Knew Him*, 1910 (New York: Books for Libraries Press, 1969), 49.

18. Since the mid-1990s, Michael Burlingame, Douglas L. Wilson, and Rodney O. Davis have explored the oral traditions of Lincoln's youth. See Michael Burlingame, ed., *An Oral History of Abraham Lincoln: John G. Nicolay's Interviews and Essays* (Carbondale: Southern Illinois UP, 1996); Douglas L. Wilson and Rodney O. Davis, eds., *Herndon's Informants: Letters, Interviews and Statements about Abraham Lincoln* (Urbana: U of Illinois P, 1998).

19. Dennis Hanks, 1877, Lincoln Papers, Manuscript Division, Library of Congress (Washington, DC: American Memory Project, 2000–2001), http://memory.loc.gov/ammen/alhtml/malhome.html (accessed October 2003); Ward H. Lamon, *Life of Abraham Lincoln: From His Birth to His Inauguration as President* (Boston: Osgood, 1872), 66–67.

20. "Contemporary Impressions of Burns," James Kinsley, ed., *The Poems and Songs of Robert Burns*, 4 vols. (Oxford: Oxford UP, 1968), 3:1534–47; second quotation from "Robert Burns," *Littell's Living Age* 7 (August 25, 1895): 528.

21. McIlvanney, *Burns the Radical*, 80, 150–51.

22. Helen Damico, "Sources of Stanza Forms Used by Burns," *Studies in Scottish Literature* 12 (January 1975): 207–19. See also "Burns Stanza" in *Princeton Encyclopedia of Poetry and Poetics*, ed. Alex Preminger, Frank J. Warnke, and O. B. Harrison Jr. (Princeton: Princeton UP, 1974), 90.

23. Herndon and Werk, *Herndon's Life of Lincoln*, 48. A good discussion may be found in Burlingame, chapter 7, "Lincoln's Anger and Cruelty," *Inner World*, 147–235.

24. Lamon, *Life of Lincoln*, 51.

25. Benjamin P. Thomas, *Abraham Lincoln* (New York: Knopf, 1952), 19; Wilson and Davis, *Herndon's Informants*, 152; Herndon and Werk, *Herndon's Life of Lincoln*, 45–48; Basler, *Collected Works*, 1:1–2.

26. Joshua F. Speed, *Reminiscences of Abraham Lincoln and Notes of a Visit to California: Two Lectures* (Louisville: Mortono, 1884), 17–18; Henry B. Rankin, *Personal Recollections of Abraham Lincoln* (New York: Putnam's, 1916), 18.

27. Gienapp, *Abraham Lincoln*, 32.

28. Paul M. Angle, *"Here I Have Lived": A History of Lincoln's Springfield, 1821–1865* (Chicago: Abraham Lincoln Book Shop, 1971), 68, 121–25.

29. Abraham Lincoln, quoted in James E. Myers, *The Astonishing Saber Duel of Abraham Lincoln* (Springfield, IL: Lincoln-Herndon, 1968), 6; Basler, "The 'Rebecca' Letter," *Collected Works*, 1:291–97.

30. Herndon and Werk, *Herndon's Life of Lincoln*, 183; J. G. Randall, *Lincoln the President: Springfield to Gettysburg*, 2 vols. (New York: Dodd, Mead, 1945), 1:62.

31. David R. Locke, in *Reminiscences of Abraham Lincoln*, ed. A. T. Rice, 442.

32. Henry C. Whitney, *Lincoln the Citizen* (1892; repr., New York: Current Literature, 1907), 47.

33. The most thorough study of this theme is Robert Bray, "The Power to Hurt: Lincoln's Early Use of Satire and Invective," *Journal of the Abraham Lincoln Association* 16 (Winter, 1995): 39–58.

34. See Reep, *Lincoln at New Salem*, and Mary Turner, "The Miller-Kelso Residence," unpublished essay written for the Illinois Historic Preservation Agency, ca. 1990, on this issue.

35. William E. Barton, *Life of Abraham Lincoln*, 1:193; Donald, *Lincoln*, 41; Gienapp, *Abraham Lincoln*, 15; Sandburg, *Abraham Lincoln*, 1:165; Helen Nicolay, *Personal Traits of Abraham Lincoln* (New York: Appleton-Century, 1939), 66.

36. Wilson and Davis, *Herndon's Informants*, 66, 74, 370, 374, 528.

37. Mary Turner, "The Miller-Kelso Residence," unpublished essay written for the Illinois Historic Preservation Agency, ca. 1990.

38. Wilson and Davis, *Herndon's Informants*, 66.

39. An excellent survey is Fern Nance Pond, "New Salem's Miller and Kelso," *Lincoln Herald* 52 (December 1950): 26–42.

40. Wilson and Davis, *Herndon's Informants*, 371–74.

41. Interview with Jim Patton, summer 2001.

42. Edgar Lee Masters, *The New Spoon River* (New York: Liveright, 1924), 260.

43. Wilson and Davis, *Herndon's Informants*, 73, 30, 90, 141, 179.

44. Maltby and Hay, quoted in Walter B. Stevens, *A Reporter's Lincoln*, ed. Michael Burlingame (Lincoln: U of Nebraska P, 1998), 280; Donald, *Lincoln*, 47.

45. James Grant Wilson, "Recollections of Lincoln," *Putnam's Magazine* 5 (February 1909): 517.

46. R. Sheldon MacKenzie to Abraham Lincoln, January 27, 1864, Lincoln Papers; Robert Crawford to Abraham Lincoln, January 23, 1864, Lincoln Papers; Alexander Williamson to Abraham Lincoln, January 24, 1865, Lincoln Papers; Basler, *Collected Works*, 8:327.

47. Michael Burlingame, ed., *At Lincoln's Side: John Hay's Civil War Correspondence and Selected Writings* (Carbondale: Southern Illinois UP, 2000), 137–38.

48. Speed, *Reminiscences*, 39.

49. John Young, *Robert Burns: A Man for All Season: The Natural World of Robert Burns* (Aberdeen: Scottish Cultural Press, 1996), ix.

50. Whitney, *Life on the Circuit*, 121.

51. Don E. Fehrenbacher and Virginia Fehrenbacher, comps., *Recollected Words of Abraham Lincoln* (Stanford, CA: Stanford UP, 1996), 180.

52. Wayne C. Temple, *Thomas and Abraham Lincoln as Farmers* (Racine: Lincoln Fellowship of Wisconsin; Historical Bulletin 53, 1996): 1–15; "Abraham Lincoln on Agriculture, 1859," in Wayne D. Rasmussen, ed., *Agriculture in the United States: A Documentary History* (New York: Random House, 1975), 1:881–88.

53. John Woods, *Two Year's Residence in the Settlement on the English Prairie in the Illinois Country, United States* . . . (London: Longman, 1922), 211, 252.

54. Alexis de Tocqueville, *Democracy in America* (New York: Harper & Row, 1966), 1:316.

55. Maurice Lindsay, ed., *The Burns Encyclopedia*, 3rd ed. (London: Hale, 1993), 282; T. Crawford, *Burns*, 43–48.

56. "High Prices for Books and Manuscripts," *Scotsman*, March 21, 1907, 8.

57. McIlvanney, *Burns the Radical*, 161.

58. James H. Matheny, quoted in Wilson and Davis, *Herndon's Informants*, 251.

59. "Burns and Abraham Lincoln," *Scotsman*, July 23, 1872, 6.

60. See Craig James Hazen, *The Village Enlightenment in America; Popular Religion and Science in the Nineteenth Century* (Urbana: U of Illinois P, 2000).

61. O. H. Browning, quoted in Burlingame, *Oral History*, 6.

62. Fehrenbacher and Fehrenbacher acknowledge that there is "soft" evidence that Lincoln attended séances (*Recollected Words of Abraham Lincoln* [Stanford, CA: Stanford UP, 1996], 11).

63. The best studies on this theme are Elton Trueblood, *Abraham Lincoln: Theologian of American Anguish* (New York: Harper and Row, 1973), and the superb Allen C. Guelzo, *Abraham Lincoln: Redeemer President* (Grand Rapids, MI: Eerdmans, 1999).

64. Douglas L. Wilson, *Honor's Voice: The Transformation of Abraham Lincoln* (New York: Knopf, 1998), 76–85. Two recent studies take almost opposite tracks. Guelzo's *Abraham Lincoln* stresses Lincoln's Calvinism, while Stewart Lance Winger, *Lincoln, Religion, and Romantic Cultural Politics* (DeKalb: Northern Illinois UP, 2002), argues that Lincoln was deeply influenced by Romanticism.

65. Louis A. Warren, "The Religious Background of the Lincoln Family," *Filson Club History Quarterly* 6 (April 1932): 79–88, esp. 84.

66. Lincoln, quoted in *Lincoln Lore*, December 19, 1955.

67. Mathew Simpson, quoted in *Building the Myth: Selected Speeches Memorializing Abraham Lincoln,* ed. Waldo W. Braden (Urbana: U of Illinois P, 1990), 82.

68. Lincoln to the Baltimore Presbyterian Synod, version 1, Basler, *Collected Works*, 6:535.

69. J. G. Randall to Professor —— [Gardner] Williams, September 20, 1947, Randall Papers, Manuscript Collection, Library of Congress, Washington, DC.

70. MacKay, *Complete Letters*, 118, 140, 153, 174, 178, 181, 199, 427, 431, 459, 466.

71. John H. Leith, "The Westminster Confession in American Presbyterianism," in *The Westminster Confession in the Church Today*, ed. Alasdair I. C. Heron (Edinburgh: St. Andrew Press, 1982), 95–100. See also the discussion of Calvinism in E. Brooks Holifield, *Theology in America: Christian Thought from the Age of the Puritans to the Civil War* (New Haven, CT: Yale UP, 203), 10–13.

72. *The Confession of Faith* (Edinburgh: Free Presbyterian Church of Scotland, 1963), 22–23, 28.

73. Basler, *Collected Works*, 5:479.

74. Shakespeare, *Hamlet*, 2.10.

75. Ronald C. White Jr., *Lincoln's Greatest Speech: The Second Inaugural* (New York: Simon and Schuster, 2002), 122–28; appendix 3, 210; Guelzo, *Abraham Lincoln*, 326–27.

76. W. C. Bitting, "Burns and Religious Matters," in *St. Louis Nichts wi Burns* (St. Louis: Burns Club of St. Louis, 1913), pamphlet, Mitchell Library of Glasgow; George T. Sermon, "The Bible on the Tongue of Lincoln," *Methodist Review* 9 (Jan. 1907): 93–99; Mark A. Noll, *America's God: From Jonathan Edwards to Abraham Lincoln* (New York: Oxford UP, 2002), 426–35.

77. See Merrill D. Peterson, *"This Grand Pertinacity": Abraham Lincoln and the Declaration of Independence* (Fort Wayne, IN: Lincoln Museum, 1991).

78. Sandburg, *Abraham Lincoln*, 2:303.

79. Basler, *Collected Works*, 1:106.

80. Elizabeth Drew, *Poetry: A Modern Guide to Its Understanding and Enjoyment* (New York: Norton, 1959), 240–41.

81. Wilson and Davis, *Herndon's Informants*, 470.

82. Basler, *Collected Works*, 1:271–79.

83. Emanuel Hertz, *Abraham Lincoln: His Favorite Poems and Poets* (n.p.: February 12, 1930); A. G. McKnight, *Lincoln and Burns* (Duluth, MN, 1943), 1–8.

84. Arvarh E. Strickland, "The Illinois Background of Lincoln's Attitude toward Slavery and the Negro," *Illinois State Historical Society Journal* 56 (Autumn 1963): 474–94.

85. Gideon Welles, "The History of Emancipation," *Galaxy* 14 (December 1872): 840. Probably the best study is Guelzo, *Lincoln's Emancipation Proclamation*. See also Kenneth Cmiel, *Democratic Eloquence: The Fight over Popular Speech in Nineteenth-Century America* (Berkeley: U of California P, 1991), 59–60.

86. Congregational Church at Patterson, New Jersey, to Abraham Lincoln, July 4, 1864, Lincoln Papers.

87. Whitney, *Life on the Circuit*, 117.

88. Philip Shaw Paludan, *The Presidency of Abraham Lincoln* (Lawrence: UP of Kansas, 1994), 158.

89. LaWanda Cox, *Lincoln and Black Freedom: A Study in Presidential Leadership* (Urbana: U of Illinois P, 1985), 14; Guelzo, *Lincoln's Emancipation Proclamation*.

90. James G. Randall and Richard N. Current, *Lincoln the President: Last Full Measure*, 1955 (Urbana: U of Illinois P, 2000), 301–2.

91. See the analysis in Harold Holzer, *Lincoln Seen and Heard* (Lawrence: UP of Kansas, 2000): 179–90. An excellent overview is Arthur Zilversmit, "Lincoln and the Problem of Race: A Decade of Interpretations," in *"For a Vast Future Also": Essays from the Journal of the Abraham Lincoln Association*, ed. Thomas F. Schwartz (New York: Fordham UP, 1999): 3–20.

92. Leonard Swett, "A Very Poor Hater," in *Lincoln As I Knew Him*, ed. Harold Holzer (Chapel Hill, NC: Algonquin Books, 1999), 81.

93. William H. Seward, quoted in Jay Monaghan, *Diplomat in Carpet Slippers: Abraham Lincoln Deals with Foreign Affairs* (Indianapolis, IN: Bobbs-Merrill, 1945), 63.

94. John Hay, quoted in Nicolay, *Personal Traits*, 291.

95. David Herbert Donald, *"We Are Lincoln Men": Abraham Lincoln and His Friends* (New York: Simon and Schuster, 2003).

96. Matthew Pinsker, *Lincoln's Sanctuary: Abraham Lincoln and the Soldiers' Home* (New York: Oxford UP, 2003), 5; Wayne C. Temple, *Alexander Williamson: Friend of the Lincolns* (Racine: Lincoln Fellowship of Wisconsin, 1997); O. H. Browning to Isaac N. Arnold, November 25, 1872, Isaac N. Arnold Papers, Chicago Historical Society, Chicago; Noah Brooks, "Personal Recollections of Abraham Lincoln," *Harper's* 31 (1865): 226.

97. Leonard Grover to Abraham Lincoln, September 8, 1863, Abraham Lincoln Papers at the Library of Congress; Leonard Grover, "Lincoln's Interest in the Theatre," *Century* 77 (April 1909): 943–95.

98. See the essays in Roy B. Basler, *A Touchstone for Greatness: Essays, Addresses, and Occasional Pieces about Abraham Lincoln* (Westport, CT: Greenwood, 1973), especially the chapter "Lincoln and Shakespeare."

99. Abraham Lincoln to William Hackett, August 17, 1863, in Basler, *Collected Works*, 6:392; see also 358–59.

100. Fehrenbacher and Fehrenbacher, *Recollected Words*, 46.

101. Isaac N. Arnold, *The History of Abraham Lincoln and the Overthrow of Slavery* (Chicago: Clarke, 1866), 76.

102. David Homer Bates, *Lincoln in the Telegraph Office* (New York: Century, 1907), 223.

103. David Bevington, ed., *The Complete Works of Shakespeare*, 4th ed. (New York: Longman, 1997), 3.2:24–28.

104. Bevington, *Complete Works*, 3.2:15–17.

105. Bevington, *Complete Works*, 3.2:155–60.

106. Bevington, *Complete Works*, 1.1:1–4.

107. Bevington, *Complete Works*, 3.3:65–69. See also Robert Berkelman, "Lincoln's Interest in Shakespeare," *Shakespeare Quarterly* 2, no. 4 (1951): 303–12.

108. William A. Slade, "Abraham Lincoln's Shakespeare," typescript, James G. Randall Papers. See also David Chambers Means, "'Act Well Your Part': Being the Story of Mr. Lincoln and the Theatre," in Means, *Largely Lincoln* (New York: St. Martin's, 1961); Frank Kenmore, *Shakespeare's Language* (London: Penguin, 2000), Harold Bloom, *Shakespeare: The Invention of the Human* (New York: Riverhead, 1998), and R. Gerald McMurtry, "Lincoln Knew Shakespeare," *Indiana Magazine of History* 31 (December 1935): 265–87. Also consult Harkness and McMurtry, *Lincoln's Favorite Poets*, 25, and Luther Emerson Robinson, *Abraham Lincoln as a Man of Letters* (New York: Putnam's, 1923), 202–3.

109. James G. Randall to William A. Slade, October 14, 1943, Randall Papers.

110. Daniel Kilham Dodge, *Abraham Lincoln: Master of Words* (Urbana: U of Illinois P, 2000); Roy P. Basler, "Abraham Lincoln's Rhetoric," *American Literature* 11 (May 1939): 167–79.

111. Nicolson, *God's Secretaries*, 77.

112. Garry Wills, *Lincoln at Gettysburg: The Words That Remade America* (New York: Simon and Schuster, 1992), 177–89.

113. Arnold, *History of Abraham Lincoln*, 61.

114. Owen Barfield, *Poetic Diction: A Study in Meaning*, 1928 (New York: McGraw-Hill, 1964), 145.

115. R. V. Bieder, "Lincoln's Power of Expression," *Methodist Review* 83 (September 1901): 695, 698, 700; Basler, *Touchstone*; Lord Charnwood, *Abraham Lincoln* (Garden City, NY: Garden City, 1917).

116. Marianne Moore, "Abraham Lincoln and the Art of the Word," in *Lincoln for the Ages,* Ralph G. Newman, ed. (Garden City, NY: Doubleday, 1960), 382.

117. Herbert Joseph Edwards and John Erskine Hankins, *Lincoln the Writer: The Development of His Literary Style* (Orono: UP of Maine, 1962).

118. Carl Schurz, *Abraham Lincoln: An Essay* (Boston: Houghton Mifflin, 1891), 104; Lucas E. Morel has used Douglass's observation as the title of his book *Lincoln's Sacred Effort: Defining Religion's Role in American Self-Government* (Lanham: Lexington Books, 2000).

119. W. S., "Abraham Lincoln a Poet," *Notes and Queries*, 3rd series, 7 (April 15, 1865): 297.

120. Theodore L. Cuyler in *Abraham Lincoln: Tributes from His Associates* (New York: Crowell, 1895), 128. See also Herbert Joseph Edwards and John Erskine Hankins, *Lincoln the Writer: The Development of His Literary Style* (Orono: UP of Maine, 1962); White, *Lincoln's Greatest Speech*; and White, *Eloquent President*.

121. I borrow this phrase from Jason Cowley's "Beautiful but Damned," *Guardian Weekly*, April 27–May 3 2000, 17.

122. Douglas L. Wilson, *Lincoln's Sword: The Presidency and the Power of Words* (New York: Knopf, 2006).

123. James M. McPherson, *Abraham Lincoln and the Second American Revolution* (New York: Oxford UP, 1990), 108.

4. Scottish Émigrés and Scottish Ideas in Lincoln's World

1. Figures from Roland Tappan Berthoff, *British Immigrants in Industrial America, 1790–1950* (Cambridge, MA: Harvard UP, 1953), 7.

2. Charlotte Erickson, *Invisible Immigrants: The Adaptation of English and Scottish Immigrants in Nineteenth-Century America* (Ithaca: Cornell UP, 1972). See also Calder, *Scots in the USA*.

3. Francis MacManus, "The Two Languages of Abe Lincoln," *Irish Press*, May 11, 1963. A good analysis of his youth may be found in Douglas L. Wilson, *Lincoln before Washington: New Perspectives on the Illinois Years* (Urbana: U of Illinois P, 1997), 133–48.

4. W. M. Butler, in Burlingame, *Oral History*, 20.

5. Basler, *Collected Works*, 1:1.

6. Basler, *Collected Works*, 3:203–4.

7. William W. Betts Jr., ed., *Lincoln and the Poets* (Pittsburgh, PA: U of Pittsburgh P, 1965), xix; Donald, *"We Are Lincoln Men,"* 68.

8. Two solid studies of this theme may be found in Robert V. Bruce, *Lincoln and The Riddle of Death* (Fort Wayne, IN: Louis A. Warren Lincoln Library and Museum, 1981), and Douglas L. Wilson, "Abraham Lincoln's Indiana and the Sprit of Mortal," *Indiana Magazine of History* 87 (June 1991): 155–70.

9. Ecclesiastes 1:9, King James Version; verse 9, "Mortality," Maurice Boyd, *William Knox and Abraham Lincoln: The Story of a Poetic Legacy* (Denver: Sage Books, 1966), vii–ix; and David J. Harkness and R. Gerald McMurtry, *Lincoln's Favorite Poets* (Knoxville: U of Tennessee P, 1959).

10. Basler, *Collected Works*, 1:378–9.

11. *Scotsman*, April 19, 1927, 11; Boyd, *William Knox and Abraham Lincoln*, xxviii.

12. *Scotsman*, June 7, 1905, 11; *Scotsman*, June 9, 1905, 7.

13. "A Century of Scottish Song," *Scotsman*, February 24, 1896, 9.

14. *Lincoln Lore*, April 5, 1937.

15. *Scotsman*, June 6, 1905, 7.

16. *Scotsman*, June 7, 1905, 11.

17. *Scotsman*, April 19, 1927, 11. For a fuller discussion of Lincoln's depressions, see Joshua Wolf Shenk, *Lincoln's Melancholy: How Depression Challenged a President and Fueled His Greatness* (Boston: Houghton Mifflin, 2005).

18. Boyd, *William Knox and Abraham Lincoln*, xxxvi.

19. Lawrence Weldon, "Leaders of the Illinois Bar," in *Reminiscences of Abraham Lincoln*, ed. A. T. Rice (New York: North American Review, 1888), 139.

20. Gerald Emanuel Stearn and Albert Fried, quoted in MacManus, "Two Languages," *Irish Press*, May 11, 1963; conversation with Wayne C. Temple, summer 2001.

21. Holzer, *Lincoln As I Knew Him*, 20–21; Basler, *Collected Works*, 1:367–70.

22. Basler, *Collected Works*, 1:386. On July 19, 1863, in response to the Battle of Gettysburg, Lincoln penned a last bit of doggerel and triumphantly showed it to secretary John Hay.

General Lee's invasion of the North written by himself—
In eighteen sixty three, with pomp
and mighty swell,
Me and Jeff's confederacy, went
forth to sack Phil-del.
The Yankees they got after us, and
give us particular hell,
And we skedaddled back again,
and didn't sack Phil-del.
(Douglas Wilson, *Lincoln's Sword*, 104)

23. Basler, *Collected Works*, 3:203.

24. Earl W. Haytes, "Sources of Early Illinois Culture," in *Transactions of the Illinois State Historical Society for 1936* (Springfield: Illinois State Historical Society, 1937): 94–95.

25. James D. Smith III, "The Pilgrimage of James Smith (1798–1871): Scottish Infidel, Southern Evangelist, and Lincoln's Springfield Pastor," *American Presbyterians* 66 (Fall 1988): 147–56.

26. *The Evidences of Christianity: A Debate between Robert Owen, of New Lanmark, Scotland, and Alexander Campbell, President of Bethany Coll., Va., Containing an Examination of the "Social System" and All the Systems of Skepticism of Ancient and Modern Times* (St. Louis, MO: Christian Board of Publication, n.d., ca. 1830).

27. James Smith, *The Christian's Defense, Containing a Fair Statement, and Impartial Examination of the Leading Objections Urged by Infidels against the Antiquity, Genuineness, Credibility and Inspiration of the Holy Scripture; Enriched with Copius Extracts from Learned Authors*, 2 vols. (Cincinnati, OH: J. A. James, 1843), ii.

28. John H. Littlefield, quoted in Holzer, *Lincoln As I Knew Him*, 76.

29. Reverend William Bishop, quoted in William E. Barton, *The Soul of Abraham Lincoln* (New York: George H. Doran, 1920), 160.

30. *Lincoln Lore*, August 1966; Barton, *Soul of Abraham Lincoln*, 165.

31. See the lengthy Smith quotation in Barton, *Soul of Abraham Lincoln*, 163.

32. James Delany to Abraham Lincoln, October 1863, Lincoln Papers. See also Noll, *America's God*. Noll finds a preeminent Calvinist presence in early America.

33. James A. Smith, quoted in *Chicago Tribune*, March 6, 1867.

34. *Chicago Tribune*, March 6, 1867.

35. *Lincoln Lore*, August 1966. The most penetrating analysis remains Harry V. Jaffa, *Crisis of the House Divided: An Interpretation of the Issues in the Lincoln-Douglas Debates* (1959; repr., Seattle: U of Washington P, 1973).

36. Don C. Seitz, *The James Gordon, Bennetts, Father and Son, Proprieters of the* New York Herald (Indianapolis, IN: Bobbs-Merrill, 1928), 171.

37. James L. Crouthamel, *Bennett's* New York Herald *and the Rise of the Popular Press* (Syracuse: Syracuse UP, 1989), 56; William A. Croffut, "Bennett and His Times," *Atlantic Monthly*, February 1931, 204.

38. Croffut, "Bennett and His Times," 199; Douglas Fermer, *James Gordon Bennett and the* New York Herald: *A Study of Editorial Opinion in the Civil War Era, 1854–1867* (New York: St. Martin's Press, 1986), 317–18.

39. Cited in Crouthamel, *Bennett's*, 79; John C. Waugh, *Reelecting Lincoln: The Battle for the 1864 Presidency* (New York: Crown, 1997), 140, 304, 324.

40. Abraham Lincoln to James G. Bennett, May 21, 1862, Basler, *Collected Works*, 5:225–26; Abraham Lincoln to Salmon P. Chase, Basler, *Collected Works*, 4:357.

41. Crouthamel, *Bennett's*, 121; Fermer, *James Gordon Bennett*, 214–15.

42. Abraham Lincoln to Abram Wakeman, July 25, 1864, Basler, *Collected Works*, 7:461.

43. Robert S. Harper, *Lincoln and the Press* (New York: McGraw-Hill, 1951), 318–24.

44. James A. Perry, *A Bohemian Brigade: The Civil War Correspondents—Mostly Rough, Sometimes Ready* (New York: Wiley, 2000), 49; 53–55.

45. See "John Watt," Mr. Lincoln's White House, at http://www.mrlincolns whitehouse.org/content-inside.asp?ID=68&csubjectID=2 (accessed February 2, 2006).

46. Jennifer Fleischner, *Mrs. Lincoln and Mrs. Keckly: The Remarkable Story of the Friendship between a First Lady and a Former Slave* (New York: Broadway Books, 2003), 223–25; Ruth Painter Randall, *Mary Lincoln: Biography of a Marriage* (Boston: Little, Brown, 1953), 254–55, 304; Basler, *Collected Works*, 5:25.

47. William Howard Russell, *My Diary North and South* (New York: Harper, 1954): 23; Washington, D.C., *Sunday Chronicle*, March 7, 1869; see the interview with Williamson, included in its entirety, in Temple, *Alexander Williamson*, 31.

48. Temple, *Alexander Williamson*, 21–31.

49. Justin G. Turner and Linda Levitt Turner, eds., *Mary Todd Lincoln: Her Life and Letters* (New York: Knopf, 1972), 260–63; Mary Todd Lincoln to Alexander Williamson, June 29, 1866, ibid., 314.

50. Mary Todd Lincoln to Alexander Williamson, June 29, 1866, in ibid., 374; see also editors' comment, 338n. The only account of Williamson's career is Temple's pamphlet *Alexander Williamson*.

51. Frank Morn's *"The Eye That Never Sleeps": A History of the Pinkerton National Detective Agency* (Bloomington: Indiana UP, 1982) is a solid biography.

52. Victor Searcher, *Lincoln's Journey to Greatness: A Factual Recount of the Twelve-Day Inaugural Trip* (Philadelphia: Winston, 1960), 249–60, believes the plot was genuine.

53. James MacKay, *Allan Pinkerton: The First Private Eye* (New York: Wiley, 1996), 97; 103.

54. Smith Stimmel, "Experiences as a Member of President Lincoln's Body Guard, 1863–65," *North Dakota Historical Quarterly* 1 (1926): 27–33.

55. Allan Pinkerton, *The Spy of the Rebellion* (1883; rpt. Lincoln: U of Nebraska P, 1989), 65–67, and passim.

56. Lawrence Weldon in *Reminiscences of Abraham Lincoln*, ed. A. T. Rice, 113; *Lincoln Lore*, October 1956; Shaw, *Abraham Lincoln*, 252–54. For an excellent collection of images, see Gary L. Bunker, *From Rail-Splitter to Icon: Lincoln's Image in Illustrated Periodicals, 1860–1865* (Kent, OH: Kent State UP, 2001), and Mark E. Neely Jr. and Harold Holzer, eds., *The Union Image: Popular Prints of the Civil War North* (Chapel Hill: U of North Carolina P, 2000).

57. Allan Pinkerton, *History and Evidence of the Passage of Abraham Lincoln from Harrisburg, PA., on the Twenty-second and Twenty-third of February: Eighteen hundred and Sixty-one* (n.p.: 1868), 10–13, 24–26 (copy, Scottish National Library).

58. For a superb history of Scotland, see T. M. Devine, *The Scottish Nation, 1700–2000* (London: Lane, Penguin Press, 1999).

59. T. M. Devine, *Scotland's Empire and the Shaping of the Americas, 1600–1815* (Washington, DC: Smithsonian Books, 2003).

60. T. C. MacMillan, "The Scots and Their Descendants in Illinois," 71–73.

61. William Todd, *The Seventy-ninth Highlanders, New York Volunteers in the War of Rebellion, 1861–1865* (Albany, NY: Press of Brandow, 1886), 6.

62. Todd, *Seventy-ninth Highlanders*, 499; United States War Department, *The War of the Rebellion: A Compilation of the Official Records of the Union*

and Confederate Armies, series 1, vol. 2 (Washington, DC: GPO, 1880), 2:314; 351; 368–70.

63. Julia Taft Bayne, *Tad Lincoln's Father* (Lincoln: U of Nebraska P, 2001), 62–63.

64. Tony Mandara, "Thank God Lincoln Had Only One 79th Highlander Regiment," *Crossfire* 67, December 2001, http://www.americancivilwar.org. uk/articles/highlanders.htm (accessed February 2, 2006).

65. Alexander Campbell, quoted in *"Him on the One Side and Me on the Other": The Civil War Letters of Alexander Campbell, 79th New York Infantry Regiment, and James Campbell, 1st South Carolina Battalion*, ed. Terry A. Johnson Jr. (Columbia: U of South Carolina P, 1999), 92. Johnson has masterfully collected the letters of the two Scots brothers in this volume; see especially 1–11. Walter J. Taylor, "Scots and the American Civil War," *Highlander* 41 (November/December 2003): 14–18; Todd, *Seventy-ninth Highlanders*, 122, 142, 160.

66. *Scottish American Journal*, April 22, 1865; April 29, 1865; May 13, 1865.

67. A succinct summary may be found in *The Oxford Companion to Scottish History*, ed. Michael Lynch (Oxford: Oxford UP, 2001), 436–437; 439–441; and Robert W. Scribner, Roy Porter, and Mikulás Teich, eds., *The Reformation in National Context* (Cambridge: Cambridge UP, 1994), 107.

68. C. B. Boynton, *Discourse by Reverend C. B. Boynton for National Thanksgiving Services Held on Thanksgiving December 7, 1865 in the Hall of the House of Representatives of the United States of America* (Washington, DC: Morrison, 1865), 14–16.

69. Marilyn J. Westerkamp, *Triumph of the Laity: Scots-Irish Piety and the Great Awakening, 1625–1700* (New York: Oxford, 1988); Leigh Eric Schmidt, *Holy Fairs: Scottish Communions and American Revivals in the Early Modern Period* (Princeton, NJ: Princeton UP, 1989).

70. J. H. Thornwell, "Our National Sins," in *Fast Day Sermons: Or the Pulpit on the State of the Country* (New York: Rudd and Carleton, 1861), 33.

71. Lowell H. Harrison, *Lincoln of Kentucky* (Lexington: UP of Kentucky, 2000), shows how Lincoln's early contacts were almost all Kentucky based. See also John F. Cady, "The Religious Environment of Lincoln's Youth," *Indiana Magazine of History* 37 (March 1941): 16–30; and Harry Thomas Stock, "Protestantism in Illinois before 1835," *Illinois State Historical Society Journal* 12 (April 1919): 1–31.

72. Kim Bauer (archivist, Illinois State Historical Library, Springfield, Illinois), discussion with the author, Summer 2001.

73. *Fast Day Sermons*, viii.

74. For example, see Alonzo Potter to Abraham Lincoln, April, 1864; William B. Edwards and M. Simpson to Abraham Lincoln, March 10, 1863; Byron Sunderland to Abraham Lincoln, May 4, 1864, Abraham Lincoln Papers.

75. Alonzo Potter to Abraham Lincoln, September 27, 1862, Abraham Lincoln Papers

76. This theme is superbly analyzed by Garry Wills, *Lincoln at Gettysburg: The Words That Remade America* (New York: Simon and Schuster, 1992), and Guelzo, *Abraham Lincoln: Redeemer President*.

77. Beale, *Diary of Edward Bates*, 393.

78. Wills, *Lincoln at Gettysburg*, 184.

79. James G. Randall Papers.

80. *Lincoln Lore*, November 25, 1929; see also Louis A. Warren, *Little Known Facts about Thanksgiving* (Fort Wayne, IN: Lincoln National Life Insurance, 1939), and George William Douglas, *The American Book of Days* (New York: Wilson, 1948), 231.

81. John A. Andrew to Abraham Lincoln, April 11, 1865; Reuben E. Fenton, April 11, 1865; Sarah J. Hale to Abraham Lincoln, September 28, 1863, Abraham Lincoln Papers.

82. *Scotsman*, April 17, 1847, 2.

83. John W. Blassingame, ed., *The Frederick Douglass Papers* (New Haven, CT: Yale UP, 1979) 1:195–241.

84. *Scotsman*, May 11, 1853, 2.

85. *Scotsman*, December 24, 1889, 5.

86. *Scotsman*, July 2, 1896, 5.

87. *Scotsman*, July 2, 1896, 5.

88. *Scotsman*, September 7, 1860.

89. *Scotsman*, September 7, 1860, 2.

90. *Scotsman*, October 28, 1863, 2.

91. *Scotsman*, November 14, 1864, 3.

92. *Scotsman*, December 14, 1864, 2.

93. Joseph Frazier Wall, *Andrew Carnegie* (1970; repr., Pittsburgh: U of Pittsburg P, 1989), 182–86; R. J. M. Blackett, *Divided Hearts: Britain and the American Civil War* (Baton Rouge: Louisiana State UP, 2001), 4.

94. Quoted in *Scottish American Journal*, January 28, 1865.

95. The Comte de Paris, "The Civil War in America," *Blackwood's Magazine*, August 1874, 221.

96. *Historical Aspects of New Milns* (Ayrshire, Scotland: Walker and Connell, 1990): 1–10.

97. Ferenc M. Szasz, "Scotland, Abraham Lincoln, and the American Civil War," *Northern Scotland* 16 (1996): 127–40.

98. Ferenc M. Szasz, "The Wisconsin Scot Reports on the American Civil War—Part 1," *Milwaukee History* 17 (Summer 1994): 34–50; "The Wisconsin Scot Reports on the American Civil War—Part 2," *Milwaukee History* (Autumn–Winter 1994): 88–103.

99. *Scotsman*, 27 November 1863, 4.

100. *Scotsman*, 27 November 1863, 2.

101. *Scotsman*, 15 October 1863, 3.

102. *Glasgow Daily Herald*, 5 May 1865, 6 May 1865.

103. *Scotsman*, 3 May 1865, 7.

104. *Glasgow Herald*, 27 May 1865.

105. *Scotsman*, 27 April 1865, 2.

106. *Glasgow Herald*, 27 April 1865.

107. *Scotsman*, 3 May 1865, 7.

108. *Glasgow Herald*, 3 May 1865.

109. *Scotsman*, 3 May 1865.

110. *Scotsman*, 4 May 1865, 6.

111. *Scotsman*, 10 May 1865, 7.

5. Burns and Lincoln in Historical Memory

1. *Scotsman*, 28 July 1884, 4.

2. *Scotsman*, 14 November 1900, 8.

3. Reinhard H. Luthin, *The Real Abraham Lincoln: A Complete One Volume History of His Life and Times* (Englewood Cliffs, NJ: Prentice-Hall, 1960), 391.

4. Joseph H. Barrett, *Life of Abraham Lincoln* (New York: Loomis National Library Association, 1888), 18, 839.

5. F. B. Carpenter, *The Inner Life of Abraham Lincoln: Six Months at the White House* (New York: Hurd and Houghton, 1869), 114.

6. Review of *The Valley of Shadows: Recollections of the Lincoln Country, 1858–1863*, by Francis Grierson, *New York Times*, August 21, 1909.

7. Barton, *Life of Abraham Lincoln*, 1:70–75; *Scotsman*, February 25, 1926, 7.

8. Hamilton Wright Mabie, "Burns, the Poet of Democracy," *North American Review* 189 (1909): 347.

9. Raymond Bentman, "Robert Burns's Declining Fame," *Studies in Romanticism* 2 (Summer 1972): 207–25.

10. Joseph H. Choate, *Abraham Lincoln and Other Addresses in England* (New York: Century, 1910).

11. *Scotsman*, November 14, 1900, 8.

12. James S. Ewing, quoted in Angle, *Abraham Lincoln by Some Men Who Knew Him*, 47.

13. "America: Lincoln Centenary," *Scotsman*, February 13, 1909.

14. *Scotsman*, February 13, 1909, 9.

15. "Tribute to Abraham Lincoln," http://www.hayleycourt.com/bruce.htm.

16. *Reader's Guide*, 1905–1909; *New Mexico Department of Education, New Mexico Common School Course of Study* (Albuquerque: Press of the Morning Journal, 1911), 127–28.

17. *Scottish American*, July 2, 1896; January 27, 1909.

18. Andrew Carnegie, *Autobiography of Andrew Carnegie* (London: Constable, 1920), 101–2; *Burns Chronicle* 22 (January 1913): 76.

19. Szasz, "Scotland, Abraham Lincoln, and the American Civil War," 136.

20. *Scots Magazine* 12 (June–November, 1893): 375.

21. *Edinburgh Evening Dispatch*, May 5, 1893.

22. "Edinburgh Memorial of American Civil War," *Scotsman*, May 31, 1912, 6; "American Editors in Edinburgh," *Scotsman*, September 17, 1918, 3.

23. "Completion of Ayr Burns Statue," *Scotsman*, August 22, 1895, 6; "The Burns Cottage Association at St. Louis Exhibition," *Scotsman*, September 2, 1902, 6.

24. *Scotsman*, February 12, 1917, 7.

25. "Lincoln Statue," *Scotsman*, July 29, 1920, 5.

26. "Burns in America," *Scotsman*, August 7, 1920, 7.

27. Duluth *Herald*, June 19, 1950.

28. Duluth *Herald*, June 1, 1935; Duluth *News Tribune*, February 1, 1928.

29. Duluth *News Tribune*, January 19, 1941.

30. Duluth *Herald*, April 6, 1934.

31. Duluth *Herald*, June 23, 1939.

32. Duluth *Herald*, June 19, 1950.

33. A. G. McKnight to Helen Nicolay, April 21, 1947, Burns folder, Lincoln Museum Research Library, Fort Wayne, Indiana.

34. A. G. McKnight to L. A. Warren, December 19, 1941, Burns folder, Lincoln National Life Library; Herbert L. Grave to James G. Randall, August 22, 1945, Lincoln National Life Library; and J. G. Randall to William A. Slade, October 14, 1943, box 10, J. G. Randall Family Papers.

35. A. G. McKnight, "Robert Burns: The Poet of Liberalism," pamphlet reprint, *Quarterly of American Interprofessional Institute* (December 1929): 12. See also A. G. McKnight, *Lincoln and Burns* (Duluth, 1943).

36. DeLancey Ferguson, *Pride and Passion: Robert Burns, 1759–1796* (1939; repr., New York: Russell and Russell, 1964), ix; Celeste Ray, *Highland Heritage: Scottish Americans in the American South* (Chapel Hill: U of North Carolina P, 2001), 52.

37. Doris H. Hamilton, "'For Auld Lang Syne'—and Robert Burns," *Hobbies*, January 1959, 111; *Robert Burns, 1759–1959, a Bicentenary List of Current Books and New Publications on or by Our National Bard, with Several Important Works Announced for the First Time* (n.p.: John Grant, 1959) (copy at Scottish National Library, Edinburgh).

38. *Scotsman*, January 26, 1959.

39. *Scotsman*, January 26, 1959.

40. J. D. Ross, *Burnsiana*, 74.

41. On this theme, see Braden, ed., *Building the Myth*; McKnight, *America's Appreciation of Robert Burns*; Paul Connerton, *How Societies Remember*

(Cambridge: Cambridge UP, 1989): 1–5, 16; *Representations* 26 (Spring 1989); and David Gross, *Lost Time: On Remembering and Forgetting in Late Modern Culture* (Amherst: U of Massachusetts P, 2000).

42. Undated newspaper clipping, scrapbook 3, Burnsiana, Shaw Collection.

43. *Weekly Scotsman*, August 15, 1936.

44. John Cairney, *On the Trail of Robert Burns* (Edinburgh: Luath Press, 2000); John G. Gray and Charles J. Smith, *A Walk on the Southside in the Footsteps of Robert Burns* (Edinburgh: Southside Museum, 1998).

45. "Children as Pilgrims to Lincoln Shrines in Springfield, Illinois, Learn Lessons of Patriotism," *Journal of the Illinois State Historical Society* 17 (January 1925): 736–40.

46. "Abraham Lincoln Birthplace," pamphlet, National Park Service.

47. Fern Nance Pond, "Lincoln's New Salem Restored," *DAR Magazine*, February 1952, 113–17; and Evelyn Taylor, *Lincoln's New Salem: A Village Reborn* (Salem, IL: New Salem Lincoln League, 1994).

48. Don Davenport, *In Lincoln's Footsteps: A Historical Guide to the Lincoln Sites in Illinois, Indiana, and Kentucky* (Madison, WI: Prairie Oak Press, 1991).

49. Ralph Gary, *Following in Lincoln's Footsteps: A Complete Annotated Reference to Hundreds of Historical Sites Visited by Abraham Lincoln* (New York: Carroll and Graf, 2001).

50. Christopher A. Thomas, *The Lincoln Memorial and American Life* (Princeton, NJ: Princeton UP, 2002), presents a thorough discussion of the monument. See also Merrill D. Peterson, *Lincoln in American Memory* (New York: Oxford UP, 1994), 214–18.

51. C. A. Thomas, *Lincoln Memorial*, xviii.

52. Mary Gilchrist, quoted in Ferenc M. Szasz, "Symbolizing the Scottish-American Connection: The Statues of Robert Burns in Denver and Cheyenne," *Annals of Wyoming* 72 (Winter 2000): 5.

53. Goodwillie, *World's Memorials*, xv.

54. *Scotsman*, October 17, 1898 (repr. Edinburgh *Evening News*, August 9, 1961).

55. Undated newspaper clipping (ca. 1920), scrapbook 3, box 1665, Burnsiana, Shaw Collection.

56. Quoted in John Cairney, ed., *Immortal Memories* (Edinburgh: Luath Press, 2003), 174.

57. "Programs of the Marches," box 551, George F. Black Collection, Special Collections, Florida State University, Tallahassee, Florida.

58. Newspaper clipping, scrapbook 3, box 551, folder 26, George F. Black Collection.

59. F. Lauriston Bullard, *Lincoln in Marble and Bronze* (New Brunswick, NJ: Rutgers UP, 1952), 1–3; *Lincoln Lore*, February 1962.

60. Frederick C. Moffat, *Errant Bronzes: George Grey Barnard's Statues of Abraham Lincoln* (Newark: U of Delaware P, 1998).

61. *Lincolnian* 23, May–June 2003, 8.

62. Robert M. Lester, *Forty Years of Carnegie Giving: A Summary of the Benefactions of Andrew Carnegie and of the Work of the Philanthropic Trusts Which He Created* (New York: Charles Scribner's, 1941), 93.

63. Tom LaMarre, "Lincoln Treasures: Numismatic Collectibles of 'Old,'" *Coins* July 1999: 46–55; Carl Sandburg, quoted in LaMarre, "Lincoln Treasures," 53.

64. Gary M. Brown (proprietor, Bisbee Coin and Paper, Bisbee, Arizona), in discussion with author, March 2006.

65. *Scottish-American Journal*, November 23, 1867.

66. Charles R. Cushman, ed., *Memorial Addresses Delivered before the Two Houses of Congress on the Life and Character of Abraham Lincoln, James Garfield, William McKinley* (Washington, DC: GPO, 1903); Richard Nelson Current, *Abraham Lincoln: The Man and His Meaning for Our Times* (Urbana: U of Illinois P, 1983).

67. Michael Davis, *The Image of Lincoln in the South* (Knoxville: U of Tennessee P, 1971), 119–20.

68. "Letter from Charleston, SC, February 12, 1866," *Farmers' Cabinet* March 1, 1866, 2, Early American Newspapers.

69. "Abraham Lincoln," *Farmers' Cabinet*, April 19, 1866, Early American Newspapers.

70. G. W. Douglas, *American Book of Days*, 92–98.

71. See also Frank J. Williams, "Lincoln Collection: What's Left?" in *Judging Lincoln*, by Frank J. Williams (Carbondale: Southern Illinois UP, 2002), 163–77.

72. "Some Burns Collectors of My Acquaintance," (1902, unsigned), box 551, folder 26, George F. Black Collection.

73. J. A. Mackay, *Complete Letters*, appendix 2, "The Forgeries of Burns Manuscripts by 'Antique' Smith," 762. Two solid accounts of this affair are J. DeLancey Ferguson, "Antique Smith and His Forgeries of Robert Burns," *Colophon* 13 (1933): 1–20, and William Roughead, *The Riddle of the Ruthvens and Other Studies* (Edinburgh: Green, 1919): 147–70.

74. Davidson Cook, *Scotsman* (ca. 1925). scrapbook 3, Shaw Collection.

75. John S. Clark, "Forgeries of Burns Manuscripts: The Cause Célèbre of 'Antique Smith,'" *Burns Chronicle and Club Directory* 41 (1941): 26; See also Henry T. Scott, *Autograph Collecting* (London: Upcott Gill, 1894), chapter 22.

76. *Evening Dispatch*, June 25, 1898; *Scottish Law Reporter* 30 (1893): 488–98, contains a record of the trial. The Edinburgh Public Library holds most of the forgeries. See also the coverage in the *Scotsman*, June 27, 1893, 7, and December 19, 1892, 8.

77. Don E. Fehrenbacher, *Lincoln in Text and Context: Collected Essays* (Stanford: Stanford UP, 1987), esp. chap. 18, "The Minor Affair: An Adventure in Forgery and Detection"; "The Discovery: A New Storehouse of Lincoln Material," *Atlantic Monthly*, December 1928, 834–37; Wilma Frances Minor, "Lincoln the Lover: 1, the Setting—New Salem," *Atlantic Monthly*, December 1928, 838–55; "2, the Courtship," January 1929, 1–14; "3, the Tragedy," February 1929, 215–25.

78. "Lincoln the Lover," *Motion Picture Magazine*, March 1914, 95–100.

79. Fehrenbacher, *Lincoln in Text*, 261; Paul M. Angle, "The Minor Collection: A Criticism," *Atlantic Monthly*, January–June 1929, 516–25.

80. *New York Times*, February 8, 1934. Some sources give Joseph Cosey's real name as Martin Coneely (1887–1950?), but that, too, is uncertain. See also *Collector*, October 1947, 665, and *Evening Bulletin*, February 11, 1967 (copy in "Forgeries" file, Lincoln National Life Foundation). See also S. Moyerman to L. A. Warren, September 20, 1940, Lincoln National Life Foundation, and *Collectors Journal*, June 1934, 496.

81. John Kobler, "Trailing the Book Crooks," *Saturday Evening Post*, March 13, 1943, 18–19, 103.

82. *New York Times*, February 8, 1934. See also Charles Hamilton, *Great Forgers and Famous Fakes*, 2nd ed. (Lakewood, CO: Glenbridge, 1996).

83. *Fort Wayne Journal-Gazette*, February 10, 1962.

84. The three best books on this phenomenon are Lloyd Lewis, *Myths after Lincoln* (New York: Press of the Readers Club, 1929), Barry Schwartz, *Abraham Lincoln and the Forge of National Memory* (Chicago: U of Chicago P, 2000), and Peterson, *Lincoln in American Memory*.

85. Rankin, *Personal Recollections*, 388–89; William Howard Taft, quoted in "Washington Mecca for Lincoln Admirers," press release 428, J. G. Randall Family Papers; Carl Sandburg, quoted in *New York Times*, December 17, 1939.

86. Goodwillie, *World's Memorials to Robert Burns*, xi; Wallace Bruce, quoted in J. D. Ross, *Burnsiana*, 19.

87. *Scotsman*, January 25, 1892; January 30, 1932.

88. Carl Van Doren, "The Poetical Cult of Lincoln," *Nation*, May 17, 1919, 777.

89. Newspaper clipping, 13 February 1964, author's collection.

90. Donald MacMillan, *Burns and the War: His Message to the Nation* (Glasgow, 1917).

91. Undated newspaper clipping, scrapbook 3, box 1665, Burnsiana, Shaw Collection.

92. Peter Esslemont, *Brithers A': A Minute a Day with Burns* (Aberdeen: Avery, 1943), preface.

93. *Scotsman*, September 9, 1935, 15.

94. Ian McIntyre, *Robert Burns: A Life* (London: Penguin Books, 2001), 433–36; 443–44.

95. Hugh MacDiarmid, "The Burns Cult," in *At the Sign of the Thistle: A Collection of Essays*, by MacDiarmid (London: Nott, 1934), 168.

96. David B. Morris, "Burns and Heteroglossia," *Eighteenth Century* 28 (1987): 3. See also Mary Ellen Brown, *Burns and Tradition* (Urbana: U of Illinois P, 1984), 140–46, and Suzanne Gilbert, "Recovering Burns's Lyric Legacy: Teaching Burns in American Universities," *Studies in Scottish Literature*, 30 (1998): 137–45.

97. Noble and Hogg, *Canongate Burns*, 1:xciv; R. Crawford, *Devolving*, 88, 89–110.

98. It is interesting to note the paucity of African American or southern White voices in Braden, *Building the Myth*.

99. Benjamin Rush Plumly to Abraham Lincoln, January 1, 1863, Abraham Lincoln Papers.

100. Charles Carleton Coffin, "Lincoln's First Nomination and His Visit to Richmond in 1865," in A. T. Rice, *Reminiscences of Abraham Lincoln*, 184–86.

101. Noah Brooks, "The Close of Lincoln's Career," *Century* 50 (May 1895): 21.

102. Gideon Welles, quoted in Richard S. West Jr., *Gideon Welles: Lincoln's Navy Department* (Indianapolis, IN: Bobbs-Merrill, 1943), 320.

103. Benjamin Quarles, *Lincoln and the Negro* (New York: Oxford UP, 1962), foreword, 245; Gabor S. Boritt, ed., *The Lincoln Enigma: The Changing Faces of An American Icon* (New York: Oxford UP, 2001), 305–6.

104. See Scott A. Sandage, "A Marble House Divided: The Lincoln Memorial, the Civil Rights Movement, and the Politics of Memory, 1939–1963," *Journal of American History* 80 (June 1993): 135–67; George M. Fredrickson, "A Man but Not a Brother: Abraham Lincoln and Racial Equality," *Journal of Southern History* 41 (1975): 39–58; Allen C. Guelzo, *Lincoln's Emancipation Proclamation: The End of Slavery in America* (New York: Simon and Schuster, 2004), 247.

105. Lerone Bennett Jr., *Forced into Glory: Abraham Lincoln's White Dream* (Chicago: Johnson, 2000).

106. B. Schwartz, *Abraham Lincoln*, 10; R. R. Wright, "Abraham Lincoln's Birthday," in Ward, *Abraham Lincoln*, 185–86.

107. Harold Holzer, *Lincoln at Cooper Union: The Speech That Made Abraham Lincoln President* (New York: Simon and Schuster, 2004), 30–31.

108. Boritt, *Lincoln Enigma*; Boritt, letter to the editor, *Washington Post* (February 22, 2003).

109. Paludan, *Presidency of Abraham Lincoln*, 19; James Oakes, *The Radical and the Republican: Frederick Douglass, Abraham Lincoln, and the Triumph of Anti-slavery Politics* (New York: Norton, 2007).

110. Guelzo, *Lincoln's Emancipation Proclamation*, 3–10.

111. Abraham Lincoln to A. G. Hodges, April 4, 1864; Basler, *Collected Works*, 7, 282.

112. See James F. Simon, *Lincoln and Chief Justice Taney: Slavery, Secession and the President's War Powers* (New York: Simon and Schuster, 2006).

113. Guelzo, *Lincoln's Emancipation Proclamation*, 7.

114. Carpenter, *Inner Life*, 90.

115. Ved Mehta, *The Fly and the Fly-bottle: Encounters with British Intellectuals* (Baltimore: Penguin, 1965), 93–161.

116. Carpenter, *Inner Life*, 208–9.

117. "Late Scenes in Richmond," *Atlantic Monthly*, June 1865, 755; Boritt, *Lincoln Enigma*, 306. Because social customs, such as, tipping one's hat or bowing, have changed so in the last century and a half, few historians have realized the implications of this seemingly simple gesture. Helen Nicolay, however, correctly interprets the gravity of Lincoln's response: "Lincoln's uncovering in answer to the sweeping obeisance of a bent and grizzled negro whose twisted limbs and white hairs betokened the labors and injustice heaped upon the race, is one of the most impressive and dramatic incidents of the war" (*Personal Traits*, 223).

Epilogue: The Dilemmas of Democratic Fame

1. James Grant Wilson, "Recollections of Lincoln," *Putnam's Magazine* 5 (February 1909): 516.

2. Charles MacKay, in *Scotland and the Americas, c. 1650–c. 1939: A Documentary Source Book*, ed. Allan I. Macinnes, Marjory-Ann D. Harper, and Linda G. Fryer (Edinburgh: Lothian, 2002), 275n1.

3. I borrow this concept from Elaine Pagels, *Beyond Belief: The Secret Gospel of Thomas* (New York: Random House, 2003), 26.

4. Leo Braudy, *The Frenzy of Reknown: Fame and Its History* (New York: Oxford UP, 1986). See also Clive James, *Fame in the 20th Century* (New York: Random House, 1993).

5. Kevin Wheeler, "Lincoln's Students Will Be at It Again," Clippings, n.d., J. G. Randall Manuscripts, Library of Congress.

6. Carl Schurz, *Abraham Lincoln: An Essay* (Boston: Houghton Mifflin, 1891), 36, 92; Robert L. Kincaid, "The New Portrait of Abraham Lincoln," *Vital Speeches of the Day* (February 15, 1948): 266; copy in Randall Manuscripts.

7. James McWhir, "Country Life in the Days of Burns," *Scotsman*, January 30, 1932, clipping file, G. F. Black Collection; Seamus Heaney, "Burns's Art Speech," in Heaney, *Finders Keepers: Selected Prose, 1971–2001* (London: Faber and Faber, 2002), 358.

8. Horace White, "Abraham Lincoln in 1854," *Putnam's Magazine*, March 1909, 726–27; Whitney, *Life on the Circuit*, 66.

9. Frank J. Williams, "Abraham Lincoln: Our Ever-Present Contemporary," in *"We Cannot Escape History": Lincoln and the Last Best Hope of Earth* (Urbana: U of Illinois P, 1995): 139–57.

10. Helen Nicolay, *Personal Traits of Abraham Lincoln* (New York: Appleton-Century, 1939), 359; 33–35.

11. Mason Brayman, quoted in Holzer, *Lincoln at Cooper Union*, 87; A. Maurice Low, "American Affairs," *National Review*, March–August 1909, 637.

12. Abraham Lincoln, quoted in John Hay and Tyler Dennert, ed., *Lincoln and the Civil War in the Diaries and Letters of John Hay* (New York: Dodd, Mead, 1939), 105, in Fehrenbacher and Fehrenbacher, *Recollected Words*, 217.

13. See his 1838 "Address before the Young Men's Lyceum of Springfield, Illinois," in Basler, *Collected Works*, 1:108–15.

14. Cited in Lamon, *Life of Abraham Lincoln*, 356.

15. "Let America Be America Again," in *The Collected Works of Langston Hughes*, ed. Arnold Rampersand (Columbia: U of Missouri P, 2001), 1:131–33.

16. Allen Dwight Callahan, *The Talking Book: African Americans and the Bible* (New Haven: Yale UP, 2006), 188–89.

17. Gabor Boritt, *The Gettysburg Gospel: The Lincoln Speech That Nobody Knows* (New York: Simon and Schuster, 2006), 177.

18. *Scottish Notes and Queries* 11 (January 1898): 105–6.

19. Sutherland and Sutherland, *At Your Own Risk*, 242.

20. Sutherland and Sutherland, *At Your Own Risk*, 184.

21. Sutherland, "Burns in Beirut," 8.

22. Interview with Frank Walker (telephone), June 25, 2007; interview with Alicia Erickson (telephone), June 28, 2007. This story is marvelously told in Andrew Ferguson, *Land of Lincoln: Adventures in Abe's America* (New York: Atlantic Monthly, 2007), 269–74.

23. J. Frank Dobie, "The Robinhooding of Sam Bass," in *I'll Tell You a Tale: An Anthology* (Austin: U of Texas P, 1981), 169.

Appendix A: Selected Burns's Verses

1. www.robertburns.org and James Kinsley, ed., *Burns: Complete Poems and Songs* (Oxford: Oxford UP, 1969); and *The Poems and Songs of Robert Burns*, 4 vols. (Oxford: Oxford UP, 1968).

Appendix B: Selected Lincoln Documents

1. "The Emancipation Proclamation, January 1, 1863," a transcription, U.S. National Archives & Records Administration, February 10, 2006, http://www. archives.gov/exhibits/featured_documents/emancipation_proclamation/ print_friendly.html?page=transcript_content.html&title=Emancipation_

Proclamation; "The Gettysburg Address," November 19, 1863, http://www. loc.gov/exhibits/gadd/images/Gettysburg-2.jpg; and "Abraham Lincoln, Second Inaugural Address, March 4, 1865," Abraham Lincoln Papers at the Library of Congress, transcribed and annotated by the Lincoln Studies Center, Knox College, Galesburg, Illinois, http://memory.loc/gov/cgis-bin/query/ r?ammem/mal:@field(DOCID+@lit(d4361300)). For a hard copy, with slight variations, see Roy P. Basler, ed., *The Collected Works of Abraham Lincoln*, 9 vols., 2 supplements (New Brunswick, NJ: Rutgers UP, 1953–90).

Bibliography

The recent creation of the newspaper *The Scotsman* archives, which currently allows access to every issue from 1817 up to 1950, has proven a marvel. In June 2005, I was poring over microfilm issues at the Scottish National Library in Edinburgh, Scotland. In February 2006, I was printing out articles from my office in Albuquerque, New Mexico. The papers of Abraham Lincoln at the Library of Congress are similarly available online. Such electronic tools have virtually revolutionized the nature of historical research.

Libraries and Archives

Aberdeen Central Library, Aberdeen, Scotland

Allen County Public Library, Fort Wayne, Indiana

Arnold, Isaac N. Papers. Chicago Historical Society, Chicago, Illinois

Black, George F. Collection. Special Collections, Robert Manning Strozier Library, Florida State University, Tallahassee, Florida

Robert Burns Room. Mitchell Library, Glasgow, Scotland

Central Library of Inverness, Inverness, Scotland

Chicago Historical Society, Chicago, Illinois

Dublin Public Library, Dublin, Ireland

Early American Newspapers, http://infoweb.newsbank.com

Edinburgh Room, Edinburgh Central Library, Edinburgh, Scotland

Illinois State Historical Library, Springfield, Illinois

Library of Congress Manuscript Room, Washington, DC

Lincoln Museum Research Library, Fort Wayne, Indiana

Lincoln National Life Foundation, Fort Wayne, Indiana

Lincoln, Abraham. Papers. Manuscript Division, Library of Congress, Washington, DC, American Memory Project, 2000–2001, http://memory.loc.gov/ammen/alhtml/malhome.html

National Poetry Library, Edinburgh, Scotland

Randall, James G., Family Papers. Manuscript Division, Library of Congress, Washington, DC

The Scotsman. http://archive.scotsman.com

Scottish Record Office (now the Scottish National Archives), Edinburgh

Shaw, John M., Collection. Special Collections, Robert Manning Strozier Library, Florida State University, Tallahassee, Florida

Special Collections, University of Aberdeen, Aberdeen, Scotland

Western Room, Denver Public Library, Denver, Colorado

Books and Articles

"Abraham Lincoln Birthplace." Pamphlet. National Park Service.

"Abraham Lincoln on Agriculture, 1859." In *Agriculture in the United States: A Documentary History*, edited by Wayne D. Rasmussen, 1:881–88. New York: Random House, 1975.

Altor, Robert. *The Art of Biblical Narrative*. New York: Basic Books, 1981.

Angle. Paul M. *Abraham Lincoln by Some Men Who Knew Him*. 1910. New York: Books for Libraries Press, 1969.

———. *"Here I Have Lived": A History of Lincoln's Springfield, 1821–1865*. Chicago: Abraham Lincoln Book Shop, 1971.

———, ed. *The Lincoln Reader*. New Brunswick, NJ: Rutgers UP, 1947.

———. "The Minor Collection: A Criticism." *Atlantic Monthly*, January–June 1929, 516–25.

Arnold, Isaac N. "Abraham Lincoln." In *The Lincoln Memorial: Album—Immortelles*, edited by Osborn H. Oldroyd, 129–69. New York: Carleton, 1883.

———. *The History of Abraham Lincoln and the Overthrow of Slavery*. Chicago: Clarke, 1866.

Baker, Jean H. *Mary Todd Lincoln: A Biography*. New York: Norton, 1987.

Barfield, Owen. *Poetic Diction: A Study in Meaning*. 1928. New York: McGraw-Hill, 1964.

Barrett, Joseph H. *Life of Abraham Lincoln*. New York: Loomis National Library Association, 1888.

Barton, William E. *The Life of Abraham Lincoln*. 2 vols. Indianapolis, IN: Bobbs-Merrill, 1925.

———. *The Soul of Abraham Lincoln*. New York: George H. Doran, 1920.

Basler, Roy P. "Abraham Lincoln's Rhetoric." *American Literature* 11 (May 1939): 167–79.

———, ed. *The Collected Works of Abraham Lincoln*. 9 vols., 2 supplements. New Brunswick, NJ: Rutgers UP, 1953–90.

———. *A Touchstone for Greatness: Essays, Addresses and Occasional Pieces about Abraham Lincoln*. Westport, CT: Greenwood, 1973.

Bassuk, Daniel. *Abraham Lincoln and the Quakers*. Wallingford, PA: Pendle Hill, 1987.

Bates, David Homer. *Lincoln in the Telegraph Office*. New York: Century, 1907.

Bayne, Julia Taft. *Tad Lincoln's Father*. Lincoln: U of Nebraska P, 2001.

Beale, Howard K., ed. *Diary of Edward Bates, 1859–1866*. Washington, DC: GPO, 1933.

Bennett, Lerone, Jr. *Forced into Glory: Abraham Lincoln's White Dream*. Chicago: Johnson, 2000.

Bentman, Raymond. "Robert Burns's Declining Fame." *Studies in Romanticism* 2 (Summer 1972): 207–25.

Berkelman, Robert. "Lincoln's Interest in Shakespeare." *Shakespeare Quarterly* 2, no. 4 (1951): 303–12.

Bernard, Kenneth A. "Lincoln and Music." In *Lincoln for the Ages*, edited by Ralph G. Newman, 338–43. Garden City, NY: Doubleday, 1960.

Berthoff, Roland Tappan. *British Immigrants in Industrial America, 1790–1950.* Cambridge, MA: Harvard UP, 1953.

Betts, William W., Jr., ed. *Lincoln and the Poets.* Pittsburgh, PA: U of Pittsburgh P, 1965.

Beveridge, Albert J. *Abraham Lincoln, 1809–1858.* 2 vols. Boston: Houghton Mifflin, 1928.

Bevington, David, ed. *The Complete Works of Shakespeare.* 4th ed. New York: Longman, 1997.

Bieder, R. V. "Lincoln's Power of Expression." *Methodist Review* 83, September 1901.

Bitting, W. C. "Burns and Religious Matters." In *St. Louis Nichts wi Burns.* St. Louis, MO: Burns Club of St. Louis, 1913. Pamphlet, held by Mitchell Library of Glasgow.

Blackett, R. J. M. *Divided Hearts: Britain and the American Civil War.* Baton Rouge: Louisiana State UP, 2001.

Blackie, John Stuart. *Life of Robert Burns.* London: Walter Scott, 1888.

Blassingame, John W., ed. *The Frederick Douglass Papers.* New Haven: Yale UP, 1979.

Bloom, Harold. *Shakespeare: The Invention of the Human.* New York: Riverhead, 1998.

Bobrick, Benson. *Wide as the Waters: The Story of the English Bible and the Revolution It Inspired.* New York: Penguin Books, 2001.

Bold, Alan. *A Burns Companion.* London: Macmillan, 1991.

"Books Lincoln Read." *Lincoln Lore*, June 20, 1932.

Boritt, Gabor S. *The Gettysburg Gospel: The Lincoln Speech That Nobody Knows.* New York: Simon and Schuster, 2006.

———. *Lincoln and the Economics of the American Dream.* Memphis, TN: Memphis State UP, 1978.

———. *The Lincoln Enigma: The Changing Faces of an American Icon.* New York: Oxford UP, 2001.

"Borrowed Books in the White House." *Lincoln Lore*, September 28, 1931.

Boyd, Maurice. *William Knox and Abraham Lincoln: The Story of a Poetic Legacy.* Denver, CO: Sage Books, 1966.

Boyle, A. M., ed. *The Ayrshire Book of Burns Lore.* 2nd ed. Darvel, Scotland: Alloway, 1996.

Boynton, C. B. *Discourse by Reverend C. B. Boynton for National Thanksgiving Services Held on Thanksgiving December 7, 1865 in the Hall of the House of Representatives of the United States of America.* Washington, DC: Morrison, 1865.

Braden, Waldo W., ed. *Building the Myth: Selected Speeches Memorializing Abraham Lincoln.* Urbana: U of Illlinois P, 1990.

Braudy, Leo. *The Frenzy of Reknown: Fame and Its History.* New York: Oxford UP, 1986.

Briggs, John Channing. *Lincoln's Speeches Reconsidered.* Baltimore, MD: Johns Hopkins UP, 2005.

Brooks, Noah. *Abraham Lincoln and the Downfall of American Slavery.* New York: Putnam's, 1894.

———. "The Close of Lincoln's Career." *Century* 50, May 1895, 21–23.

———. "Personal Recollections of Abraham Lincoln." *Harper's* 31, 1865, 222–30.

Brougham, Henry, Lord. *Letter by the Right Honorable Lord Brougham, on the Occasion of the Burns' Centenary Festival, 25th January 1859 to the Honorable Lord Ardmillan in the Music Hall, Edinburgh, Printed for Those Who Attended the Banquet.* Edinburgh: 1859.

Brown, Mary Ellen. *Burns and Tradition.* Urbana: U of Illinois P, 1984.

Browne, Ray B., ed. *Lincoln-Lore: Lincoln in the Popular Mind.* 2nd ed. Bowling Green, OH: Bowling Green State U Popular P, 1996.

Bruce, Robert V. *Lincoln and the Riddle of Death.* Fort Wayne, IN: Louis A. Warren Lincoln Library and Museum, 1981.

Bruce, Wallace. "The Influence of Robert Burns on American literature." *Annual Burns Chronicle* 1 (1892): 45–50.

Buchan, James. *Crowded with Genius. The Scottish Enlightenment: Edinburgh's Moment of the Mind.* New York: HarperCollins, 2003.

Buchanan, W. W., and W. F. Kean. "Robert Burns's Illness Revisited." *Scottish Medical Journal* 27 (1982): 75–88.

Bullard, F. Lauriston. *Lincoln in Marble and Bronze.* New Brunswick, NJ: Rutgers UP, 1952.

Bunker, Gary L. *From Rail-Splitter to Icon: Lincoln's Image in Illustrated Periodicals, 1860–1865.* Kent, OH: Kent State UP, 2001.

Burlingame, Michael. ed. *An Oral History of Abraham Lincoln: John G. Nicolay's Interviews and Essays.* Carbondale: Southern Illinois UP, 1996.

———. *At Lincoln's Side: John Hay's Civil War Correspondence and Selected Writings.* Carbondale: Southern Illinois UP, 2000.

———, ed. *The Inner World of Abraham Lincoln.* Urbana: U of Illinois P, 1994.

Burns, Robert. *The Complete Poems and Songs of Robert Burns.* New Lanark, MD: Geddes and Grossett, 2001.

———. *The Complete Works of Robert Burns . . . with a Memoir by William Gunnyon.* Edinburgh: Nimmo, 1892.

Burns Centenary: Are Such Honors Due to the Ayrshire Bard? Glasgow: privately printed, 1859.

Burns Centenary: Being an Account of the Proceedings and Speeches at the Various Banquets and Meetings throughout the Kingdom, with a Memoir and Portrait of the Poet. 2nd. ed. Edinburgh: Nimmo, 1859.

"The Burns Centennial in New York." In *St. Louis Burnsians: Their Twentieth Anniversary and Some Other Burns Nights.* St. Louis: Burns Clubs, 1926.

"Burns Festival." *Littell's Living Age* 60, January 1859, 740–49.

Burnsiana: Speeches of Professor John Wilson. Washington, DC: Gibson, 1877.

Cady, John F. "The Religious Environment of Lincoln's Youth." *Indiana Magazine of History* 37 (March 1941): 16–30.

Cairney, John, ed. *Immortal Memories.* Edinburgh: Luath Press, 2003.

———. *On the Trail of Robert Burns.* Edinburgh: Luath Press, 2000.

Calder, Jenni. *Scots in the USA.* Edinburgh: Luath Press, 2006.

Carnegie, Andrew. *Autobiography of Andrew Carnegie.* London: Constable, 1920.

Carpenter, F. B. *The Inner Life of Abraham Lincoln: Six Months at the White House.* New York: Hurd and Houghton, 1869.

Carswell, Catherine. *The Life of Robert Burns.* 1930. Edinburgh: Canongate Classics, 1990.

Carwardine, Richard J. *Lincoln: Profiles in Power.* Harrow, England: Pearson Longman, 2003.

Catalogue of the Robert Burns Collection: The Mitchell Library, Glasgow. Glasgow: Glasgow City Libraries and Archives, 1996.

Celebration of the Centennial Anniversary of the Birth of Robert Burns by the Burns Club of Washington City, D.C., at the National Hotel, January 25, 1859. Washington, DC: Shillington, 1859.

Charnwood, Lord. *Abraham Lincoln.* Garden City, NY: Garden City, 1917.

"Children as Pilgrims to Lincoln Shrines in Springfield, Illinois, Learn Lessons of Patriotism." *Journal of the Illinois State Historical Society* 17 (January 1925): 736–40.

Choate, Joseph H. *Abraham Lincoln and Other Addresses in England.* New York: Century, 1910.

Clay, Cassius M. *Reminiscences of Abraham Lincoln by Distinguished Men of His Time,* ed. Allen Thorndike Rice, 293–306. 1885. New York: North American Review, 1888.

Clive, John, and Bernard Bailyn. "England's Cultural Provinces: Scotland and America." *William and Mary Quarterly* 11 (April 1954): 200–213.

Cmiel, Kenneth. *Democratic Eloquence: The Fight over Popular Speech in Nineteenth-Century America*. Berkeley: U of California P, 1991.

Coffin, Charles Carleton. "Lincoln's First Nomination and His Visit to Richmond in 1865." In A. T. Rice, *Reminiscences of Abraham Lincoln*, 161–84.

Comte de Paris. "The Civil War in America." *Blackwood's Magazine*, August 1874.

Confession of Faith, The. Edinburgh: Free Presbyterian Church of Scotland, 1963.

Connecticut Wits, The. New York: Crowell, 1954.

Connerton, Paul. *How Societies Remember*. Cambridge: Cambridge UP, 1989.

Cox, LaWanda. *Lincoln and Black Freedom: A Study in Presidential Leadership*. Urbana: U of Illinois P, 1985.

Crawford, Robert. *Devolving English Literature*. 2nd ed. Edinburgh: Edinburgh UP, 2000.

———, ed. *Robert Burns and Cultural Authority*. Edinburgh: Edinburgh UP, 1997.

Crawford, Thomas. *Burns: A Study of the Poems and Songs*. 1960. Edinburgh: Canongate Academic, 1994.

Croffut, William A. "Bennett and His Times." *Atlantic Monthly*, February 1931, 196–206.

Cromek, R. H. *Reliques of Robert Burns*. London: Cadell and Davis, 1813.

Crouthamel, James L. *Bennett's New York Herald and the Rise of the Popular Press*. Syracuse, NY: Syracuse UP, 1989.

Cunningham, Joseph, ed. *The Birthday of Robert Burns, as Celebrated by the Burns Club of the City of New York, Tuesday, January 25, 1859*. New York: Laing and Laing, 1860.

Cuomo, Mario M. *Why Lincoln Matters: Today More Than Ever*. Orlando, FL: Harcourt, 2004.

Cuomo, Mario, and Harold Holzer, eds. *Lincoln on Democracy*. New York: HarperCollins, 1990.

Current, Richard Nelson. *Speaking of Abraham Lincoln: The Man and His Meaning for Our Times*. Urbana: U of Illinois P, 1983.

Currie, James C. *The Entire Works of Robert Burns; with His Life and a Criticism on His Writings*. 1800. 4 vols. Glasgow: George Brookman, 1823.

Cushman, Charles R., ed. *Memorial Addresses Delivered before the Two Houses of Congress on the Life and Character of Abraham Lincoln, James Garfield, William McKinley*. Washington, DC: GPO, 1903.

Daiches, David. "The Facets of Genius." *Scotland's Magazine*, January 1959, 45–48.

———. *The Paradox of Scottish Culture: The Eighteenth-Century Experience*. London: Oxford UP, 1964.

————. *Robert Burns and His World*. 1953. London: Thames and Hudson, 1971.

————. *Robert Burns the Poet*. 1950. Edinburgh: Saltire Society, 1994.

Damico, Helen. "Sources of Stanza Forms Used by Burns." *Studies in Scottish Literature* 12 (January 1975): 207–19.

Davenport, Don. *In Lincoln's Footsteps: A Historical Guide to the Lincoln Sites in Illinois, Indiana, and Kentucky*. Madison, WI: Prairie Oak Press, 1991.

Davis, Cullom, ed. *The Public and the Private Lincoln: Contemporary Perspectives*. Carbondale: Southern Illinois UP, 1979.

Davis, Michael. *The Image of Lincoln in the South*. Knoxville: U of Tennessee P, 1971.

Dick, James C. *The Songs of Robert Burns*. London: Henry Frowde, 1903.

"Discovery: A New Storehouse of Lincoln Material." *Atlantic Monthly*, December 1928, 834–37.

Dodge, Daniel Kilham. *Abraham Lincoln: Master of Words*. New York: Appleton, 1924.

————. *Abraham Lincoln: The Evolution of His Literary Style*. Introduction by James Hart. Urbana: U of Illinois P, 2000.

Donald, David Herbert. *Lincoln*. New York: Simon and Schuster, 1995.

————. *"We Are Lincoln Men": Abraham Lincoln and His Friends*. New York: Simon and Schuster, 2003.

Douglas, George William. *The American Book of Days*. New York: Wilson, 1937.

Douglas, Hugh. *Robert Burns: The Tinder Heart*. Gloucestershire, England: Sutton, 1998.

Dow, John G. "Burns in America." *Robert Burns: The Critical Heritage*. Edited by Donald A. Low. London: Routledge, 1974.

Drew, Elizabeth. *Poetry: A Modern Guide to Its Understanding and Enjoyment*. New York: Norton, 1959.

Drummond, Robert Blackley. *The Religion of Robert Burns: A Lecture*. Edinburgh: Mathers, 1859.

Duncan, John M. *Travels through Part of the United States and Canada in 1818 and 1819*. Glasgow: Glasgow University Press, 1823.

Duncan, Kunigunde, and D. F. Nickols. *Mentor Graham: The Man Who Taught Lincoln*. Chicago: U of Chicago P, 1944.

Edwards, Herbert Joseph, and John Erskine Hankins. *Lincoln the Writer: The Development of His Literary Style*. Orono: U of Maine, 1962.

Egerer, J. W. *A Bibliography of Robert Burns*. Carbondale: Southern Illinois UP, 1964.

Elliott, Ebenezer. "The Character of Robert Burns." *Harper's New Monthly Magazine*, 1850, 114–20.

Emerson, Ralph Waldo. *The Complete Works of Ralph Waldo Emerson*. New York: Houghton Mifflin, 1911.

Epstein, Daniel Mark. *Lincoln and Whitman: Parallel Lives in Civil War Washington*. New York: Ballantine, 2004.

Erickson, Charlotte. *Invisible Immigrants: The Adaptation of English and Scottish Immigrants in Nineteenth-Century America*. Ithaca, NY: Cornell UP, 1972.

Esslemont, Peter. *Brithers A': A Minute a Day with Burns*. Aberdeen, Scotland: Avery, 1943.

Evidences of Christianity: A Debate between Robert Owen, of New Lanmark, Scotland, and Alexander Campbell, President of Bethany Coll., Va. Containing an Examination of the "Social System" and All the Systems of Skepticism of Ancient and Modern Times. St. Louis, MO: Christian Board of Publication, n.d., ca. 1830.

Eyre-Todp, George, ed. *Scottish Ballad Poetry*. Glasgow: William Hodge, 1893.

Fehrenbach, T. R. *Lone Star: A History of Texas and the Texans*. New York: Macmillan, 1968.

Fehrenbacher, Don E. *Lincoln in Text and Context: Collected Essays*. Stanford: Stanford UP, 1987.

Fehrenbacher, Don E., and Virginia Fehrenbacher, comps. *Recollected Words of Abraham Lincoln*. Stanford, CA: Stanford UP, 1996.

Ferguson, Andrew. *Land of Lincoln: Adventures in Abe's America*. New York: Atlantic Monthly Press, 2007.

Ferguson, J. DeLancey. "Antique Smith and His Forgeries of Robert Burns." *Colophon* 13 (1933): 1–20.

———. *Pride and Passion: Robert Burns, 1759–1796*. 1939. Reprint, New York: Russell and Russell, 1964.

Fermer, Douglas. *James Gordon Bennett and the New York Herald: A Study of Editorial Opinion in the Civil War Era, 1854–1867*. New York: St. Martin's Press, 1986.

Fleischner, Jennifer. *Mrs. Lincoln and Mrs. Keckly: The Remarkable Story of the Friendship between a First Lady and a Former Slave*. New York: Broadway Books, 2003.

Forney, John W., ed. *Anecdotes of Public Men*. New York: Harper, 1894.

Fox, Everett. *The Five Books of Moses*. New York: Schocken, 1997.

Fredrickson, George M. "A Man but Not a Brother: Abraham Lincoln and Racial Equality." *Journal of Southern History* 41 (1975): 39–58.

Fry, Michael. *How the Scots Made America*. New York: Dunne Books, 2003.

Gary, Ralph. *Following in Lincoln's Footsteps: A Complete Annotated Reference to Hundreds of Historical Sites Visited by Abraham Lincoln*. New York: Carroll and Graf, 2001.

Gienapp, William E. *Abraham Lincoln and Civil War America: A Biography*. New York: Oxford UP, 2002.

Gilbert, Suzanne. "Recovering Burns's Lyric Legacy: Teaching Burns in American Universities." *Studies in Scottish Literature* 30 (1998): 137–45.

Goodwillie, Edward. *The World's Memorials of Robert Burns*. Detroit, MI: Waverley, 1911.

Goodwin, Doris Kearns. *Team of Rivals: The Political Genius of Abraham Lincoln*. New York: Simon and Schuster, 2005.

Gray, John G., and Charles J. Smith. *A Walk on the Southside in the Footsteps of Robert Burns*. Edinburgh: Southside Museum, 1998.

Gross, David. *Lost Time: On Remembering and Forgetting in Late Modern Culture*. Amherst: U of Massachusetts P, 2000.

Grover, Leonard. "Lincoln's Interest in the Theatre." *Century* 77 (April 1909): 943–95.

Guelzo, Allen C. *Abraham Lincoln: Redeemer President*. Grand Rapids, MI: Eerdmans, 1999.

———. *Lincoln's Emancipation Proclamation: The End of Slavery in America*. New York: Simon and Schuster, 2004.

Hamilton, Doris H. "'For Auld Lang Syne'—and Robert Burns." *Hobbies*, January 1959.

Hamm, Charles. *Yesterdays: Popular Song in America*. New York: Norton, 1979: 42–60.

Harkness, David J., and R. Gerald McMurtry. *Lincoln's Favorite Poets*. Knoxville: U of Tennessee P, 1959.

Harper, Robert S. *Lincoln and the Press*. New York: McGraw-Hill, 1951.

Harrison, Lowell. *Lincoln of Kentucky*. Lexington: UP of Kentucky, 2000.

Hawthorne, Nathaniel. "Some of the Haunts of Burns: By a Tourist without Imagination or Enthusiasm." *Atlantic Monthly*, October 1860, 385–95.

Hayter, Earl W. "Sources of Early Illinois Culture." In *Transactions of the Illinois State Historical Society for the Year 1936*, 43.81–96. Springfield: Illinois State Historical Society, 1937.

Hecht, Hans. *Robert Burns: The Man and His Work*. 1936. Ayr, Scotland: Alloway, 1991.

Herd, David. *Ancient and Modern Scottish Songs, Heroic Ballads, etc.* 2 vols. Edinburgh: John Witherspoon, 1876.

Herndon, William, and Jesse W. Werk. *Herndon's Life of Lincoln: The History and Personal Recollections of Abraham Lincoln*. 1888. New York: Boni, 1936.

Heron, Robert. *A Memoir of the Life of the Late Robert Burns*. Edinburgh: Brown, 1797.

Hertz, Emanuel. *Abraham Lincoln: His Favorite Poems and Poets*. N.p., February 12, 1930.

———. *The Hidden Lincoln: From the Letters and Papers of William H. Herndon*. New York: Viking, 1938.

Historical Aspects of New Milns. Ayrshire, Scotland: Walker and Connell, 1990.

Holifield, E. Brooks. *Theology in America: Christian Thought from the Age of the Puritans to the Civil War*. New Haven: Yale UP, 2003.

Holzer, Harold, ed. *Dear Mr. Lincoln: Letters to the President*. Reading, MA: Addison-Wesley, 1995.

———, ed. *Lincoln As I Knew Him*. Chapel Hill, NC: Algonquin Books, 1999.

———. *Lincoln at Cooper Union; The Speech That Made Abraham Lincoln President*. New York: Simon and Schuster, 2004.

———. *Lincoln Seen and Heard*. Lawrence: UP of Kansas, 2000.

Hook, Andrew. *From Goose Creek to Gandercleugh, Studies in Scottish-American Literary and Cultural History*. East Linton: Tuckwell Press, 1999.

Houser, M. L. *Lincoln's Education*. New York: Bookman, 1957.

Jaffa, Harry V. *Crisis of the House Divided: An Interpretation of the Issues in the Lincoln-Douglas Debates*. 1959. Seattle: U of Washington P, 1973.

James, Clive. *Fame in the 20th Century*. New York: Random House, 1993.

Jefferson, Joseph. *The Autobiography of Joseph Jefferson*. Cambridge, MA: Belknap Press of Harvard University, 1964.

Johnson, Terry A., Jr., ed. *"Him on the One Side and Me on the Other": The Civil War Letters of Alexander Campbell, 79th New York Infantry Regiment, and James Campbell, 1st South Carolina Battalion*. Columbia: U of South Carolina P, 1999.

Keckley, Elizabeth. *Behind the Scenes, or, Thirty Years a Slave, and Four Years in the White House*. 1868. New York: Oxford UP, 1988.

Keith, Thomas. "A Discography of Robert Burns 1948 to 2002." *Studies in Scottish Literature* 33–34 (2004): 387–412.

Keneally, Thomas. *Abraham Lincoln*. New York: Lipper/Viking, 2003.

Kenmore, Frank. *Shakespeare's Language*. London: Penguin, 2000.

Kincaid, Robert L. "The New Portrait of Abraham Lincoln." *Vital Speeches of the Day* 14, no. 9 (February 15, 1948): 265–69.

Kinsley, James, ed. *Burns: Complete Poems and Songs*. Oxford: Oxford UP, 1969.

———. *The Poems and Songs of Robert Burns*. 4 vols. Oxford: Oxford UP, 1968.

Knapp, John. "National Poetry." *North American Review* 8 (December 1818): 169–76.

Kobler, John. "Trailing the Book Crooks." *Saturday Evening Post*, March 13, 1943, 18–19.

Kunhardt, Philip B., Jr., Philip B. Kunhardt III, and Peter W. Kunhardt. *Lincoln: An Illustrated Biography*. New York: Knopf, 1992.

LaMarre, Tom. "Lincoln Treasures: Numismatic Collectibles of 'Old.'" *Coins* 46, July 1999, 46–55.

Lamon, Ward H. *The Life of Abraham Lincoln: From His Birth to His Inauguration as President*. Boston: Osgood, 1872.

"Late Scenes in Richmond." *Atlantic Monthly*, June 1865, 755–57.

Lee, Katie. *Ten Thousand Goddam Cattle*. Albuquerque: U of New Mexico P, 2001.

Legman, G., ed. *The Merry Muses of Caledonia*. New Hyde Park, NY: University Books, 1965.

Leith, John H. "The Westminster Confession in American Presbyterianism." In *The Westminster Confession in the Church Today*, edited by Alasdair I. C. Heron, 95–100. Edinburgh: St. Andrew Press, 1982.

Lester, Robert M. *Forty Years of Carnegie Giving: A Summary of the Benefactions of Andrew Carnegie and of the Work of the Philanthropic Trusts Which He Created*. New York: Charles Scribner's, 1941.

Lewis, B. Roland. *Creative Poetry: A Study of Its Organic Principles*. Stanford, CA: Stanford UP, 1931.

Lewis, Lloyd. *Myths after Lincoln*. New York: Press of the Readers Club, 1929.

Lincoln, Abraham. "The Emancipation Proclamation, January 1, 1863." Transcription, U.S. National Archives and Records Administration, February 10, 2006. http://www.archives.gov/exhibits/featured_documents/emancipation_proclamation/print_friendly.html?page=transcript_content.html&title=Emancipation_Proclamation.

———. "The Gettysburg Address." November 19, 1863. Library of Congress. http://www.loc.gov/exhibits/gadd/images/Gettysburg-2.jpg.

———. "Abraham Lincoln, Second Inaugural Address, March 4, 1865." Abraham Lincoln Papers, Library of Congress. Transcribed and annotated by the Lincoln Studies Center, Knox College, Galesburg, Illinois. http://memory.loc.gov/cgis-bin/query/r?ammem/mal:@field(DOCID+@lit(d4361300)).

"Lincoln's Background of Borrowed Books." *Lincoln Lore*, October 31, 1949.

Lindsay, Joyce, and Maurice Lindsay, eds. *The Burns Quotation Book*. London: Hale, 1994.

Lindsay, Maurice, ed. *The Burns Encyclopedia*. 1959. 3rd ed. London: Hale, 1995.

Locke, David R. In A. T. Rice, *Reminiscences of Abraham Lincoln*, 439–53.

Lockhart, John Gibson. *Life of Burns*. Edinburgh: Constable, 1828.

Loesberg, John. *The Scottish Songs of Robert Burns*. Cork, Ireland: Ossian, 1995.

Longfellow, Samuel, ed. *Life of Henry Wadsworth Longfellow*. 3 vols. New York: AMS Press, 1966.

Lorant, Stefan. *Lincoln: A Picture Story of His Life*. Rev. ed. New York: Harper, 1957.

Low, Donald A., ed. *Critical Essays on Robert Burns*. London: Routledge, 1975.

——. *Robert Burns*. Edinburgh: Scottish Academic Press, 1986.

Luthin, Reinhard. *The Real Abraham Lincoln: A Complete One Volume History of His Life and Times*. Englewood Cliffs, NJ: Prentice-Hall, 1960.

MacDiarmid, Hugh. "The Burns Cult." *At the Sign of the Thistle: A Collection of Essays*. London: Nott, 1934.

MacKay, Charles. *Scotland and the Americas, c. 1650–c. 1939: A Documentary Source Book*. Ed. Allan I. Macinnes, Marjory Harper, and Linda G. Fryer. Edinburgh: Lothian, 2002.

MacKay, James. *Allan Pinkerton: The First Private Eye*. New York: Wiley, 1996.

MacKay, James A., ed. *The Complete Letters of Robert Burns*. 1987. Ayrshire, Scotland: Alloway, 1990.

——. "New Developments in Burns Biography." *Studies in Scottish Literature* 30 (1998): 291–301.

——. *RB: A Biography of Robert Burns*. Edinburgh: Mainstream, 1992.

MacLaine, A. H. "Burns Stanza." In *Princeton Encyclopedia of Poetry and Poetics*, edited by Alex Preminger, Frank J. Warnke, and O. B. Hardison Jr., 90. Princeton, NJ: Princeton UP, 1974.

MacManus, Francis. "The Two Languages of Abe Lincoln." *Irish Press*, May 11, 1963.

MacMillan, Donald. *Burns and the War: His Message to the Nation*. Glasgow, Scotland, 1917.

MacMillan, Thomas C. "The Scots and Their Descendants in Illinois." *Transactions of the Illinois State Historical Society*, 26:31–85. Springfield, IL: Phillips, 1919.

Mandara, Tony. "Thank God Lincoln Had Only One 79th Highlander Regiment." *Crossfire* 67, December 2001. http://www.americancivilwar.org. uk/articles/highlanders.htm (accessed February 2, 2006).

Manning, Susan. *Fragments of Union: Making Connections in Scottish and American Writing*. New York: Palgrave, 2002.

——. *The Puritan-Provincial Vision: Scottish and American Literature in the Nineteenth Century*. Cambridge: Cambridge UP, 1990.

Mauchline Memories of Robert Burns. 1985. Ayrshire, Scotland: Ayrshire Archaeological and Natural History Society, 1996.

McCoy, C. M. "'Auld Lang Syne.'" *Metropolitan Review* 2 (July 1927): 10–12.

McCrorie, Thomas S. "My Experiences at the Burns House." *Burns Chronicle*, 3rd series, 7–8 (1958–59), 12–14.

McGrath, Alister. *In the Beginning: The Story of the King James Bible and How It Changed a Nation, a Language, and a Culture*. New York: Anchor Books, 2001.

McGuirk, Carol, ed. *Critical Essays on Robert Burns*. New York: Hall, 1998.

———. "Haunted by Authority: Nineteenth-Century American Constructions of Robert Burns and Scotland." In *Robert Burns and Cultural Authority*, edited by Robert Crawford, 136–58. Edinburgh: Edinburgh UP, 1997.

———. *Robert Burns and the Sentimental Era*. Athens: U of Georgia P, 1985.

———, ed. *Robert Burns: Selected Poems*. New York: Penguin Books, 1993.

McIlvanney, Liam. *Burns the Radical: Poetry and Politics in Late Eighteenth-Century Scotland*. East Linton, Scotland: Tuckwell Press, 2002.

McIntyre, Ian. *Robert Burns: A Life*. London: Penguin Books, 1995.

McKnight, A. G. *America's Appreciation of Robert Burns*. Minneapolis: N.p., 1924.

———. *Lincoln and Burns*. Duluth, MN: N.p., 1943.

———. "Robert Burns: The Poet of Liberalism." *Quarterly of American Interprofessional Institute*, December 1929.

McMunn, Thomas. "My Thirty-Three Years at the Burns Cottage." *Burns Chronicle*, 3rd series, 7–8 (1958–59): 15–17.

McMurtry, R. Gerald. "Lincoln Knew Shakespeare." *Indiana Magazine of History* 31 (December 1935): 265–87.

McNie, Alan, compiler. *The Illustrated Life and Works of Robert Burns*. Rowandean, Beles, Jedburgh, Scotland: Cascade, 1995.

McPherson, James M. *Abraham Lincoln and the Second American Revolution*. New York: Oxford UP, 1990.

———, ed. *"We Cannot Escape History": Lincoln and the Last Best Hope of Earth*. Urbana: U of Illinois P, 1995.

Means, David Chambers. *Largely Lincoln*. New York: St. Martin's, 1961.

Mehta, Ved. *The Fly and the Fly-bottle: Encounters with British Intellectuals*. Baltimore, MD: Penguin, 1965.

Miers, Earl Schenck, ed. *Lincoln Day by Day*. 3 vols. Washington: Lincoln Sesquicentennial Commission, 1960.

Miller, William Lee. *Lincoln's Virtues: An Ethical Biography*. New York: Knopf, 2002.

———. *President Lincoln: The Duty of a Statesman*. New York: Knopf, 2008.

Minor, Wilma Frances. "Lincoln the Lover: 1, the Setting—New Salem," *Atlantic Monthly*, December 1928, 838–55; "2, The Courtship," January 1929, 1–14; "3, the Tragedy," February 1929, 215–25.

Moffatt, Frederick C. *Errant Bronzes: George Grey Barnard's Statues of Abraham Lincoln.* Newark: U of Delaware P, 1998.

Monaghan, Jay. *Diplomat in Carpet Slippers: Abraham Lincoln Deals with Foreign Affairs.* Indianapolis, IN: Bobbs-Merrill, 1945.

Moore, Marianne. "Abraham Lincoln and the Art of the Word." In *Lincoln for the Ages,* edited by Ralph G. Newman, 378–83. Garden City, NY: Doubleday, 1960.

Morel, Lucas E. *Lincoln's Sacred Effort: Defining Religion's Role in American Self-Government.* Lanham, MD: Lexington Books, 2000.

Morn, Frank. *"The Eye That Never Sleeps" A History of the Pinkerton National Detective Agency.* Bloomington: Indiana UP, 1982.

Morison, David. "Burns and the Scots Tongue." *Scotland's Magazine* 55 (January 1959): 40–42.

Morris, David B. "Burns and Heteroglossia." *Eighteenth Century: Theory and Interpretation* 28 (1987): 3–27.

Murr, J. Edward. "Lincoln in Indiana." *Indiana Magazine of History* 13 (December 1917): 307–48, and 14 (March 1918): 13–75, 148–82.

Murray, Charles Augustus. *Travels in North America.* 1839. New York: Da Capo, 1974.

Myers, James E. *The Astonishing Saber Duel of Abraham Lincoln.* Springfield, IL: Lincoln-Herndon, 1968.

Neely, Mark E., Jr., ed. *The Abraham Lincoln Encyclopedia.* New York: McGraw-Hill, 1982.

———. *The Last Best Hope of Earth: Abraham Lincoln and the Promise of America.* Cambridge, MA: Harvard UP, 1993.

Neely, Mark E., Jr., and Harold Holzer, eds. *The Union Image: Popular Prints of the Civil War North.* Chapel Hill: U of North Carolina P, 2000.

New Mexico Department of Education, New Mexico Common School Course of Study. Albuquerque: Press of the Morning Journal, 1911.

Nicolay, Helen. *Personal Traits of Abraham Lincoln.* New York: Appleton-Century, 1939.

Nicolson, Adam. *God's Secretaries: The Making of the King James Bible.* New York: HarperCollins, 2003.

Noble, Andrew, and Patrick Scott Hogg, eds. *The Canongate Burns.* 2 vols. Edinburgh: Canongate Books, 2001.

Noll, Mark A. *America's God: From Jonathan Edwards to Abraham Lincoln.* New York: Oxford UP, 2002.

Norton, Charles Eliot, ed. *Letters of James Russell Lowell.* 1893. New York: Harper, 1947.

Nye, Russel B. *The Cultural Life of the New Nation.* New York: Harper and Rowe, 1963.

Oakes, James. *The Radical and the Republican: Frederick Douglass, Abraham Lincoln, and the Triumph of Anti-slavery Politics.* New York: Norton, 2007.

Oates, Stephen B. *With Malice toward None: the Life of Abraham Lincoln.* New York: Harper and Row, 1977.

O'Hara, Arnold, compiler, *As Burns Said.* Darvel, Scotland: Alloway, 1995.

Ong, Walter J. *Orality and Literacy: The Technologizing of the Word.* London: Routledge, 1982.

———. *The Presence of the Word: Some Prolegomena for Cultural and Religious History.* New Haven, CT: Yale UP, 1963.

O'Rourke, Donny. *Ae Fond Kiss: The Love Letters of Robert Burns and Clarinda.* Edinburgh: Mercat Press, 2000.

Orth, Ralph H., ed. *The Poetry Notebooks of Ralph Waldo Emerson.* Columbia: U of Missouri P, 1986.

Pagels, Elaine. *Beyond Belief: The Secret Gospel of Thomas.* New York: Random House, 2003.

Paludan, Philip Shaw, ed. *Lincoln's Legacy: Ethics and Politics.* Urbana: U of Illinois P, 2008.

———. *The Presidency of Abraham Lincoln.* Lawrence: UP of Kansas, 1994.

Parrington, Vernon L., ed. *The Connecticut Wits.* New York: Thomas Y. Crowell, 1969.

Perret, Geoffrey. *Lincoln's War: The Untold Story of America's Greatest President as Commander in Chief.* New York: Random, 2004.

Perry, James A. *A Bohemian Brigade: The Civil War Correspondents—Mostly Rough, Sometimes Ready.* New York: Wiley, 2000.

Peterson, Merrill D. *Lincoln in American Memory.* New York: Oxford UP, 1994.

———. *"This Grand Pertinacity": Abraham Lincoln and the Declaration of Independence.* Fort Wayne, IN: Lincoln Museum, 1991.

Pinkerton, Allan. *History and Evidence of the Passage of Abraham Lincoln from Harrisburg, PA., on the Twenty-second and Twenty-third of February: Eighteen Hundred and Sixty-one.* N.p.: 1868.

———. *The Spy of the Rebellion.* 1883. Reprint, Lincoln: U of Nebraska P, 1989.

Pinsker, Matthew. *Lincoln's Sanctuary: Abraham Lincoln and the Soldiers' Home.* New York: Oxford UP, 2003.

Pond, Fern Nance. "Lincoln's New Salem Restored." *DAR Magazine,* February 1952, 113–17.

Quarles, Benjamin. *Lincoln and the Negro.* New York: Oxford UP, 1962.

Randall, James G. *Lincoln the President: Springfield to Gettysburg.* 2 vols. New York: Dodd, Mead, 1945.

Randall, James G., and Richard N. Current. *Lincoln the President: Last Full Measure*. Urbana: U of Illinois P, 1955; 2000.

Randall, Ruth Painter. *Mary Lincoln: Biography of a Marriage*. Boston: Little, Brown, 1953.

Rankin, Henry B. *Personal Recollections of Abraham Lincoln*. New York: Putnam's, 1916.

Ray, Celeste. *Highland Heritage: Scottish Americans in the American South*. Chapel Hill: U of North Carolina P, 2001.

"Recollections of Lincoln: Three Letters of Intimate Friends." *Bulletin of the Abraham Lincoln Association* 25 (December 1931): 6–12.

Reep, Thomas P. *Lincoln at New Salem*. N.p.: Old Salem League, 1927.

Rice, Allen Thorndike, ed. *Reminiscences of Abraham Lincoln by Distinguished Men of His Time*. New York: North American Review, 1888.

Rice, C. Duncan. *The Scots Abolitionists, 1833–1861*. Baton Rouge: Louisiana State UP, 1981.

"Robert Burns." *Littell's Living Age* 7 (August 25, 1895): 528–33.

Robinson, Luther Emerson. *Abraham Lincoln as a Man of Letters*. New York: Putnam's, 1923.

Ross, Ishbel. *The President's Wife: Mary Todd Lincoln, a Biography*. New York: Putnam's, 1973.

Ross, John D., comp. *Burnsiana: A Collection of Literary Odds and Ends Relating to Robert Burns, Six Volumes in One*. London: Gardner, 1892.

———, comp. *A Little Book of Burns Lore*. 1926. Clydebank: Lang Syne, 1991.

Roughead, William. *The Riddle of the Ruthvens and Other Studies*. Edinburgh: Green, 1919.

Roy, G. Ross, ed. *The Letters of Robert Burns*. 2nd ed., rev. Oxford: Oxford UP, 1985.

———, ed. *Robert Burns and America: A Symposium*. Columbia, SC: Cooper Library, 2001.

———. "Robert Burns: Editions and Critical Works 1968–1982." *Studies in Scottish Literature* 19 (1984): 216–51.

———. "Some Notes on Scottish Chapbooks." *Scottish Literary Journal* 1 (1974): 50–60. http://www.sc.edu/library/spcoll/brit lit/cbooks2.html.

Russell, William Howard. *My Diary North and South*. New York: Harper, 1954.

S., W. "Abraham Lincoln a Poet." *Notes and Queries*, 3rd series, 7, April 15, 1865.

Sandage, Scott A. "A Marble House Divided: The Lincoln Memorial, the Civil Rights Movement, and the Politics of Memory, 1939–1963." *Journal of American History* 80 (June 1993): 135–67.

Sandburg, Carl. *Abraham Lincoln*. 6 vols. New York: Scribner's, 1940.

"Satire." In *The New Princeton Encyclopedia of Poetry and Poetics*, edited by Alex Preminger, T. V. F. Brogan, Frank J. Warnke, O. B. Hardison Jr., and Earl Miner, 1114–17. Princeton, NJ: Princeton UP, 1993.

Scharnhorst, Gary. "Whitman on Robert Burns: An Early Essay Recovered." *Walt Whitman Quarterly Review* 13 (Spring 1996): 217–20.

Schmidt, Leigh Eric. *Holy Fairs: Scottish Communions and American Revivals in the Early Modern Period*. Princeton, NJ: Princeton UP, 1989.

Schurz, Carl. *Abraham Lincoln: An Essay*. Boston: Houghton Mifflin, 1891.

Schwartz, Barry. *Abraham Lincoln and the Forge of National Memory*. Chicago: U of Chicago P, 2000.

Searcher, Victor. *Lincoln's Journey to Greatness: A Factual Account of the Twelve-day Inaugural Trip*. Philadelphia, PA: Winston, 1960.

Seitz, Don C. *The James Gordon, Bennetts, Father and Son, Proprieters of the New York Herald*. Indianapolis, IN: Bobbs-Merrill, 1928.

Sermon, George T. "The Bible on the Tongue of Lincoln." *Methodist Review* 9 (January 1907): 93–99.

Shairp, Principal. *Robert Burns*. New York: Harper, 1900.

Sharp, Cecil J. *English Folk Songs from the Southern Appalachians*. 2 vols. London: Oxford UP, 1932.

Shaw, Albert. *Abraham Lincoln: The Year of His Election*. New York: Review of Reviews, 1930.

Shaw, Archer H., ed. *The Lincoln Encyclopedia*. New York: Macmillan, 1950.

Shaw, John Mackay, and Frederick Korn. *Robert Burns: An Inventory of Burnsiana in the John M. Shaw Collection*. Tallahassee: Florida State University, 1982.

Shenk, Joshua Wolf. *Lincoln's Melancholy: How Depression Challenged a President and Fueled His Greatness*. Boston: Houghton Mifflin, 2005.

Simon, James F. *Lincoln and Chief Justice Taney: Slavery, Secession and the President's War Powers*. New York: Simon and Schuster, 2006.

Simpson, Kenneth, ed. *Burns Now*. Edinburgh: Canongate Academic, 1994.

———, ed. *Love and Liberty, Robert Burns: A Bicentenary Celebration*. East Lothian: Tuckwell Press, 1997.

———. *Robert Burns*. Aberdeen: Association for Scottish Literary Studies, 1994.

Sloan, Douglas. *The Scottish Enlightenment and the American College*. New York: Teachers' College Press, 1971.

Smith, Graham. *Robert Burns, the Exciseman*. Ayr, Scotland: Alloway, 1989.

Smith, James. *The Christian's Defense, Containing a Fair Statement, and Impartial Examination of the Leading Objections Urged by Infidels against the Antiquity, Genuineness, Credibility and Inspiration of the Holy Scripture;*

Enriched with Copius Extracts from Learned Authors. 2 vols. Cincinnati, OH: James, 1843.

Smith, James D., III. "The Pilgrimage of James Smith (1798–1871): Scottish Infidel, Southern Evangelist, and Lincoln's Springfield Pastor." *American Presbyterians* 66 (Fall 1988): 147–56.

Smith, Sidney. Review. *Edinburgh Review* 33 (January 1820): 69–80.

Snyder, Franklyn Bliss. *Robert Burns: His Personality, His Reputation and His Art.* 1936. Reprint, Port Washington, NY: Kennikat Press, 1970.

Speed, Joshua F. *Reminiscences of Abraham Lincoln and Notes of a Visit to California: Two Lectures.* Louisville, KY: Mortono, 1884.

Sprott, Gavin. *Robert Burns: Farmer.* Edinburgh: National Museums of Scotland, 1990.

———. *Robert Burns: Pride and Passion: The Life, Times and Legacy.* Edinburgh: National Library of Scotland, 1996.

Stevens, Walter B. *A Reporter's Lincoln.* Edited by Michael Burlingame. Lincoln: U of Nebraska P, 1998.

Stimmel, Smith. "Experiences as a Member of President Lincoln's Body Guard, 1863–65." *North Dakota Historical Quarterly* 1 (1926): 27–33.

Stock, Harry Thomas. "Protestantism in Illinois before 1835." *Illinois State Historical Society Journal* 12 (April 1919): 1–31.

Strawhorn, John. *The Scotland of Robert Burns.* Darvel, Scotland: Alloway, 1995.

Strickland, Arvarh E. "The Illinois Background of Lincoln's Attitude toward Slavery and the Negro." *Illinois State Historical Society Journal* 56 (Autumn 1963): 474–94.

Striner, Richard. *Father Abraham: Lincoln's Relentless Struggle to End Slavery.* New York: Oxford UP, 2006.

Sutherland, Tom. "Burns in Beirut." *Studies in Scottish Literature* 30 (1998): 1–8.

Sutherland, Tom, and Jean Sutherland. *At Your Own Risk: An American Chronicle of Crisis and Captivity in the Middle East.* Golden, CO: Fulcrum, 1996.

Swett, Leonard. "A Very Poor Hater." In *Lincoln as I Knew Him: Gossip, Tributes and Revelations from His Best Friends and Worst Enemies,* edited by Harold Holzer. Chapel Hill, NC: Algonquin, 1999.

Szasz, Ferenc Morton. "Jefferson Davis's 1869 and 1871 Visits to Scotland: Cultural Symbols of the Old and New Souths." *Northern Scotland* 14 (1994): 47–54.

———. "The 1958/59 Comic Book Biographies of Abraham Lincoln." *Journal of Popular Culture,* forthcoming.

———. "Scotland, Abraham Lincoln, and the American Civil War." *Northern Scotland* 16 (1996): 127–40.

———. *Scots in the North American West, 1790–1917.* Norman: U of Oklahoma P, 2000.

———. "Symbolizing the Scottish-American Connection: The Statues of Robert Burns in Denver and Cheyenne." *Annals of Wyoming* 72 (Winter 2000): 2–5.

———. "The Wisconsin Scot Reports on the American Civil War—Part 1." *Milwaukee History* 17 (Summer 1994): 34–50.

———. "The Wisconsin Scot Reports on the American Civil War—Part 2." *Milwaukee History* (Autumn–Winter 1994): 88–103.

Tarbell, Ida M. *All in the Day's Work: An Autobiography.* New York: Macmillan, 1939.

———. *In the Footsteps of the Lincolns.* New York: Harper, 1929.

———. *The Life of Abraham Lincoln.* 2 vols. New York: Lincoln Memorial Association, 1895.

Taylor, Evelyn. *Lincoln's New Salem: A Village Reborn.* New Salem, IL: New Salem Lincoln League, 1994.

Taylor, Walter J. "Scots and the American Civil War." *Highlander* 41 (November/December 2003): 14–18.

Temple, Wayne C. *Abraham Lincoln: From Skeptic to Prophet.* Mahomet, IL: Mayhaven, 1995.

———. *Alexander Williamson: Friend of the Lincolns.* Racine: Lincoln Fellowship of Wisconsin, 1997.

———. *Thomas and Abraham Lincoln as Farmers.* Racine: Lincoln Fellowship of Wisconsin; Historical Bulletin 53, 1996.

Thomas, Benjamin P. *Abraham Lincoln: A Biography.* New York: Knopf, 1952.

———. *Lincoln's New Salem.* Carbondale: Southern Illinois UP, 1954.

———. *Portrait for Posterity: Lincoln and His Biographers.* New Brunswick, NJ: Rutgers UP, 1947.

Thomas, Christopher A. *The Lincoln Memorial and American Life.* Princeton, NJ: Princeton UP, 2002.

Thornwell, J. H. "Our National Sins." In *Fast Day Sermons: Or the Pulpit on the State of the Country.* New York: Rudd and Carleton, 1861.

Tocqueville, Alexis de. *Democracy in America.* New York: Harper and Row, 1966.

Todd, William. *The Seventy-ninth Highlanders, New York Volunteers in the War of Rebellion, 1861–1865.* Albany, NY: Press of Brandow, 1886.

Turner, Justin G., and Linda Levitt Turner, eds. *Mary Todd Lincoln: Her Life and Letters.* New York: Knopf, 1972.

"Tribute to Abraham Lincoln." http://www.hayleycourt.com/bruce.htm.

Tripp, C. A. *The Intimate World of Abraham Lincoln.* New York: Free Press, 2005.

Trueblood, Elton. *Abraham Lincoln: Theologian of American Anguish.* New York: Harper and Row, 1973.

United States Information Agency. *Abraham Lincoln (1809): 16th President of the United States of America.* Washington, DC: GPO, 1959.

United States War Department. *The War of the Rebellion: A Compilation of the Official Records of the Union and Confederate Armies.* Series 1. Vol. 2. Washington, DC: GPO, 1880–1901. 130 vols.

Wagenknecht, Edward. *James Russell Lowell: Portrait of a Many-sided Man.* New York: Oxford UP, 1971.

Wall, Joseph Frazier. *Andrew Carnegie.* 1970. Reprint, Pittsburgh, PA: U of Pittsburgh P, 1989.

Walsh, Robert. "Foreign Literature." *American Review of History and Politics* (January 1811): 166–75.

Ward, William H., ed. *Abraham Lincoln: Tributes from His Associates.* New York: Crowell, 1895.

Warren, Louis A. *Lincoln's Youth: Indiana Years, 1816–1830.* Indianapolis: Indiana Historical Society, 1991.

———. *Little Known Facts about Thanksgiving.* Fort Wayne, IN: Lincoln National Life Insurance, 1939.

———. "The Religious Background of the Lincoln Family." *Filson Club History Quarterly* 6 (April 1932): 79–88.

Waugh, John C. *Reelecting Lincoln: The Battle for the 1864 Presidency.* New York: Crown, 1997.

Weldon, Lawrence. "Leaders of the Illinois Bar." In A. T. Rice, *Reminiscences of Abraham Lincoln,* 197–215.

Welles, Gideon. "The History of Emancipation." *Galaxy* 14 (December 1872): 840–47.

West, Richard S., Jr. *Gideon Welles: Lincoln's Navy Department.* Indianapolis, IN: Bobbs-Merrill, 1943.

Westerkamp, Marilyn J. *Triumph of the Laity: Scots-Irish Piety and the Great Awakening, 1625–1700.* New York: Oxford, 1988.

White, Ronald C., Jr. *The Eloquent President: A Portrait of Lincoln through His Words.* New York: Random House, 2005.

———. *Lincoln's Greatest Speech: The Second Inaugural.* New York: Simon and Schuster, 2002.

Whitney, Henry Clay. *Life on the Circuit with Lincoln.* 1892. Caldwell, ID: Caxton, 1940.

———. *Lincoln the Citizen.* 1892. New York: Current Literature, 1907.

Wilkie, George Scott. *Understanding Robert Burns: Verse, Explanation and Glossary.* Glasgow, Scotland: Neil Wilson, 2002.

Williams, Frank J. *Judging Lincoln.* Carbondale: Southern Illinois UP, 2002.

Wills, Garry. *Lincoln at Gettysburg: The Words That Remade America.* New York: Simon and Schuster, 1992.

Wilson, Douglas L. "Abraham Lincoln's Indiana and the Spirit of Mortal." *Indiana Magazine of History* 87 (June 1991): 155–70.

———. *Honor's Voice: The Transformation of Abraham Lincoln.* New York: Knopf, 1998.

———. *Lincoln before Washington: New Perspectives on the Illinois Years.* Urbana: U of Illinois P, 1999.

———. *Lincoln's Sword: The Presidency and the Power of Words.* New York: Knopf, 2006.

———. "What Jefferson and Lincoln Read." *Atlantic Monthly,* January 1991: 51–62.

Wilson, Douglas L., and Rodney O. Davis, eds. *Herndon's Informants: Letters, Interviews and Statements about Abraham Lincoln.* Urbana: U of Illinois P, 1998.

Wilson, James Grant. "Recollections of Lincoln," *Putnam's Magazine,* February 1909, 515–29.

Winger, Stewart Lance. *Lincoln, Religion, and Romantic Cultural Politics.* DeKalb: Northern Illinois UP, 2002.

Winkle, Kenneth J. *The Young Eagle: The Rise of Abraham Lincoln.* Dallas: Taylor Trade, 2001.

Woods, John. *Two Years' Residence in the Settlement on the English Prairie in the Illinois Country, United States.* London: Longman, 1922.

Woodward, C. Vann, and Elisabeth Muhlenfeld, eds. *The Private Mary Chestnut: The Unpublished Civil War Diaries.* New York: Oxford UP, 1984.

Wright, R. R. "Abraham Lincoln's Birthday." In *Abraham Lincoln: Tributes from His Associates,* edited by William H. Ward. New York: Crowell, 1895.

Young, John. *Robert Burns: A Man for All Seasons: The Natural World of Robert Burns.* Aberdeen, Scotland: Scottish Cultural Press, 1996.

Zilversmit, Arthur. "Lincoln and the Problem of Race: A Decade of Interpretations." In *"For a Vast Future Also": Essays from the Journal of the Abraham Lincoln Association,* edited by Thomas F. Schwartz. North's Civil War Series, 10. New York: Fordham UP, 1999.

Index

Harvard Classics, 13
"Has the Lincoln Theme Been Exhausted?" (Randall), 9
Hawthorne, Nathaniel, 39–40
Hay, John, 8, 65, 73, 77, 80
Hay, Milton, 63, 77
Heany, Seamus, 155
Hearst, William Randolph, 132
Herndon, William A., 2, 8, 55, 60, 72, 98
Heron, Robert, 27
Hertz, Emanuel, 77
Highland clans, 15
Highland clearances, 27
Highland Heritage (Ray), 129
Hillyer, Robert, 146
historical memory, 122–23; birthday celebrations, 139–40; 1909 birthday celebrations, 124–26; collectors and forgers, 140–43; first comparisons, 123–24; heroic statues, 133–37; national icons, 143–45, 153; opposition and shift in reputations, 145–52, 153; spokesmen of Lincoln-Burns connection, 126–30; stamps and coins, 137–39; of "the people," 130–34. See also Lincoln-Burns connection
Hogg, Patrick Scott, 7, 147
Holmes, Oliver Wendell, 46
Hopkins, Lemuel, 33
Houser, M. L., 51, 61
Howells, William Dean, 63
Humphreys, David, 33
Hunter, David, 77, 101
Hyde, George, 29

Illinois, Nineteenth Voluntary Infantry, 107–8
Ingersoll, Robert G., 40–41
Irish immigration, 35–36
Irving, Washington, 42

Jackson, Andrew, 36, 99
Jacobite rising of 1745, 15
Jefferson, Thomas, 29, 92
"John Anderson, My Jo" (Burns), 20–22, 35, 43; parodies of, 36–38

Johnson, Andrew, 139
Johnson, James, 4, 27
Johnson, Lyndon B., 145
Johnston, John, 66
Johnston, Sarah Bush, 66
Journal of the Abraham Lincoln Association, 11
Juneteenth, 151

Kelso, John (Jack), 61–63, 80
Kennedy, John F., 145
Kennedy, John S., 141
Kincaid, Robert L., 154
King, Martin Luther, Jr., 145, 148–49
King James Version of Bible, 16, 54, 58, 80–81, 84
Knapp, John, 33
Know-Nothing Party, 44
Knox, John, 90, 110
Knox, William, 12, 89–94

Laird-Tenant relationship, 110
Lamon, Ward Hill, 8, 67, 107
Land of Lincoln, Illinois as, 4
language: Doric Scots, 15–16, 22, 41–42, 43, 64; frontier dialect, 77; power of words, 4, 52, 58; simplicity of, 56–57, 155–56
"Last Moments of Lincoln, The" (Miller), 104
Lauder, Henry, 135
Library of Congress, 11
Life of Abraham Lincoln, The (Barton), 123–24
Life of Lincoln (Herndon), 2, 8
Life of Robert Burns, The (Carswell), 7, 25
Life of Wallace, A (Blind Harry), 25
Lincoln, Abraham: African American views of, 125, 131, 136, 139, 144–45, 147–48, 150, 152; assassination of, 81, 98, 104, 110–11, 120–21, 148; Baltimore assassination plot, 105–7; biographies of, 2, 8–11, 49–50, 114, 123–24, 133, 144–45, 154–55; brief biography, 49–50; Burns, fascination with, 3, 11, 50–

Ferenc Morton Szasz was a Regents' Professor of History at the University of New Mexico and on appointment as an Honorary Research Fellow in the School of Divinity, History, and Philosophy at the University of Aberdeen, Scotland. He wrote or edited eleven books, including *Scots in the North American West, 1790–1917*, *The Day the Sun Rose Twice, The Story of the Trinity Site Nuclear Explosion, July 16, 1945*, and *The Divided Mind of Protestant America: 1880–1930*. For a commemoration of his life see *Ferenc Morton Szasz: A Celebration and Selected Writings*, edited by Mark T. Banker (2018).